AMERICAN VENICE

The Epic Story of San Antonio's River

Early Morning on the San Antonio River at
Mill Bridge, Julian Onderdonk (1919)

AMERICAN VENICE
THE EPIC STORY OF SAN ANTONIO'S RIVER

Lewis F. Fisher

Foreword by Irby Hightower

MAVERICK PUBLISHING COMPANY

Maverick Publishing Company
P. O. Box 6355, San Antonio, Texas 78209

Library of Congress Cataloging-in-Publication Data

Fisher, Lewis F.
American Venice : the epic story of San Antonio's river / Lewis F. Fisher;
foreword by Irby Hightower.
pages cm
Includes bibliographical references and index.
ISBN 978-1-893271-65-4 (alkaline paper)
1. San Antonio River (Tex.)–History. 2. Paseo del Rio (San Antonio, Tex.)–History.
3. Urban parks–Texas–San Antonio–Design and construction–History.
4. River life–Texas–San Antonio–History. 5. San Antonio (Tex.)–History.
6. San Antonio (Tex.)–Description and travel. I. Title.
F392.S19L565 2014
976.4'351–dc23
2014034645

Printed in China

1 3 5 4 2

Book and Jacket design by
Janet Brooks / janetbrooks.com

CONTENTS

PREFACE

San Antonio's Alamo and the River Walk jockey for the crown of top Texas travel destination. Both rank high in national and even international listings. But when it comes to the written record, books about the Alamo could fill a library. The number of books devoted to the River Walk can be counted on one hand.

To be sure, the Battle of the Alamo was a cataclysmic event with long-reaching consequences, and well deserves its thorough analysis and ongoing new perspectives. The saga of the River Walk, by comparison, occurred so gradually and so far beneath the radar that it seems hardly anyone was paying attention to the process, much less writing about it. When the River Walk suddenly came to everyone's awareness, half-remembered stories were stitched together to explain its existence, however fragmentary or contradictory the tales may have been. To this day they confuse many San Antonians, visitors, historians and travel writers.

Yet the evolution of the River Walk has elements of a great epic. Its roots are in tragedy—a long series of floods that, despite heroic rescues, drowned some six dozen San Antonians, more than a third the number of Texans killed at the Alamo, depending on which battle tally you use. The flood control project that first addressed the problem and made the River Walk possible was the subject of fierce debates from the 1840s until everyone finally agreed to build it after the disastrous flood of 1921.

In the meantime, periodic civic outbursts were guiding preservation of the future River Walk's setting, unaware though citizens were of where their steps would lead. Before and after the 1921 flood grand plans were proposed and discarded. Politicians sometimes supported river improvements and sometimes opposed them, sometimes prevailed and sometimes were thwarted. In 1940 the creator of the River Walk was fired halfway through the project. His concept was rescued decades later by the group whose leaders had urged his dismissal. Citizens happened to lock in rules to guide the River Walk's development just as it was abruptly launched to greatness by a World's Fair.

The multiple overlays left from its halting development has created a world-renowned urban linear park. Few other parks achieve so much: environmental preservation and restoration, water conservation, neighborhood renewal, historic preservation, inspired public art. Its picturesque setting is not only ideal for dining and shopping but also for sightseeing, hiking, biking, canoeing. And all of this along fifteen miles of sidewalks and paths that lay bare the spectrum of a city's soul. Along the River Walk one can reach the tallest downtown buildings and the countryside, a shopping center and a performing arts center, centuries-old center-city plazas, the churches and fields of four historic Spanish missions.

My own experience with the River Walk dates from 1964, when I came to San Antonio from Rochester, New York, for U.S. Air Force officer training. It was still winter back home. But beside the San Antonio River evenings were mild as I discovered Mexican food at an outdoor table. I returned as a journalist five years later with my San Antonio-born wife, Mary. In the mid-1990s, between years as a suburban newspaper publisher and then as a publisher of regional books, I found myself writing *Saving San Antonio: The Precarious Preservation of a Heritage*, commissioned by the San Antonio Conservation Society. For it I began asking questions about how the River Walk truly came to be. Answers were published in greater detail in my *Crown Jewel of Texas* (1996) and the expanded *River Walk* (2007). *American Venice* revises the earlier work, adds many historical images that have since to come to light and includes the new sections of the River Walk, recently lengthened from three to fifteen miles.

In addition to persons credited earlier, I am especially grateful to those who have gone the extra mile in providing support for this work. They include Steven Schauer and Clint Marzec at the San Antonio River Authority; architect Irby Hightower, longtime San Antonio River Oversight Committee co-chair and author of the foreword, who also kindly reviewed part of the text and made suggestions, as did Steven Schauer; Stuart Johnson at the San Antonio River Foundation; Tom Shelton, photo archivist at the University of Texas at San Antonio Institute of Texan Cultures; photographer Mark Menjivar; photography collector Robin Stanford of Houston; San Antonio Conservation Society Librarian Beth Standifird; my wife Mary, at her best in guiding me through some editorial tough spots and in taking photographs; our son William, who translated from Spanish a dramatic report of an encounter during the flood of 1921; and our son Maverick, who drew from his editing skills to help smooth it all out.

FOREWORD

People have been visiting the San Antonio River for at least ten thousand years, and I am one of them. Like most, my first experience was as a tourist, as a child on a 1968 family vacation to HemisFair. The River Walk was the nicest place I had seen in a Texas city. The river starts some three miles north of downtown at a series of springs and an artesian "blue hole" and remains tiny through downtown. It's on a child's scale. With idiosyncratic stairs, arcades, little bridges, fountain cascades, tropical plants and meandering walkways, it is a fun and fanciful place to walk.

On my first visit, the River Walk was still mostly an undeveloped park. It had not fulfilled its planned purpose of creating an area for businesses that would generate enough tax income to pay for improvements and upkeep. But that was about to change, for 1968 marked the end of another recurring cycle.

San Antonio's River Walk did not suddenly leap from overgrown, underutilized creek to widely acclaimed, innovative urban linear park. It was a renovation of an existing park, and it wasn't considered a success for decades. The conversation and debate we had with the River Improvements Project in 1999 and 2000 turned out to be very similar to the debate in the 1930s, even in the 1910s: What should we do with this little river? Why should we bother? How can we get anything done? There were always more questions: Should the river be urban or natural, should it be highly protected or should people be allowed to experience it, how does the river fit into the broader context of the city, why should we pay for such a big project when there are so many other needs?

It can take twenty, thirty, forty years to find a workable solution to these questions, but the process seems to occur in a similar way. At a grassroots level, we decide what should happen. With the help of architects and engineers we establish a community vision. The business community eventually figures out why it's a good idea. Finally, elected leaders step forward to accomplish the desired outcome. It is not an easy evolution. The professionals are usually volunteers, business leaders have a hard time convincing others and elected leaders have to make risky choices.

The only time we have not followed this process was in the mid-twentieth century after yet another devastating flood. We didn't bother asking a complex set of questions. We just grabbed available federal money and channelized the river north and south of downtown into an efficient floodway. That came at the expense of the river's ecosystem and, for those sections, eliminated any semblance of being anything but a drainage ditch. It was an odd choice for a city that had so successfully dealt with the two miles of the river through downtown, though the immediate benefit was indeed improved flood control. But as awareness of the severity of damage to the river began to dawn, the long cycle of answering why do anything, what to do, why and how had to begin anew. Decades later, by 2014, the solution was at last nearly complete—for now.

When the Spanish arrived, they knew how to make use of the river. They built small dams, diverted some water into irrigation ditches that fed farmland and managed the system to ensure equal access to water along the entire length of the river. The system worked for a hundred and fifty years and made the most of the slender resource while doing little to harm to it. Then, in the latter 1800s, industrially drilled wells at last provided a stable source of drinking water for the city, but they also dramatically changed the spring flows that fed the river. That's when the process of questions, controversies and solutions began.

For nearly three hundred years we have slowly changed the river's path. We have changed the amount of water in it and its ability to sustain animal and plant life. We have seen how quickly it can go from a small stream to a devastating torrent. Though we know San Antonio exists only because of the river, it is a small and limited resource. It would be easy to ignore it, keep taking the water from the aquifer that supplies the springs, let the river dry up and deal with the occasional severe flood caused by runoff from central Texas thunderstorms simply by replacing the river channel with an efficient floodway. But most San Antonians love their river, and have had none of it.

As passionate as we are about the river, we have also been passionate about the wonderful tale of how the River Walk happened: a small group of like-minded people, concerned with tradition and preservation, rallying against a city government seeking modernity and efficiency. The story rings true, and has a very happy ending: the grassroots group wins, the river is saved and people flock from throughout the world to see the beautiful—not to mention profitable—result.

We loved the story so much that no one bothered to check its accuracy. When Lewis Fisher called to discuss a few facts for his earlier version of this book he told me he'd gone back through original documents and newspaper stories and told me the results. All I could say was, "Lewis, they're going to run you out of town." Several years earlier, in 1999, I had received a similar warning. "You need to check your homeowner's insurance to see if it covers civil unrest," a noted local newspaper columnist announced at a neighborhood party. "Irby is being appointed co-chair of a river oversight committee. When his house is fire-bombed, it might spread to yours," he chuckled. My house is still standing, and the $358 million San Antonio River Improvements project is nearly finished. But, as an expert city observer, the columnist knew how viscerally many San Antonians react to any hint of change to their river or to its mythology.

The real story is a bit less Hollywood but far more interesting. The river was not in danger from a city government bent on destroying it but benefited from a city government quite amenable to saving it. The grassroots effort certainly existed, though focused more broadly than on just the river. But the commonly held story and the real story both end in how the local, specific solutions to problems facing many cites created a unique asset. With a growing number of cities facing issues of water supply, urban runoff, flooding and ways of rebuilding better after a disaster, the San Antonio River Walk remains a great example of getting it right.

Irby Hightower, FAIA, Co-Chair
San Antonio River Oversight Committee

There were few bridges to cross the meandering San Antonio River in 1873, when Augustus Koch drew an overview of the city looking southeast, shown in this detail. Many bends have since been removed. One was the horseshoe bend below left center, below Travis Park, straightened to become the site of the Municipal Auditorium/Tobin Center for the Performing Arts. Also straightened, to the right of the Great Bend at above right center, was the bend creating the narrow peninsula called Bowen's Island, the site of what is now known as the Tower Life Building.

·1·
San Antonio's River

Passing Spaniards happened upon the headwaters of the San Antonio River in 1691, and took notes. They would be useful.

For ten thousand years Native Americans had hunted, fished and camped by the springs. Bones of ancient mastodons and giant bison were buried in the mud, the graves shaded by dense groves of mossy oaks.

But now these fertile hunting and fishing grounds were wedged between competing European empires. In 1691 Domingo Terán de los Ríos and Father Damian Massanet passed through while leading Spanish soldiers and priests across the northern frontier of New Spain to the Louisiana border, where the French were stirring up Native American tribes and casting longing eyes on Spanish silver mines in northern Mexico, unprotected across the Texas vastness. Native Americans called this spot Yanaguana, often translated as "place of refreshing waters." But on the Spanish calendar it was June 13, the feast day of St. Anthony of Padua. The Spaniards named it San Antonio de Padua, and moved on.

Two decades later, the French were still misbehaving. Spanish planners consulted the report of the passersby of 1691 and picked San Antonio as the site for a defensive way station between Spanish settlements on the Rio Grande at the south and the Spanish border with French Louisiana to the northeast.

The San Antonio Springs were the finest in this part of the southern edge of the upthrust known as the Balcones Escarpment. Freed from the overbearing rock of the thick escarpment, water escaped through crevices in limestone that reflected light such that the largest spring became known as the Blue Hole. But the neighborhood was heavily wooded and boggy. There was firmer ground around San Pedro Springs, two miles west.

And so it was to San Pedro Springs that a handful of Spanish soldiers under Governor Martín de Alarcón came on May 1, 1718, to build a presidio. Nearby, Franciscans under Father Antonio de San Buenaventura y Olivares established Mission San Antonio de Valero. Three years later, presidio and mission moved to better sites, two miles southeast where San Pedro Creek flowed near the convoluted bends of the San Antonio River.

The narrow San Antonio Valley was fertile but shallow. It sloped so gently that the river meandered thirteen miles to reach a point six miles distant. Through town the river was usually less than twenty feet wide and rarely more than fifteen feet deep, too weak to power more than small industry. Its 180-mile course southeast to the Gulf of Mexico was often choked with logs and brush. Stuck at the head of a spring-fed, un-navigable river and having to suffer through dry summers, its modest supply of surface water seemed to doom San Antonio to remain a small, isolated outpost strung along the banks of the two streams.

But Moors from North Africa had taught the Spanish how to tease small supplies of water into nourishing large communities. Spanish engineers designed a network of acequias, narrow gravity-driven canals that branched from the San Antonio River and San Pedro Creek to reach homes many blocks away. As acequias wound about and the river frequently doubled back on itself, a density of homes and fields could be laid out in long, narrow lots that could touch both a water source and a street. Acequias supported five Spanish missions as well.

This medieval water system supplied a colorful community for more than a century and a half, until growth exceeded the river's ability to support it. Isolated San Antonio gained an amalgam of foreign tongues and cultures as cowboys and trail drivers mingled with natives and a host of immigrants newly arrived from

The San Antonio River's headwaters spring, known as the Blue Hole, below, was a favorite picnic spot in the 1870s, though its wooded surroundings were still as boggy as when the site was rejected for settlement by San Antonio's founders. That choice went to the firmer ground around San Pedro Springs, below right, in the 1870s a public park with a lake for boaters.

Europe. Central plazas became points of arrival and embarkation for travelers and wagon trains. Ox-drawn wagon convoys lumbered to and from distant places on the western frontier of Texas and northern Mexico.

San Antonio's fortunes as a trade and transportation hub rose and fell through a rapid succession of parent governments—from Spain to Mexico in the 1820s, to the Republic of Texas in the next decade, to the United States in the decade after that and, with the Civil War, to the Confederacy, then back to the United States. Its population—2,000 at the end of the Spanish era—dropped to 800 before Texas joined the United States. Although San Antonio could be reached from the outside world only by a days-long overland journey by horse or stagecoach from the coast, by 1870 political stability helped swell the population past 12,000.

In the 1850s nearly half of all San Antonians were foreign-born. The dominant language was German. When landscape architect Frederick Law Olmsted passed through in 1856, before returning to New York to lead the design of Central Park, he famously wrote of San Antonio's "jumble of races, costumes, languages, and buildings" that lent San Antonio an "odd and antiquated foreignness."[1]

Visitors were charmed by the river. "Rich blue and as pure as crystal," Olmsted observed. "One could lean for hours over the bridge rail." Poet Sidney Lanier thought it "a lovely milky-green." He wrote on of "winding vistas of sweet lawns running down to the water, of weeping willows kissing its surface, . . . combing the long sea-green locks of a trailing water-grass which sends its waving tresses down the center of the current."[2]

Grasses and trees lined the riverbanks beside the Ursuline Academy, above left, in a scene drawn for readers of New York's *Harper's Monthly Magazine* in 1879. Two years earlier, rail service had ended San Antonio's isolation and replaced freight trains of wagons drawn by oxen, shown above lumbering down Commerce Street.

Acequias for San Antonio

For more than a century and a half, San Antonians depended for their water on a medieval system utilizing techniques brought to Spain from North Africa by the Moors, and with roots in Roman times. The system was ideal for a place lacking strong rivers and tributaries with a constant flow.

To extend the waters of the San Antonio River and San Pedro Creek, Spanish engineers designed acequias, derived from the Arabic al-saqiya and pronounced a-SAY-key-ah. The fifty-mile network of narrow irrigation canals was perhaps the most extensive of its type within the present-day United States, and served as San Antonio's water system for more than 150 years.

Acequias diverged from their sources down slight grades often invisible to the untrained eye, maintaining an unbroken flow by re-entering river or creek downstream. Engineers used a variety of specialized tools and surveying instruments to measure angles and build such construction features as diversion dams to raise water sources to flow into acequias, head gates at the water sources and hollowed logs or stone aqueducts to carry acequias over low points or streams. Lateral channels to fields or homes were fed through gates that controlled seasonal use and the users' specified water allotments.

Allowing individual homes and fields to have access to water caused the laws of gravity to trump the planning dictates of a distant Spanish king. Streets paralleling acequias' irregular downward paths disrupted the official orderly street grid. Even today they confound pedestrians and drivers trying to decipher their tortuous routes through central San Antonio.

Such a water system could serve only an area downhill from its source at river or stream. As San Antonio grew following the Civil War, acequias could not be extended uphill into new neighborhoods. Their waters were inadequate for fighting fires. Good drinking water was available only from private wells or a few riverside springs. Then came the knowledge that impure water spread disease, like the cholera epidemic that killed 300 residents in 1866.

Growth certain to follow arrival of the railroad in 1877 caused city officials to finally yield to demands for a modern water system. In mid 1878 the San Antonio Water Works Company began pumping from below the river's headwaters into a system with underground pipes and a hilltop reservoir. Some acequias were maintained for a time as storm drains, but those in town were eventually filled in. Farther south, farm cooperatives maintained acequias to irrigate fields near missions San Juan and Espada, where a 1740s stone acequia aqueduct, still in use, is part of San Antonio Missions National Historical Park.

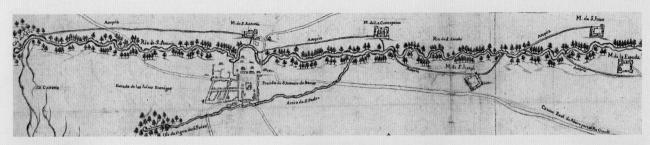

The present-day River Walk parallels the fifteen-mile length of the Spanish acequia system, shown at top in a detail from Captain Don Luis Antonio Menchaca's map of 1764. What is now called the Museum Reach stretches from near the San Antonio River's headwaters at left—north— to the town, where the original River Walk is centered around the Great Bend. To the right—south—along today's Mission Reach, acequias are shown serving the four missions on alternate sides of the river.

The painting at upper left, sometimes attributed to Robert Onderdonk, shows at its lower left the type of gate that controlled the flow of water through acequia channels and their lateral ditches for irrigation or household use, as for doing the day's wash, left. The 1740s aqueduct, above, that carried Mission Espada's acequia over a creek is still in use.

An auxiliary element in San Antonio's early water system was the wooden waterwheel propelled by the flow of the river at the southern edge of town to lift irrigation water for farmland on Bowen's Island.

San Antonians delighted in the confusion of visitors who crossed bridges—two dozen by the end of the nineteenth century—and wondered each time if they were crossing a different stream. "You cannot escape it," marveled one visitor of the river. "You think you have left it behind you, and there it is before you."[3]

Adequate bridges, however, were a hard-won amenity in frontier San Antonio. Early on, an everyday challenge was simply getting across the river.

The first recorded bridge was built in the 1730s, a makeshift pedestrian bridge of logs at the end of Commerce Street crossing from the main settlement to the final location of Mission San Antonio de Valero—later known as the Alamo—on a bluff on the far side. The crossing could not be depended upon, however, for a priest would occasionally decide that access to the town made mission converts too worldly and order the bridge taken down. A block north, where Crockett Street now crosses, Francisco Calaorra in 1786 was using his boat as a public ferry in return for a Spanish land grant.[4]

The city's first wagon bridge was built at Commerce Street in 1842. It was a community effort. A decree required "all voters" to help fill in a low approach to the bridge, adding that "every person having carts shall furnish them one day with yoke of oxen to haul dirt and every lone man shall present himself with a pick and spade." To be certain that dirt did not sift out in transit, all wagon floorboards were to be covered with hides.[5]

But the completed bridge was too low, and in a few years washed out in a flood. A higher bridge was built. In 1860, contractor John H. Kampmann was hired to replace that one with a more sturdy wooden structure, "the old red bridge," its trestle substructure luring boys to crawl beneath and nab pigeons. Given all the factors involved in bridge construction, it is no surprise that at this time there was still only one more wagon bridge in town, at Houston Street. Elsewhere, horses and wagons forded the river as best they could.[6]

Pedestrian crossings could be tricky. Those unwilling or unable to wade or afraid to slip on stepping-stones could cross an assortment of flimsy, narrow plank bridges that floated on empty, airtight barrels, often with waist-level ropes or

The earliest known photo of the San Antonio River, top right, taken in about 1860, looks west past Commerce Street's 1842 wagon bridge. Contemplative scenes in the early 1880s show the Convent Street Bridge, top left; St. Mary's Church and the John Twohig house, lower left; and, at lower right, Houston Street's 1871 iron bridge.

Pedestrians once crossed the river on footbridges of varying stability. Some, like that below right, had railings, others none, like that propped up across from John Twohig's home to a building fronting Commerce Street, bottom left. Many pedestrian bridges floated atop barrels, like the private bridge, below, supporting a fisherman kept by a security door from reaching the far side. Footbridge locations were so familiar in the 1860s that one could be used to identify where on Main/Commerce Street to find the food merchants who supplied William Menger's hotel.

boards attached for hand grips. How far one had to step up or down to get on or off a bridge depended upon how high the water was at the time. To keep floating footbridges from being swept away by high water in a storm, they were chained to trees or posts. During swiftly rising water, the chain on one side was released so the bridge could swing into the current, then be pulled back and re-chained when the water lowered.

Some children delighted in the experience. "We would jump up and down on the footbridge and get ourselves thoroughly splashed with water," recalled Maria James. Others did not get as excited. "I always hated to cross this bridge," remembered another. "I crawled across it in rainy weather holding on tight on each side. At other times I always stayed right in the middle."[7]

If so many rickety footbridges were an oddity in America at the time, floating bathhouses were even more curious. Without indoor plumbing and with no ponds

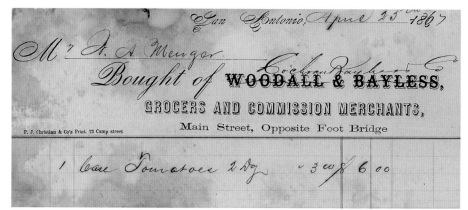

or lakes nearby, San Antonians' obvious place to bathe was in the river. By the 1840s, however, visitors with Victorian sensibilities were shocked by "quite a startling spectacle to see here, just above the bridge in the heart of the city, a number of Mexican women and girls bathing entirely naked, unconcerned about our presence." The solution was enclosed bathhouses that shielded bare skin from prying eyes.[8]

Yielding to the prevailing primness, in the 1850s the city council outlawed nude public bathing altogether in both the river and San Pedro Creek, except at fords during certain hours. Open bathing remained unregulated outside city limits, where the less inhibited, "manifesting not the slightest regard for the curious glances of the passersby," could still bathe "without the annoyance of dresses."[9]

Like floating footbridges, most bathhouses were secured atop barrels on the river or on parts of San Pedro Creek, though some were built at ground level to straddle acequias. A framework, perhaps ten feet square, was sheathed in strips of muslin or canvas and covered by a roof—muslin stretched flat across or a pitched roof with shingles—so that those on the shore or in buildings above could not peer in. After stepping inside, bathers fastened the fabric door and hung their clothes on pegs. Benches were on a floor of wooden slats that could be raised or lowered to keep adults and children at a safe depth. Men usually bathed early in the morning or late at night, women and children following the afternoon siesta, though this was not always the case. "It was not unusual any time of day," according to one report, "to see a lady or gentleman making their way to the river with a towel, a bar of soap and a change of clothes under their arm."[10]

There were larger bathhouses for girls and nuns at the Ursuline Academy and for the Turners—a German fraternal group—at Bowen's Island.[11] A public

"Street scene" was the title given *Harper's Monthly* readers for a sketch, above left, of boats and bathhouses floating in the San Antonio River. A long commercial bathhouse drew bathers to the crossing beside Nat Lewis's stone mill, a corner of which shows at the far left in the above 1870s view. The steeple of the original St. John's Lutheran Church rises to the right of homes in La Villita. In the foreground may be a self-portrait of photographer W. H. Metcalf with his horse and equipment wagon.

Trees and shrubs were handy places to dry clothes on washday beside the San Antonio River at the present site of the Navarro Street/Mill Bridge. At the right in this 1860s view is the frame mill and large iron millwheel later replaced with a stone mill by Nat Lewis and, years afterward, by Hotel Contessa. On the skyline toward the left is the San Fernando Church tower.

Undershot waterwheels took what force they could from the gently falling San Antonio River to power small mills. Tallest was the five-story stone Laux Mill, right, shown across from a floating bathhouse. Two mills were built farther downstream by German immigrant C. H. Guenther, one in 1860—shown at far right next to the family home that was later enlarged and then converted to a restaurant—and the other, lower left, in 1868. Piled stones formed a dam to direct water toward turning a water wheel to power belt-driven equipment in a ramshackle iron foundry, lower right.

bathhouse at San Pedro Springs Park used the rock base around the springs as its floor. The earliest commercial bathhouse was a long affair, at first without roof or floor, put in near what is now the Navarro Street/Mill Bridge in 1852 by Sammy Hall. The lively entrepreneur and a fellow kilted Scotsman drew crowds by playing bagpipes and dancing the Highland Fling.[12]

On washdays, women found it more convenient to bring clothes to the river than to carry wash water up the banks. Clothes were hung to dry on nearby brush. A favorite laundering spot was the widest part of the river, on the southern leg of the Great Bend below the present-day Navarro Street/Mill Bridge, where water was shallow enough to provide the most popular ford for wagons and carriages. Nearby, baptisms could be counted upon to bring up "a chorus of hallelujahs" following immersions.[13]

Two bird sellers targeted potential customers on a sidewalk of the iron Navarro Street bridge across the northern leg of the Great Bend.

Mixed in between all the fishermen, floating footbridges, hidden bathers, drying clothes and hallelujahs were small industries.

From its headwaters to the southern edge of downtown, the river dropped only a gradual thirty-five feet, generating insufficient force to power major mills and factories. But at one point the river did support a half dozen grist mills, two ice factories, a tannery and two iron foundries, one of which created such a racket with its screeching water wheels and hammering that the city council declared the foundry a public nuisance and required it to move.[14]

Most notable among mills in the Civil War era were the 1845 William Small/ Nat Lewis Mill with its landmark water wheel, on the site of Hotel Contessa; the five-story stone 1860s Laux Mill, later converted to a boarding house, on the site of the Milam Building; and, south of downtown at the end of King William Street, two separate mills built—in 1860 and 1868—by the young German immigrant Carl Hilmar Guenther which grew into a family-owned international food conglomerate, San Antonio-based C. H. Guenther & Son.[15]

Two 70-horsepower boilers were used by the San Antonio Ice Company in manufacturing ice in a plant on the site of the Hyatt Regency Hotel.

Ice was a rare luxury in frontier San Antonio. What little was first available— usually harvested in Massachusetts—was hauled overland from ships docking at the Texas coast, an expensive and cumbersome operation requiring a large volume of insulation. In the late 1860s J. B. LaCoste opened the city's first successful ice manufacturing plant beside the river on Losoya Street, on the present site of the Hyatt Regency Hotel. A day's supply of ice resembling frozen snow was sold to the city's leading hotel, the Menger, for $50.[16]

The river itself froze rarely. On February 12, 1899, it froze for the first time in thirty years. This put an end to ribbing by his fellow officers of one Fort Sam Houston lieutenant, Samuel D. Rockenbach, later the general commanding Allied tank forces in World War I. Lt. Rockenbach had brought ice skates from his previous assignment in Montana. He skated that day in triumph on the river.[17]

As its growth perked up following the Civil War, the inconvenience of un-bridged river crossings finally forced the city to pay whatever it took to install at least three iron bridges. One replaced the wide ford by the Lewis Mill on the southern leg of the Great Bend with a double span bridge from Ohio's King Iron Bridge and Manufacturing Company in Cleveland, at the site of the present Navarro Street/Mill Bridge. A single span took Navarro Street across the northern leg of the Great Bend. The third iron bridge crossed the river at Houston Street.

First to arrive—in 1871—was the iron bridge at Houston Street. Its parts were cast in St. Louis, sent by train to New Orleans and by boat to the Texas port of Indianola. "Some of the material was forty feet long and so heavy that it could only be transported on the largest wagons," remembered August Santleben, the German-born freighting veteran who got the job of hauling the parts from the coast. It took fourteen wagons. For his leg of the bridge's journey Santleben was paid $3,250, today's equivalent of $64,000.[18]

Abruptly, in February 1877, San Antonio's connection with the coast was cut from days to hours by a railroad line east from Houston. Retail goods and heavy

The wooden bridge built over Commerce Street in 1860 began to sway in the center and its trestle substructure caught flood debris, causing it to be replied with an iron bridge in 1880.

construction materials began rolling in, as did hordes of tourists and new residents. San Antonio's population spiked more than eighty percent by the end of the decade, to more than 20,000 in 1880. The next year a rail line was built through from the north and on south to the Mexican border. In another two years more rails reached westward across the continent to California.

Isolated, odd and antiquated San Antonio was thrust into a modern world. In hardly a decade its dusty Spanish plazas—Military, Main and Alamo—would be landscaped and adorned with large public buildings. Outdoor vendors were moved into a public market. Streets were paved and mule-drawn streetcars were replaced with ones powered by electricity. New subdivisions spread outward over brushy pastures.

The modernizing process set in motion a transformation of the San Antonio River as well.

At Commerce Street, the "old red bridge" had withstood floods but was beginning to sway in the center, and "shook from end to end every time a heavily loaded wagon crossed it." Circus elephants parading into town from the train station instinctively tested the bridge with their front feet before beginning to cross.[19]

The bridge was replaced in 1880 with a stronger iron bridge, arriving by rail from East Berlin, Connecticut, where the Berlin Bridge Company was expanding its reach throughout the West. The bridge's parabolic spans on either side and the stylish iron spires at each corner declared the importance of passage down the city's main business street. It achieved fame through onetime San Antonio resident O. Henry's story "A Fog in Santone," about a tuberculosis sufferer who "wanders into the fog, and, at length, finds himself upon a little iron bridge," below which "the small tortuous river flows."[20]

The ease of shipping by rail brought two major breweries to the river north of downtown, the City Brewery (1881)—later the Pearl Brewing Company—and the Lone Star Brewing Company (1883), its founders including St. Louis brewer Adolphus Busch. But for its rail siding to cross the river at Grand /Jones Avenue,

"Walk Your Horse. . . And to The Right," riders were advised on corner signs of San Antonio's first iron bridge, top. It was made in St. Louis, and hauled from a costal port on fourteen wagons to be assembled across the river at Houston Street in 1871. Signature spires adorned the Connecticut-built iron bridge that carried Commerce Street across the river from 1880 to 1914, when it was taken apart and reassembled at Johnson Street.

The St. Mary's Street bridge captured in the glow of sunrise in 1883 by Ida Weisselberg Hadra, above, was replaced seven years later by San Antonio's most elaborate iron bridge. At its dedication, above right, Connecticut's Berlin Bridge Company had a fifteen-ton steamroller on hand to demonstrate the bridge's strength.

Lone Star needed a bridge of sufficient strength to support barrel-laden freight cars. Economy-minded city officials obliged in 1885 by moving up the sturdy decade-old iron bridge from Houston Street, replacing it with a less expensive wooden bridge that could handle the lighter traffic there.[21]

As improvements swept through the city, four more handsome Berlin bridges were added across the river in 1890–91, their substructures able to support concrete pavement and bear the weight of the new electric streetcars. The new iron bridge for St. Mary's Street was so wide it required supporting overhead trusses, made high enough to not obstruct floats in parades. Plaques between the decorative grillwork arching each end prominently bore the name of the incumbent mayor, Bryan Callaghan, painted in gilt. Cost-conscious opponents attacked him for extravagance. Callaghan was barely re-elected in what became known as "The Letters of Gold Campaign."[22]

The exuberance of the new era set imaginations free. The river may be no Mississippi, and San Antonio was not New Orleans, but why couldn't it have steamboats, too? The man who made that happen was Finis Foster Collins, whose plant at the northeast corner of Houston Street and the river—later the site of the Texas Theater—assembled tanks, steam boilers, windmills and other equipment for ranchers throughout Texas and Mexico. It was a short step for him to take a rowboat, rig it up with a small steam boiler to power paddlewheels on either side and launch the only steam sidewheeler known to have operated on the San Antonio River.

Collins named his craft the *Hilda* in honor of his wife, ran it daily and on Sundays made trips every twenty minutes. "The water was crowded with other pleasure craft as well," one newspaper reported, "but the steamer lorded it over the whole river."[23]

When the river was sufficiently high and unobstructed Collins also operated a barge. Seven miles downstream at Berg's Mill, the San Antonio and Aransas Pass Railroad depot was close enough to the river for Collins to conveniently access rail freight service for his equipment without having to deal with sending horse-drawn wagons to a depot across town.[24]

While the railroads may have sparked an impressive overlay of stylish and long overdue infrastructure, the benefits came at great cost.

One resulted from new development that covered much more of the watershed; with less open ground to absorb rainwater, it flowed more quickly into the river. Periodic flooding became more serious. Dry tributary creek beds with distant watersheds having little vegetation compounded the problem. The San Antonio River was particularly vulnerable to sudden runoff from the usually dry Olmos Creek, which drains thirty-four square miles from the northwest into the river below the headwaters. To the west, Alazan, Apache and Martinez creeks crossing western San Antonio have a combined drainage area of twenty-three square miles.

San Antonio's earliest recorded equivalent of a hundred-year-flood came in July 1819, when what was reported as a *culebra de agua*—a serpent of water or cloudburst—fell into the drainage area of Olmos Creek. Waters surged into the San Antonio River, already swollen by rain. They joined floodwaters overflowing San

New utility poles marched down Houston Street past its 1885 wooden bridge, left. In the view's upper left corner is one of the more unusual profiles to adorn San Antonio's skyline, the windmill marking the location of Finis F. Collins's farm and ranch equipment supply plant beside the river. Collins rigged a small steam engine with side paddlewheels to power the *Hilda*, below, the only "steamboat" to ply the San Antonio River.

GEORGE WASHINGTON BRACKENRIDGE

George Washington Brackenridge (1832–1920) was San Antonio's top financier during the Gilded Age and the city's leading philanthropist of the time. He had not planned on becoming a major player in moving the city's water system from dependence on the San Antonio River. Born in Indiana and a Harvard Law School alumnus who moved to East Texas, he was a Union loyalist during the Civil War. He found San Antonians more forgiving—or unaware—of his past loyalties than were his ex-Confederate neighbors to the east.

In 1869, three years after organizing San Antonio National Bank, George Brackenridge bought 217 scenic acres that included the headwaters of the San Antonio River. Ownership of the headwaters was still a controversial subject. Although granted to the city by the King of Spain, the city sold them in 1852 to an incumbent alderman, James Sweet, over the strenuous objections of City Engineer Francois Giraud and others.

Brackenridge took an interest in Jean B. LaCoste's San Antonio Water Works Company, opened in 1878 on leased city-owned land downstream from the headwaters. He became involved financially and in 1883, with a few close friends, bought out the founders. At his headwaters home he kept a telescope to monitor the water level at the hilltop reservoir a mile away, put the Water Works on a sound financial footing and expanded the system.

He gave little heed to those who thought growing water shortages were caused by a cluttered riverbed or clogged springs. Brackenridge believed the problem was simply lack of available water, which could be addressed by the new artesian wells. He tried drilling one beside the reservoir, but the elevation hampered its success. Hoping for better luck at a lower elevation, in 1891 the Water Works purchased land where Market Street meets the river. There, at a depth of 890 feet, Brackenridge's drillers struck water with such pressure that it spouted fifteen to twenty feet into the air and blew out rocks, according to witnesses, "as large as a man's head." The well began producing three million gallons of water a day.[1]

Increasing numbers of artesian wells provided vitally needed water, but lowered the water table to the extent that the headwaters springs and the river sometimes ceased to flow. Brackenridge sought regulation of artesian drilling, but was unsuccessful. Discouraged by the appearance of the headwaters, he wrote a friend: "I have seen this bold, bubbling, laughing river dwindle and fade away. This river is my child and it is dying, and I cannot stay here to see its last gasps. . . . I must go."[2]

In 1897 Brackenridge sold the headwaters and his surrounding estate to the Sisters of Charity of the Incarnate Word for their motherhouse and academy. The land became the campus of the University of the Incarnate Word. He sold the Water Works in 1906, seven years after donating 199 acres of riverside land that became the nucleus of Brackenridge Park.

[1] McLean, *Romance of San Antonio's Water Supply*, 9–10.
[2] Sibley, *Brackenridge*, 141.

Financier George W. Brackenridge, far left, eliminated the city water system's dependence on the San Antonio River. The lower pump house of his San Antonio Water Works, left, built in 1885, is better known for its later use as the studio where sculptor Gutzon Borglum designed his models for Mount Rushmore.

Two years before a group led by George Brackenridge purchased the San Antonio Water Works Company, Dr. Ferdinand Herff, its treasurer, issued Brackenridge this check for $67,000— today's equivalent of $1.5 million—to settle an earlier purchase of Water Works bonds.

By the 1880s flood control efforts included some retaining walls like this along the Great Bend behind the Twohig House, later site of the Drury Inn & Suites Riverwalk.

Pedro Creek and rampaged through Main and Military plazas, washing away a dozen adobe and stone buildings. Water rose five feet within San Fernando Church. Afterward, the parish priest presided over funerals for sixteen flood victims, ten of them indigenous children. Antonio María Martínez, the last governor of Texas under Spain, moved soldiers from the wreckage of their barracks on Military Plaza five blocks east to La Villita, soon recognized for its higher elevation as one of the finer places in town to live.[25]

Scarcely a quarter century later, in 1845, San Antonio was struck by a less disastrous but still severe flood. Mayor Edward Dwyer made an ambitious proposal: build a dam near the end of Olmos Creek to hold back the worst of the floodwaters. Dwyer's successor brought up the idea again seven years later, when more flooding sent the river eight feet above its normal level and into the streets.[26]

But it took yet another flood before the city even went so far as to form a study committee. That happened after a flood on March 26, 1865, when at least three people drowned. Albert Maverick, then eleven, remembered wading "everywhere" after the flood and seeing the wooden Houston Street Bridge "like an island" in the receding floodwaters. Caught behind its midstream supports was "a great mass of driftwood forming a dam and backing up the water." Although there was the same level of rainfall as in the flood of 1845, increased runoff caused floodwaters to rise six feet higher than before, and losses were greater. Once again building a dam on Olmos Creek came up.[27]

A committee of three engineers faulted the number of obstructions built within channels better left open for runoff. The engineers recommended that walls narrowing the channels of the river and of San Pedro Creek be taken down. Approaches to bridges would be better supported by stand-alone pillars rather than by solid earthen ramps, and, they said, bridges should have no midsection supports to hold back debris and act as dams. The new midtown stone diversion dam for the Concepción acequia "should be removed at once" and the acequia's flow preserved by relocating its uppermost section eastward to branch from the Alamo acequia instead. Many recommendations went unheeded, but the acequia fix was completed in 1869. A low dam preserved a pond above Nat Lewis's mill.[28]

It was long apparent that San Antonio's antiquated Spanish-era water system had become inadequate. Acequias could not be expected to defy gravity and reach new neighborhoods at higher elevations. Months after the first railroad arrived a new water system was authorized. It was in operation by mid-1878. A half-mile below the headwaters, river water was pumped eastward to a five-million-gallon hilltop reservoir, now an amphitheater on the grounds of the San Antonio Botanical Gardens. The downhill flow into the new network of underground pipes was augmented seven years later by a booster pump farther down the river, near what became the entrance to the Brackenridge Park golf course.

Filling the reservoir with water pumped from the river had limitations, however. In August 1887 the river suffered "an almost unprecedented lack of water" when drought depleted its springs, and there was widespread alarm. Waterworks officials pleaded for limits to commercial and industrial water use and the watering of lawns and gardens.[29]

Many seized on the cause of the drought as not lack of rainfall but of riverbed undergrowth and debris, which they believed blocked water from flowing up through springs beneath the river. The city council came up with $3,000 to clear logs and growth. The San Antonio *Light* editorialized against such "artificial

A low dam remained near Nat Lewis's mill after a higher acequia diversion dam was removed for flood control in 1869. Despite addition of the double span Navarro Street/Mill Bridge shortly thereafter, wagons still crossed at the old ford, giving horses a chance to drink and allowing water to expand wooden wheels tightly against their iron rims.

obstructions" as dams, trash and "natural obstructions"—brush, trees, and accumulations of silt. Flushing sewage downstream with less water was another problem. The *Light* counted more than 200 privies discharging their contents into the river and called the river "not an open sewer" but "an obstructed sewer." Efforts to scour the riverbed to yield more water, however, had no effect.[30]

Residents longed for the bountiful flow that once let John Blankenship, "the old lone fisherman of San Antonio," bring up from below the Commerce Street bridge not only a regular supply of fish but, on occasion, a six-foot eel, the times when crawfish were common and small alligators made cameo appearances.[31]

During these dark days, however, artesian wells in California and elsewhere in the West were yielding seemingly unlimited supplies of new water. By the mid-1880s there were 200 wells into aquifers around Fort Worth. They required no pumping; the water "just flowed over the top." In 1887–88, San Antonio's first two artesian wells were drilled into the Austin limestone aquifer near the West End subdivision, and filled the new body of water now known as Woodlawn Lake. Nearly a dozen more such wells were drilled in surrounding Bexar County.[32]

Meanwhile, local icemakers found that more slowly flowing river water was lowering the quality of their ice. In 1888–89, the first documented well into the

Edwards Aquifer was drilled by the Crystal Ice Company, operating in the former Alamo Mill near the river at Avenue B and Eighth Street. The drilling took five months. The company drilled three more wells. In 1891 George

When the declining river caused poorer water quality in manufactured ice, the Crystal Ice Company, far right, near the river at Avenue B and Eighth Street, found a new water source by drilling the first artesian well into the Edwards Aquifer, in 1888–89. Drillers like those at right at first hit gushers that, when capped, required no pumping.

Brackenridge's San Antonio Water Works drilled a well at the southwest corner of Market Street and the river so successfully that eight more were drilled at the site, which still produces and stores water for the San Antonio Water System. Others were drilled beside the two upstream riverside pump houses, less used since the headwaters declined.[33]

By 1896 there were seventy artesian wells in Bexar County. Together, their pumping further lowered the water table and worsened effects of a drought that began in spring 1897. The headwaters springs flow, 24,000 cubic feet per minute when the waterworks opened, dropped to as low as 2,000 cubic feet per minute, and began drying up. Downstream, the river dwindled to a trickle through the slime of refuse no longer swept away by a swift current.[34]

Despite the hand-wringing over the declining river, there were those who could look beyond the slime and the silt to another day. Why, wondered an anonymous writer to the San Antonio *Express* in the dry August of 1887, shouldn't the riverbanks become a park?

The banks "could be converted into flowerbeds, and pleasure boats [could] afford recreation to hundreds," thought the writer. "Many of our citizens are prone to look entirely upon the utility side of every question, and the river as an ornament would be likely to excite ridicule, but . . . our river would be the crown jewel of Texas."[35]

Despite the increasing periods of declines in the river level, residents by the end of the nineteenth century sensed the potential of the banks as a park. Even through overgrowth, soon after 1900 a burst of flowering yuccas could create a scenic view through the Navarro Street/Mill Bridge to the beehive dome of the county courthouse and, to its right, the clock tower of city hall. Farther upstream and around the bend, banana trees lent a semitropical lushness to the riverbanks below the Oblate Fathers' Home beside St. Mary's Catholic Church.

Horse-drawn and motor-driven vehicles mix on Crockett Street above San Antonio's new river park, completed in 1914, as seen looking west from the Navarro Street bridge west to St. Mary's Street.

·2·

Building the River Park

The twentieth century dawned on a San Antonio reveling in its new world. Freed by railroads from eccentric isolation, longtime residents were having to look twice to believe the capacious city hall, county courthouse and post office buildings that had so suddenly sprung in splendid modernity on the once dusty frontier plazas. As San Antonio's population swept past 50,000, new pride came from recapturing the crown of largest city in the largest state from Galveston.

An increasing frustration, however, was the appearance of the San Antonio River, so visible through the fast-modernizing downtown. The headwaters springs had not run for most of the drought of 1897–99. They were revived by a rainstorm in January 1900 that sent river waters rising through town, but were dry again by the summer. Only runoff from the two major breweries north of downtown kept any water in the river at all. Without flow to carry off garbage and refuse accumulating on the muddy bottom, city sanitary inspectors ordered those piping wastewater into the river to stop. More calls came to clean things up.[1]

Things began to look better when a rainy period began in November 1902, but three months later those rains culminated in a flood. The only warning came in a 2 a.m. phone call on February 26, 1903, when the engineer on duty at a waterworks pump house upstream rang up Fire Chief William G. Tobin to report floodwaters from Olmos Creek were surging past and heading toward town. The warning gave Tobin enough time to mobilize firemen for rescues, and there were no drownings. But basements were flooded, a number of small homes were swept away and water reached a depth of two and a half feet on St. Mary's Street. Floodwaters caused less damage than in the most recent major flood, in 1865, though they briefly reached within twenty-five inches of the record set that year.[2]

The next year the river was drying up yet again. With brush overhanging the dry riverbed making it look worse, street workers were sent to open it up. But in a pioneering protest at city hall, many residents accused trimmers in their zeal of destroying landmark trees. The newly organized Civic Improvement Association was instrumental in having the job transferred from the street department to the parks department, headed by the respected hotelier Ludwig Mahncke. City officials promised "to beautify the stream and protect it in every manner possible." Penalties were soon set for unauthorized cutting of riverside trees and shrubs, and authorities prepared to defend the city's river property line against encroachments.[3]

A lone carriage crossed the river between the Mill Bridge and the county courthouse during a flood in 1900, but three years later the worst flood since 1865 flooded the lower level of the Clifford Building beside the Commerce Street bridge and rose into streets elsewhere in downtown San Antonio.

Some thought the dry river was simply caused by clogged springs and layers of debris. They recalled stories passed down from Spanish days, when droughts threatened the river's flow into acequias. At such times, it was said, families assembled at assigned places. "With all manner of agricultural and farm implements known in that day," they scraped away accumulations of mud down to the gravel riverbed, and springs once more bubbled from the bottom. Figuring that was worth a try, firemen took their hoses and gave the riverbed a scouring. The river gradually rose, whether from the cleaning or from new rains. Weekend boaters again plied the river, its banks overhung with "boughs, cresses and ferns."[4]

As he took charge of beautifying the river, Parks Commissioner Ludwig Mahncke made a decision that has yielded a signature element of today's central River Walk, the towering cypresses that line its banks. The two "magnificent" willows so recently turned into stumps may have been scenic, but Mahncke did not like having willows beside the river. "I can tell you that if Mr. Mahncke had his way he would cut down all the willows on the river," said Fire Chief William G. Tobin. He added that willow roots "reach out into the water and collect sediment and fill up rivers," and even "give an awful stench when they fall into the water and decay."[5]

24 • American Venice

Thus did Mahncke instead plant cypresses, with deep root structures that hold soil without disrupting streams. He ordered 300 cypress saplings from Gustav Schattenberg in neighboring Kendall County in the Texas Hill Country, where the trees flourish on the banks of the Guadalupe River and Cypress Creek. It took Schattenberg's two nephews a week to dig up the saplings at streamside farms and pack them with wet hay in their wagon, then a few more days to haul them to the parks commissioner in San Antonio. Mahncke paid with a personal check for $300, saying there was no money in the parks account at the time.[6]

Heavy growth over a slowly flowing river led to overzealous trimming and an uproar that brought significant upgrades in river improvement.

San Antonians began making the river part of their spring festivities, notably the fiesta that has evolved into a ten-day April extravaganza of parades and events. The festival traditionally began with a masked king's arrival at a railroad station to greet the public. But in 1905, on the evening of April 24, the king arrived on the river. Waters from heavy rains subsided in time to permit a safe voyage for a flower-bedecked, torchlit flotilla, its royal barge decorated in silver and gold. It was San Antonio's first river parade.

In a scene "not unlike the ancient glories of the Bosphorous in the day of the Caesars," a steady blast of trumpets heralded the fleet's arrival at the landing along Tobin Terrace, the newly-landscaped banks below Crockett Street between St. Mary's and Navarro streets believed named for Fire Chief William Tobin, whose crews had cleaned the river. Crowds cheered as the king was greeted by the commodore of the whimsically named Alamo Yacht Club and ascended with his entourage to the street for an illuminated parade.[7]

In May 1905, the Tobin Terrace landing was the setting for a Memorial Day service organized by the Women's Relief Corps in honor of deceased sailors. "At the proper time during the exercises, a number of children led by a little boy holding an American flag aloft stepped on a floating barge," one newspaper reported. "As the barge glided gently along with the rippling current, the children showered flowers upon the water, and those along the bank did likewise."[8]

Although the spring festival skipped the river the next year, in 1907 even grander plans were made for a gala riverside Carnival of Venice. But a temporary dam built to raise water to a sufficient level for boats was washed out by a cloudburst the

Had their been any doubt of San Antonians' affection for their river, it was dispelled when citizens rose up in August 1904 to take overzealous municipal tree trimmers and their superiors to task.

This was the first time city officials had faced such an outpouring of support for preservation of the riverbanks.

"Two magnificent willow trees" that reached across a picturesque bend of the river north of the Navarro Street/Mill Bridge had been reduced to a pile of logs and two stumps, and citizens were incensed. Proclaimed one newspaper headline: "Street Commissioner's Men Ruthlessly Lay Axe to Immense Willow Trees That Made the Mill Bridge View Famous." The recently formed Civic Improvement Association sounded an alarm.

Two days later, the new group delivered to city council chambers "a full hundred citizens of the staid, sober and substantial kind that does not venture out except upon occasions of real merit."

Mayor Pro Tem Vories P. Brown was quick to assure the crowd that before the incident he had warned Street Commissioner Pat Stevens "not to cut any trees except those that were absolutely necessary." Stevens parried that he had the trees cut "at the request of the owner of the land." Fire Chief William G. Tobin said the foreman reported "that he had not cut down a single long-lived tree, except one." Tobin tried blaming the media for the uproar, suggesting that the situation "had not been so bad as the press made it."

A reporter asked Stevens what happened to all the wood. Stevens admitted he had taken one load, but swore that all the rest "would be stacked on the banks and offered to the city public schools."

One speaker suggested the job of cleaning the riverbanks be given to Parks Commissioner Ludwig Mahncke. The mayor pro tem thought that was a fine idea, and promised to take care of it.

The Civic Improvement Association, which signed up a number of new members at the session, thanked the mayor pro tem and praised the press "for its efforts in behalf of preserving the river which has made San Antonio noted abroad."

"Magnificent trees at Mill bridge chopped down by river gang" was the caption in this newspaper sketch of the scene. Mayor Pro Tem Vories Brown faced citizens' ire. The street commissioner was skewered for going off with a personal load of firewood. An ax-wielding Street Commissioner Pat Stevens was caricatured under the heading "Lumbering in city limits."

day of the parade. Events were postponed for three days while the Alamo Yacht Club's boats, damaged in the washout, were repaired and the dam was rebuilt.

Finally, on April 19, 1907, thousands gathered to watch the parade from bridges and banks. Strings of colored lights criss-crossed the river and glowed in its trees from Houston Street to the Mill Bridge. Each of the dozen skiffs, lit with strings of Japanese lanterns, carried costumed "Indians and their squaws," who appeared "very grotesque" in the light of the torches. A searchlight in the lead boat played on the crowds and on the river. The barge of the masked king—later revealed to be real estate broker John H. Kirkpatrick—drew up to the Tobin Terrace landing. Other boats passed in review, then turned back toward Houston Street. A band played "See the Conquering Hero Comes," fireworks on the riverbank went off, "and the crowd shouted itself hoarse."[9]

The undependable river level may have discouraged more parades for some time, but the river was not ignored during fiestas. In April 1910, "many thousands of tri-colored electric globes" were strung over the river and along its banks in the business district. As its float in the street parade, the Civic Improvement League built a twenty-foot canoe with "rowers" symbolizing progress emphasized by a banner proclaiming "What the Civic Improvement League is going to do with the San Antonio River."[10]

True to a headline declaring "Public Wants River To Receive First Attention," the league began to spruce up three sections with new grass, flowers, and shrubs. Permanent lighting was planned. An island below the Mill Bridge was to become a garden of roses and ferns and the riverbed was to be smoothed to a uniform depth for a more even flow. Public baths would make up for the loss of deep swimming holes.[11]

Some riverbanks were being improved by landowners. At the headwaters, the Sisters of Charity of the Incarnate Word were able to maintain high enough water for boating near their college campus. A short distance downstream, the parks commissioner was fencing preserves at the new Brackenridge Park so picnickers

In 1905, officials on a beautified section of the riverbanks named Tobin Terrace, at left of center above, reviewed the first spring festival river parade. On Memorial Day soon after, children scattered flowers there in memory of deceased sailors from San Antonio, a pioneering event shown below in a slightly blurred newspaper photo.

For the cover of a 1911 travel promotion publication, the Missouri Kansas & Texas Railway chose this view of the riverbanks at the St. Mary's Street Bridge, below the Oblate Fathers' home that stood next to St. Mary's Catholic Church.

could enjoy seeing buffalo, deer and elk, able to soak in the river on hot days.

During the dry summer of 1910, the river slowed to a trickle once more. Farmers along the two surviving acequias south of town fell to quarreling over what little water there was. It took a judge to decide that since the Spanish water grant for the San Juan Acequia was dated one day before that for the Espada Acequia, sixty percent of the river's water would be diverted to San Juan and forty percent to Espada.[12]

Sanitation concerns increased. One resident complained that in a mile downriver he counted eight privies emptying into the river, which he estimated "is about one foot deep in water and another foot deep in filth and muck and slime." If the Publicity League was spending $50,000 to bring people to San Antonio "for health and recreation and pleasure," he suggested that the group "spend a little more money and give the people what they came here for."[13]

By now it was becoming obvious that makeshift efforts dealing with the river were not going to be sufficient. Moreover, many saw the river as a key local element in the sort of municipal vision evolving nationally in the City Beautiful movement. Though they had no formal organization, reformers in major American cities had united around a City Beautiful agenda combining civic and environmental activism with political reform to improve the surroundings. The idea was that in an ordered, beautiful environment, citizens would be happier and workers more productive, and thereby the economy would be improved. Proponents developed, in the process, many principles of modern city planning.[14]

To progressive San Antonians it was obvious that to join the ranks of a modern Kansas City, Denver, Seattle, even Dallas, San Antonio needed a stately civic center, parks and boulevard systems. Streets needed to be paved, billboards restrained, trees planted, playgrounds established—and the perplexing case of the dismal riverbed had to be solved. As elsewhere, local advocates knew that the improvements could be paid for only through municipal bonds and that the ability to get those bonds approved could come only through political reform. Political action became part of the agenda.

Soon a formidable number of San Antonians, led by recent arrivals, launched perhaps the most broadly targeted reform movement in the city's history.

A primary goal would have to be unseating tight-fisted Mayor Bryan Callaghan, who had dominated San Antonio politics for twenty-five years. He had kept taxes low and held few bond elections. Callaghan's response to reformers was that the city's growth was about to stop, so the city should not overextend itself with costly obligations. If San Antonians wanted more paved streets, new gas and sewer lines or other amenities, residents could come up with ways to pay for them privately. They would get no help from city hall.[15]

With that, a political reform committee was organized in 1909 and set out to change the city charter. Ward-based aldermen would be replaced with at-large commissioners, each assigned to specific urban services. Reformers pledged to "knock into smithereens the cloud of Callaghanism which has hovered over San Antonio for the past quarter of a century."[16]

A record 80 percent of San Antonio voters turned out for the charter election in February 1911. Of 14,000 votes cast, the proposed charter was defeated by a margin of only 160.[17]

The narrow defeat sent reformers into even higher gear. A host of ad hoc improvement groups arose and began work. A Playground and Recreation Association raised funds to purchase and equip a Buena Vista Street plot as a playground. A Civic Improvement Art League was formed. A Coliseum

In Brackenridge Park, a herd of elk, bottom left, took refuge in the river from a hot summer in 1906, while ladies below chose a site for a picnic. At bottom right, a dam on what became the campus of the University of the incarnate Word created a pond for boating. The postcard scene was sent home by an Irish-born nun with the message "You will find auntie on the steps."

Elk in San Antonio River, at Brackenridge Park. San Antonio, Tex.

San Antonio River - College Grove.
College and Academy of the Incarnate Word. Alamo Heights. San Antonio. Texas.

Residents in the early 1900s continued to be concerned over the dismal appearance of the riverbanks through downtown, as in this scene of the start of Great Bend showing the Twohig House at right and, at left, the rear of buildings fronting Commerce Street.

League began raising funds for a 12,000-seat coliseum. The Woman's Club and the Chamber of Commerce proposed a coordinating Civic Improvement Federation "to promote the health and beauty of the city." The Alamo Film Company planned a movie to show internationally, "giving the widest publicity to the general plan for keeping San Antonio sanitary and attractive." The City Federation of Women's Clubs gained a measure of success against "the billboard nuisance" by persuading city council to pass an ordinance curtailing the growing epidemic of billboards.[18]

In the midst of it all, battle lines were drawn over the very downtown existence of the San Antonio River. On one side were advocates of a dramatically beautified river—even including a river walk—led by progressive citizens and the two daily newspapers. On the other were businessmen armed with an engineering report declaring that the river could be buried in a tunnel beneath downtown. They would convert the former river channel to prime real estate.

River advocates ratcheted up their efforts early in 1911 with the support of both daily newspapers. Editorialized the *Express*: "Few cities possess so great a natural asset as a winding, tree-shaded stream such as the San Antonio River. Its sinuous course through the city . . . elicits the admiration of visitors, even though the stream has dwindled to a sluggish current running through neglected banks over a riverbed covered with slime and silt." But with "its banks beautified, dredged and made a clear, swift stream as it was in 'the old days,' it would be the chief factor in the San Antonio Beautiful."[19]

The river, however, was not making an appealing solution any easier. That summer it went dry not only at the headwaters but also all the way to the city. Deep cracks opened in the dried mud. Runoff from the two breweries kept some water flowing through downtown, but the most visible stretch of the river, between Houston and Commerce streets, was branded one of the worst looking areas of the city. "Day by day," reported the *Light*, "it offends the eyes of thousands of people as they cross the Houston Street bridge."[20]

Opponents of river beautification sensed it was time to strike.

Shortening the path of a declining river had been discussed for years. After the flood in 1903, architect Francis Bowen suggested a new channel cut straight through the heart of the city, eliminating the Great Bend. This would not only improve runoff, "it would do away with a circuitous dirty river as well . . . and give a great deal of space to some better purpose." As time passed, the idea grew in some quarters that the river, by then "little more than a creek," should be "closed up and transformed into a driveway."[21]

In the late summer of 1911, downtown businessmen hungry for new space for development unveiled a study by the young engineer Willard Simpson, commissioned to examine the matter.[22] Simpson concluded that most of the river through downtown could be filled in, and that the river and its floodwaters could be carried through an underground conduit from Travis Street north of downtown past Nueva Street to the south. The ugly stretch between Houston and Commerce streets would disappear, as would the entire Great Bend. Nine high-maintenance bridges, six of them crossing the bend, could be eliminated. A strip of land some seventy feet wide and more than a mile long could be sold for commercial development.[23]

A crew of boys beneath the Navarro Street/Mill Bridge cleaned carriages while giving water an opportunity to expand the wooden wheels and tighten them against the metal rims.

Beautification advocates countered quickly. The number of respected businessmen in their ranks indicated that the business community was hardly unanimous in wanting the river buried. On the evening of September 26, 1911, three dozen citizens gathered at Chamber of Commerce headquarters to organize the San Antonio River Improvement Association. Banker Thomas L. Conroy declared there had to be a way to revive the river, "and it must be found." The president of the City Federation of Women's Clubs, Emma (Mrs. M. J.) Bliem, promised the help of her constituency in beautifying the river. The new River Improvement Association president, hotelier M. B. Hutchins, assured city council that his group had "no intent to inject politics into the movement;" members simply wanted to show that people were "deeply interested" in seeing water back in the river and in having the river cleaned and beautified.[24]

The plan to bury the river faded into the background. Mayor Callaghan approved installation of a fifty-horsepower pump at an abandoned artesian well by the river at the northern end of Brackenridge Park, albeit at no cost to the city. The mayor refused to allow the city to pay for a shelter over the pump and vetoed a $500 prize for plans for a series of dams, floodgates, and flushing devices. He did authorize city laborers to clear fallen trees and undergrowth from the dry upper riverbed.[25]

From the new water level six feet below the surface, 500 gallons a minute were soon being pumped into the riverbed, then 1,000 gallons, then 1,500. The pump ran for two and a half hours at a stretch, then ten, then twenty. Curious San Antonians flocked to the site as water slowly filled the riverbed's deep holes and cracks. Long-dormant springs began to reappear. But the millions of gallons were not reaching the river's downtown banks, nor even a half mile north of Josephine Street, "Page's fishing hole," which nevertheless on its own suddenly brimmed once more with "beautiful blue water."[26]

Miles downstream, farmers who had given up their crops for lost saw water inexplicably fill the two old mission acequias they used. A reporter dispatched to the scene found that it "brought out the greenness and changed the appearance of everything in this valley." Workers said they were too busy harvesting to speculate on the apparent reason, that the water must have flowed through an unknown underground channel starting near Brackenridge Park.[27]

But other than getting some water into the river, reformers were having little luck with their broad agenda against a recalcitrant city hall. City council defeated a street-paving ordinance by a vote of seven to five. A plan to dredge the river and remove accumulated refuse met with familiar equivocations, as did proposals for the city to pay for continued pumping and to dam the river and make a park along its banks within city limits.[28]

Instrumental in establishing the river park in 1913–14 were the city's river commissioner, George Surkey, far left, who supervised plantings and building channel walls. The project was made possible by election in 1911 of a reform mayor, Augustus H. Jones, left.

Suddenly, in mid-1912, halfway through his seventh term in office, Mayor Bryan Callaghan died. Six weeks later, reform candidate Augustus H. Jones, a rancher and financial backer of the new St. Anthony Hotel, was elected mayor. The old political machine was out. The Citizen's League was in.

Mayor Jones wasted little time. Less than two weeks after his inauguration, he took what one newspaper termed "the first big step to make this a City Beautiful and a greater San Antonio." He appointed a City Plan Committee. Boston, Chicago, Denver, Cleveland, and several dozen other cities already had municipal plans. Why shouldn't San Antonio? "San Antonio can be made the most beautiful place in the country," Jones said, "and when that is done there will be a rush of homeseekers from all parts of the country."[29]

To chair the City Plan Committee the mayor picked rising young architect Atlee B. Ayres. Reformer Thomas Conroy was made vice chairman. Members agreed with Civic Improvement League director T. Noah Smith, who insisted, "No complete plan could be adopted that would not include the preserving and beautifying of the river. The river cannot be beautiful through the business district if buildings line its course to the water's edge. . . . No city plan will be complete that does not include space along its banks for flowers, colonnades, pergolas, etc. in addition to the parks and plazas we now have [elsewhere]."[30]

The challenge was understood by River Commissioner George Surkey, who charged that the river, despite city ordinances, "has become a dumping ground." He asked the Plan Committee, "How can the river be kept clean when each day everything from an old whip to a horse blanket is thrown into it?"[31]

Ayres made river beautification his top priority along with upgrading facilities and rescuing dying trees in Brackenridge and San Pedro parks. The day after his appointment he declared the river's width should be made uniform with walls, its banks terraced and planted with flowers and trees. There were to be footpaths along the river, and they were to be lighted at night. Concrete bridges "built along classic lines" would eliminate the maintenance costs of iron bridges. The project would be like those "carried out with a wonderfully gratifying effect throughout Europe."[32]

Four days later, the committee unanimously endorsed a plan unveiled by one of its members, Harvey L. Page, another leading San Antonio architect, who proposed a system of concrete slabs to line the riverbed plus dams and monumental bridges. The *Express* endorsed Page's proposals with enthusiasm: "The San Antonio River may again be the pride of all San Antonio, and this stream may be made the most unique in the United States. . . . The famous canal of Venice will not compare with the San Antonio River, and tourists will come thousands of miles to see this city and this stream." Predicted one headline: "City Beautiful In Sight."[33]

In the first months of the Augustus Jones administration, it seemed hard not to get carried away over the reforms seeming to lie just ahead. Instead of quibbling over costs, the council summarily appropriated $1,000 to restore a pump beside the river in Brackenridge Park. Harvey Page and two others went to work on beautifying the river below the Mill Bridge. T. N. Smith took charge of a committee to reform the structure of city government. For a master plan, the City Plan Committee recommended hiring George E. Kessler, one of the nation's leading planners and City Beautiful advocates, then at work on plans for Kansas City and Dallas. A $6,000 public fund was set up to pay his fee. Mayor Jones contributed the first $50.[34]

True to his promise, soon after taking office Augustus Jones authorized the first major beautification project on the San Antonio River. It would be carried out by the new river commissioner, George Surkey, a Missouri-born one-time railroad fireman, engineer, and roundhouse foreman who had been a city councilman before going into real estate. With city funds, Surkey began a version of Page's plan, scaled down in scope and cost despite the initial excitement. Low concrete-covered rock walls—dubbed the "Surkey Sea Walls"—established a uniform width for the downtown channel. Next would come sodding and planting. Surkey sought a new artesian well to double the river's flow.[35]

The city considered straightening the river at opposite ends of downtown. Where the southern leg of the Great Bend doubled back to define Bowen's Island, a developer got permission to dig a cutoff channel to eliminate part of the switchback. The old section would remain filled with water as "a large natatorium and

River beautification projects proposed during the municipal reform enthusiasm of 1911 anticipated the completed River Walk by three decades.

London-born Alfred Giles, already one of San Antonio's best-known architects, envisioned the overgrown river between Houston and Commerce streets as a landscaped promenade, with sidewalks on both sides and boats filled with tourists on the waters. The *Light* praised his drawing as showing "in a striking manner how easily one of the ugliest spots in the city can be converted into one of the most attractive."

Harvey L. Page, who earlier practiced architecture in his native Washington, D.C., and in Chicago, made a detailed proposal for a thirteen-mile stretch of the river. To line the riverbed, Page suggested interlocking, "indestructible" reinforced concrete slabs four inches thick, four feet in width and eight feet in height. Their slope toward the channel's center would create a faster current and speed floodwaters through the city. Page estimated the panels could be built on site and hoisted into place for no more than the cost of a sidewalk of similar size. Dams to maintain the water level would include small locks for dredge boats to maintain "an

absolutely sanitary stream" and "do away with all chances of breeding disease."

In addition, streets crossing the river would get decorative concrete bridges. Benches would turn the banks into "a vast park," while "at night myriads of electric bulbs will shine from the trees while Mexicans dressed in the garb of Aztec Indians will paddle canoes, filled with tourists. . . . [and] stopping at picturesque mission landings for refreshments. . . . Firefly lights playing in the trees and in the shrubbery along the banks, with here and there a moonlight effect from a larger lamp, . . . [will] make the San Antonio River a bit of fairyland and unlike anything in the world." Page estimated his plan would cost no more than $1 million—$25.3 million today—and could be repaid by canoe concession fees. As an added benefit, the value of taxable private riverside property would rise.

Similar concepts came up, notably one illustrated by James N. Converse for real estate man Alvah B. Davis. It envisioned lighted sidewalks twelve feet wide on both sides of the river between Houston and St. Mary's streets, a walkway of the sort Davis accurately foresaw would make river-level frontage at least as valuable as frontage on the streets above.

A flurry of plans in 1912 suggested how an enhanced river might look. Architect Alfred Giles foresaw walks along landscaped banks, left, while Harvey Page suggested a river bottom of interlocking concrete slabs and monumental concrete bridges, center. Developer Alvah Davis's plan, right, recommended wide, lighted sidewalks shaded by palms.

wading pool" for the Sans Souci Amusement Park, to be "one of the south's most elaborate and best-equipped." The erstwhile riverbank would become a beach.[36]

Not as well received was the proposal by developer Paul Knittel to shorten a circuitous bend just north of Travis Park downtown and gain title to the former riverbed for the proposed coliseum. Knittel also dared to suggest eliminating the Great Bend, not with a buried conduit but with a canal following the course originally planned for the north-south conduit. Said he: "Just think of the improvement that would follow the filling up of the riverbed all round that long sweep that channel now follows."[37]

Less than eight months after it began, the Jones administration ended with the unexpected death of the 53-year-old mayor. But river planning went on. Mayor Pro Tem Albert Steves left office nearly two months later having advocated both continuing beautification of the river and a dam on Olmos Creek both for flood control and as a reservoir.[38]

Despite the absence of the popular mayor, the Citizen's League made a clean sweep in the next election, winning every council seat in a victory seen as a mandate for a long-awaited bond issue. The mayor-elect, former district attorney Clinton L. Brown, traveled to study municipal improvements in Kansas City, Dallas and Fort Worth, and returned to advocate such upgrades in San Antonio. A $3.5 million bond package soon passed, including provision for new bridges over the river.

As River Commissioner George Surkey continued work on his "sea walls," though, his budget request was cut by nearly half. He ran out of material in mid-1913. Surkey gained a new supply by recycling stones from buildings being shortened in the widening of Commerce Street, once the city's main thoroughfare, as its businessmen tried to catch up with the appeal of the newer and wider Houston Street. Commerce Street was being broadened by shearing off fronts of buildings along the southern side of the street and building new facades several feet back.[39]

Achievement of San Antonio Beautiful goals was meeting with varying degrees of success. The commission form of city government was adopted, but a city planner was not hired. An irrigation system in San Pedro Park saved its ancient trees, and a new pump started its springs flowing again and raised the lake to its old level. But the Boulevard Committee was unsuccessful in getting a mile-long San Pedro Boulevard constructed along the banks of the creek southward from the springs nearly to Houston Street.[40]

Then, during the last three months of 1913, San Antonians were distracted from work on Commerce Street and the river, and from just about everything else, when not one but two major floods sent water up into downtown streets for the first time in ten years.

 Heavy rains began creating problems on the last day of September 1913. Cities in central and east Texas were isolated by floodwaters and railroad bridges were washed out, disrupting train service into San Antonio. On October 1, a record twenty-four-hour rainfall of 7.08 inches sent waters of the San Antonio River and San Pedro and Alazan creeks rising two to four feet an hour.[41]

Floodwaters rushing south jumped the then-sharp bend below Fourth Street and surged down a straighter path to turn St. Mary's Street into a river through downtown to Nueva Street, where the river channel once again headed

Astonished spectators gathered on the Houston Street Bridge on October 1, 1913 saw floodwaters roiling downstream.

more directly southward. By 2:30 p.m. on October 1 St. Mary's Street was "a surging mass of muddy waters," filling basements of homes and businesses along the way.

At the main downtown corner of St. Mary's and Houston streets, water poured into the basement of the Gunter Hotel from sidewalk grates and air shafts "with a roar like that of Niagara Falls." Within half an hour the hotel's boiler room was flooded, electric lights were out and the hotel's barbershop, wine room and baggage rooms were inundated. As water in the

Sightseers lined Crockett Street to watch Great Bend floodwaters rise up Tobin Terrace below them and into buildings of St. Mary's College on the far side.

basement rose within inches of the floor of the lobby overhead, lobby furniture was moved upstairs.[42]

A call from Mayor Clinton Brown to the commander at Fort Sam Houston met with an immediate response. Within thirty minutes, a cavalry troop and field artillery unit with wagons and ambulances were on the scene. Fire Chief Phil Wright abandoned his auto and a buggy and then wore out three horses as he directed the rescue effort and made rescues himself. Marooned families got on the phone to city hall, giving the mayor and city officials based there "a mighty big job." In one of the more unusual rescue efforts, a wire net was stretched above the dam forming West End Lake—now Woodlawn Lake—to keep hundreds of fish from being swept downstream.[43]

Floodwaters held their crest of three feet at Houston and St. Mary's streets for two hours, then began to subside. Crowds watched from bridges and individuals waded and romped in water-filled streets. Steam fire engines began pumping out basements. Total damage was estimated at $250,000. Despite frequent reports of drownings there were only four casualties in Bexar County, a mother and her three young children swept away while fleeing their home far downstream near San José mission.[44]

San Antonio had hardly recovered when, two months later, heavy rain began falling across south and central Texas. Though rainfall was lighter than in October, the ground was already saturated by two weeks of rain, and damage was more severe.[45]

In San Antonio, rain fell gently through the evening of December 3, then at one o'clock the next morning turned into an hour-long downpour. Rainfall slowed, then intensified again. High waters coursing down Olmos Creek caught the attention of residents of Alamo Heights, who telephoned warnings downstream to the fire and police chiefs. Fort Sam Houston soldiers again were called in. Two companies of the Texas National Guard were mobilized.[46]

As in October, the San Antonio River overflowed its banks to take the shortcut down St. Mary's Street. Many basements along the way had been left empty since the October flood, and others were emptied quickly.

Floodwaters in October 1913 turned St. Mary's Street into a river. Clockwise from top, boys caught fish beside the Gunter Hotel, streetcars slowed at the Houston Street intersection, a traffic jam occurred at Travis Street and horses galloped past the Victoria Hotel.

In October the Gunter Hotel had prided itself in staying open by moving its lobby and restaurant upstairs—even though water ultimately hadn't reached above the basement—and regained power by running a line from the generator at the St. Anthony Hotel, on higher ground nearby. This time the higher water knocked out electricity at the St. Anthony as well. The St. Anthony lit "hundreds of candles" in the lobby and remained open. But the Gunter, with water this time above its basement and running into the ground floor, had to call horse-drawn buses to evacuate guests.[47]

When the deluge of October 1, 1913 ceased, floodwaters rippled down St. Mary's Street past the Gunter Hotel, above, and created a lake at St. Mary's and Travis streets across from the Telephone Building and Fire Station No. 2, above right. The San Antonio Fire Department used a steam pumper to drain basements and pump the water back into the river.

The only rail line still able to provide regular service was the San Antonio, Uvalde & Gulf, which did not serve flood-stricken areas. Several carloads of newsprint destined for the *Express* could not reach San Antonio on the Southern Pacific, forcing the newspaper to print its December 6 edition and part of the next day's on the pink newsprint normally reserved for the sports section.[48]

December 1913 flooding caused 177 deaths and damage exceeding $8.5 million throughout south and central Texas. In San Antonio, lessons of the October flood were fresh and the city was better prepared. The only drowning victim in city or county was a man swept off Culebra Road and carried down Leon Creek. Estimated losses downtown did not exceed $50,000, though county bridges suffered extensive damage.[49]

Less than a year later, however, a third flood—on October 23, 1914—left nine San Antonians drowned and 2,000 homeless. That flood, sparing downtown, centered to the west on the watersheds of San Pedro, Alazan and Apache creeks. Four of the dead were Mrs. Katrina Liebe, 38, and her four children—the youngest born the day before—swept away after their house toppled into Alazan Creek. Rescue attempts were hampered by tangles of barbed wire, debris and live electrical wires until the house hit an obstacle in the torrent and disintegrated. Wagonloads of food and clothing headed for a clinic on South Laredo Street, where County Judge James R. Davis was directing relief work.[50]

After all the floods came the usual talk of building a dam at the end of Olmos Creek. By this time, however, it was dawning on local officials that outside professional help might be needed. An engineer already working on the city's sewer system, Samuel M. Gray of Providence, Rhode Island, was asked to investigate

In December 1913 floodwaters again surged down St. Mary's Street, overflowing onto Travis Street at top left and top right before reaching the St. Mary's Street Bridge, in background at top center. Spectators, above, viewed the scene on College Street.

Cavalrymen next to the Gunter Hotel kept an eye on traffic able to negotiate Houston Street while the Gunter evacuated guests. Furniture had already been moved upstairs from the hotel lobby as guests gathered and then departed in horse-drawn buses.

MOVING PEOPLE FROM GUNTER HOTEL, DEC. 4. 1913.

the situation and make a report. He submitted one a month later, acknowledging the problems but concluding that he did not have sufficient data to reach sound conclusions and more study would be needed. The *Light*'s disapproval of Gray's $800 fee did not give the city much encouragement to pay for an in-depth study any time soon.[51]

As the river returned to its banks after the floods, River Commissioner George Surkey set about repairing his riverbank walls. He had lost tools, a temporary work bridge was washed away and the stone retaining wall beside St. Mary's College had to be replaced altogether. As completion neared, sod, shrubs, and palm trees were set in along the narrow strips between the new channel and high banks below street level.[52]

Work also resumed on widening Commerce Street and removing its landmark iron bridge, reassembled to cross the river downstream at Johnson Street. Excavations for the concrete bridge turned up a small brass cannon and other military artifacts immediately assumed to date from the siege of the Alamo.[53]

Plans were upgraded with help from Italian-born sculptor Pompeo Coppini. The bridge was widened on either side by street-level alcoves, supported by pillars decorated with concrete reliefs to be viewed from the new river park below. For the northern alcove, Coppini designed a bronze statue of a seated Augustus Jones, though it was never cast and the alcove remained empty. For the southern alcove, Coppini's student Waldine Tauch designed in imitation granite a figure called "The First Inhabitant," which wore a head-dress and held "two fountains of bubbling water" to represent the gift of the river below. On the alcoves' far corners, cast concrete pilasters tapered upward to morph into the relief of an Indian's face. Clusters of lighted globes atop each pilaster illuminated the bridge.[54]

More heavy rains in October 1914 centered over the watersheds of San Pedro, Alazan and Apache creeks, devastating poor neighborhoods in western San Antonio and causing nine drownings.

On November 21, 1914, daylong festivities along Commerce Street hailed completion of the street and river park projects. Nearly 50,000 San Antonians were reported as gathering in the evening for ceremonies at the new bridge, dedicated as Jones Bridge in memory of the late mayor. Celebrants cheered as Mayor Clinton Brown recognized River Commissioner George Surkey for his work. The touch of a switch lit up the newly beautified and channeled riverbanks, extending from the bridge a block south to Market Street and north around the Great Bend and beyond to Houston Street. The colored lights strung across the river were a project of the two-year-old Rotary Club of San Antonio. Rotarians presented the city with twelve pairs of swans to grace the river.[55]

In modernizing its streets San Antonio was playing catch-up with other cities, but in beautifying its river San Antonio was out in front. The Chamber of Commerce was not shy in making that known. It commissioned noted scenic artist Herbert Barnard, who had just moved to town, to do an illustration of the river park for the front of the chamber's new promotion booklet, for 1915. For perhaps the first time in local tourism history, the expected front cover illustration of the Alamo was relegated to the back.

The chamber's booklet was addressed "To you who would escape the rigors of winter with its snow and ice attended by bad colds, danger of pneumonia and other discomforts." San Antonio, "unlike the average American city of a hundred

One of the last views of the 1880 Commerce Street Bridge before it was moved elsewhere included, below in left foreground, a newly constructed park wall, the river segment behind it soon to be filled and the new bank landscaped. At right the bridge was gone, as preparations began for a wider bridge of concrete as part of the 1913–14 widening of Commerce Street.

A sculpture of "The First Inhabitant" wearing a headdress and holding two drinking fountains adorned the alcove on the south side of the Jones Bridge, dedicated at Commerce Street with the River Park in November 1914. The decorative corner lights disappeared in the 1950s.

thousand people," was the best place to escape to, now not the least because of its winding river, "its blue waters rippling between banks that are being parked into green esplanades of flowering shrubs and plants."[56]

Even before the park was completed, riverbanks below the heavily-walked Houston Street Bridge were hosting the first river-level businesses, however short lived. A steel stairway led down from the street to a billiards parlor in the basement of the Book Building, at the southwest corner of the bridge and river. It was later upgraded to the Riverside Athletic and Social Club. Beside it, rowboats and increasingly popular motorboats were rented "by the trip, hour or day." By 1920 the space was used by The Coffee House, the first bistro at the river level.

Down a wooden stairway across the river, the Blue Bird Boat Company opened as an agent for Michigan's Detroit Boat Company, a major motorboat manufacturer and distributor established in 1906. Blue Bird rented boats and canoes and took reservations for "private launch parties."

Above, in 1918 the street-level Riverside Restaurant gained the first construction specifically to address a beautified river. From its street-level interior, a vaguely Oriental-style enclosed balcony was built safely above the usual flood line so diners could view the newly landscaped banks. When the former restaurant building was razed for Hotel Valencia, the balcony, with its tile roof and ornamental concrete railing, was detached and mostly reconstructed at a lower level in 2003 as an outdoor feature of the hotel's Acenar Restaurant.[57]

Capitalizing on the appeal of the river park, the Riverside Restaurant at the Houston Street Bridge built a balcony so diners could overlook the river. On the other side at the river level of the Book Building by 1920 was The Coffee House, which catered to domino players.

As word spread of San Antonio's beautified river, *Architectural Record* sent a writer from New York, I. T. Frary, to assess the project. His report in the April 1919 issue summarized the essence and import of what had been achieved against so many odds.[58]

"Few municipalities recognize the possibilities for civic improvement which are to be found in even a small stream of water," Frary wrote. "Fewer still develop these possibilities when they are recognized. Occasionally there is a city, however, in which a stream is appreciated and is regarded as something more than part of a drainage system. Among these may be recorded the name of San Antonio, Texas.

"To be sure, the stream which San Antonians dignify as a river would be referred to as a creek or brook in a more humid climate, but streams of any size or variety are not sufficiently common in the great Southwest to be trifled with. Even so, the majority of cities would fail to recognize the desirability even of a little stream writhing erratically through the downtown district and withholding from commercial use many acres of valuable real estate. The average City Council would have built an intercepting sewer, the stream would have disappeared from

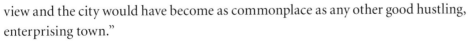

A crowd gathered along the Houston Street Bridge, top left, to watch a parade on the river. Below the bridge, boats could be rented at the lower level of the Book Building, left, or, above, across the river at the Blue Bird Boat Company, an agent for Michigan's Detroit Boat Company.

view and the city would have become as commonplace as any other good hustling, enterprising town."

The writer praised San Antonio leaders for their foresight, which—unknown at the time—would prove vital to preparing the palette for the River Walk. Easy though it would have been simple to bury their "tiny" river, officials "neither condemned it to solitary confinement in a brick sewer nor straightened its course,"

This aerial view looking west over the Great Bend in about 1920 was taken from an angle close to that of the top of today's HemisFair Tower. The river park's channel walls turn into the bend at top right of center. The park continues around the sharp corner just out of view below far right center, then extends beneath the concrete Commerce Street Bridge and the iron Market Street Bridge. The park ends just before the sharp turn enfolding waterworks buildings inside the next bend.

Beyond, past the bridges of Villita, Navarro and South St. Mary's streets, the river makes a U-turn around the open peninsula called Bowen's Island before turning left out of view. The buildings of La Villita cluster below left center.

Graphic artists were quick to portray the newly landscaped river. Edwin C. Burritt designed sheet music, far left, for a song titled "San Antonio" by publicist J. Frank Davis and musicians Alva Davis and his wife. Herbert Bernard did the cover for a 1915 Chamber of Commerce tourism booklet, center. E. C. Prixotto sketched a boat passing beneath the Commerce Street Bridge, above, to accompany his October 1916 article on the city in *Scribner's Magazine.*

but instead allowed it to "follow its own sweet way, gave it a wider bed than it demanded, and then made of this bed an attractive little parkway contentedly following the stream's windings and insinuating itself into the most unexpected corners of the downtown district."

Simplicity and serenity were the park's signatures. "No attempt has been made to produce elaborate effects," wrote Frary. "Its banks have been simply grassed over; trees form archways above its course, and flowers here and there brighten it up and add a touch of charm and color, although with but little more of sophistication than nature would employ. Winding about as it does, it passes under a myriad of bridges, each bridge affording the passersby delightful vistas of fresh, green foliage and quiet waters, a welcome relief from the torrid heat and scorching sun of southern summer days."

Stunned San Antonians take in the flood devastation
around the St. Mary's Street Bridge and St. Mary's Catholic
Church on the morning of Saturday, September 10, 1921.

· 3 ·
The Flood of 1921

Winds gusting to ninety-five miles per hour lashed the eastern coast of Mexico as the second tempest of the season hit south of Tampico on September 7, 1921. Inland, as the tempest swerved sharply north, its intensity lowered to that of a tropical storm, then weakened again. In the night it swung northeastward into Texas near Laredo and headed directly for San Antonio, still packing high winds with violent, heavy thunderstorms.[1]

Hurricane watches were as yet unknown, and San Antonians seemed blissfully unaware that such a storm was heading their way. They did have a vague idea that something resembling the massive storm of 1819 could happen again, for only nine months earlier a professional flood prevention study had warned that such a disaster "is just as likely to occur next year as at any other time."[2]

After the two major floods of 1913 and another less than a year later, city hall had dithered over homegrown proposals to address the flooding issue. There was as yet no state or federal funding to help such efforts, and traditionally tight-fisted San Antonio officials were loath to investigate what a true solution might cost. But finally, after the river nearly overflowed its banks in 1918 and yet again in 1919, in 1920 the city hired a top national engineering firm for advice. Officials moved forward with due speed on the recommendations.

But the price of the earlier years of hesitation was the greatest cataclysm in San Antonio's history.

Since the two floods of 1913, and one less than a year later, local engineers had steadily advanced ideas for dealing with floodwaters that surged down from Olmos Creek. One engineer recommended slowing them with "a wall pierced by openings" between two low bluffs across the eastern end of Olmos Basin, now the route of Hildebrand Avenue. Another urged digging a channel to send floodwaters around downtown—not westward to Alazan Creek, as proposed in the past, but eastward to Salado Creek. Based "unequivocally upon his record as a drainage engineer," the proposer of this plan dismissed straightening the river channel as "idle talk and out of the question." The channel was "a product of nature," and tampering with it, he said, would only make matters worse.[3]

Another engineer, E. A. Giraud, thought such a channel to Salado Creek was both unnecessary and impractical, since it would require a cut a half-mile deep and a tunnel more than a mile long. Giraud did agree that straightening the river would be "almost impracticable" financially and would "destroy the natural beauty of the river." He suggested instead "a monolithic concrete dam" between two high bluffs near the mouth of Olmos Basin. Former City Engineer Aaron Pancoast thought this proposal "the best by far" of any plan yet advanced.[4]

While these engineers would address floodwaters near their source, others worried more about fixing overflows downstream. Encroachments and obstructions should be removed, streets raised, bridges made higher so they would not become dams. River Commissioner George Surkey wanted an underground spillway from Navarro Street to Nueva Street to carry overflow beneath downtown. Fire Chief Phil Wright thought there should be two underground spillways, one starting at St. Mary's Street and the other along a northern portion of Navarro Street then known as Romana Street.[5]

Occasional droughts shifted attention to the opposite question—how to deal with the problems of less water. Erosion was silting the channel above the river park. In the absence of heavy rains, the channel had to be flushed out again with fire hoses. The city engineer, Norwegian immigrant Hans R. F. Helland, thought silting from erosion could be stopped by lining the banks for the five blocks from Navarro Street to Houston Street with twenty-two-foot-high retaining walls of pine planks with cypress pilings. Suction pumps could remove whatever silt made it into the channel. Parks and Sanitation Commissioner Ray Lambert agreed, adding that climbing vines could turn those walls into "an object of beauty." But bids in 1917 came in too high, and the plan was scrapped.[6]

Wooden retaining walls were built north of Pecan Street in 1920 in an attempt to combat flooding.

Two years later, several flood issues were addressed in a successful, wide-ranging bond issue that included $200,000 for "widening, deepening, altering and changing" the river channel to prevent flooding. Lumber walls were built the next year along the winding one-block segment between Travis and Pecan streets. Other funds authorized new bridges and a straight channel to eliminate the convoluted bend at the northern edge of downtown, permitting construction of the long-awaited Municipal Auditorium on the site of the bend.[7]

But while lumber walls and a straighter channel might reduce some problems, city commissioners finally had to admit that they alone could not accurately sort through the surfeit of proposals, counter-proposals and random projects and half-projects to cure major flooding. It was time to call in experts from out of town. On June 9, 1920, the city signed on with the nationally recognized Boston firm Metcalf & Eddy. Partner Leonard Metcalf was a native of Galveston and knew San Antonio well, having done four technical reports for the San Antonio Water Works Company.

Boston engineer Leonard Metcalf walked "practically every foot" of the San Antonio River and San Pedro Creek through San Antonio in 1920 as his firm prepared flood control recommendations.

Engineers led by Metcalf and an associate, Charles W. Sherman, spent nearly six months studying local conditions and meeting with officials from Mayor Sam C. Bell to River Engineer Albert Marbach to Citizens Flood Prevention Committee President L. J. Hart. City data on the river and its tributaries was considered "too limited to enable safe conclusions," so the engineers pored over U.S. Weather Bureau and U.S. Geological Survey data. They walked "practically every foot" of the river through the city as well as the length of San Pedro Creek, and explored the usually dry drainage basins of Alazan, Martinez, and Apache creeks.[8]

On December 6, 1920, Metcalf & Eddy presented city commissioners with a 348-page report. There were thirty tables of data and sixty diagrams, drawings, and maps. Maintenance may have become more regular, and the lumber retaining walls helped, but the report concluded the basic problems remained: the narrow width of the river, lack of a dam and riverbed obstructions. Measures already taken would not prevent another flood like that of December 1913, which sent 6,000 cubic feet of water per second through downtown. The greater danger was a hundred-year flood like that of 1819, which could deliver a brutal 22,000 cubic feet or more per second.[9]

The Boston engineers concluded that building a new channel to carry flood-waters through downtown was impractical and unnecessary. Instead, the existing channel could be improved by eliminating six bends. That would shorten the river by more than a mile and a half and increase its capacity to 12,000 cubic feet per second, twice the volume of the second 1913 flood. The remaining waters of a hundred-year flood could be held back in the retaining basin of a dam between the high bluffs near the mouth of Olmos Creek.[10]

Contrary to later misconceptions, Metcalf & Eddy did not recommend a cut-off channel to eliminate the Great Bend, either above or below ground. Metcalf & Eddy were given Willard Simpson's 1911 engineering report recommending an underground cutoff, which would allow the bend to be filled in and developed. The Boston engineers at first agreed with that proposal, but by the time they finished

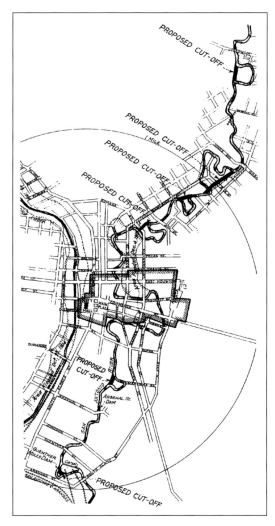

Six circuitous bends in the San Antonio River were marked for elimination between Josephine and South Alamo streets in a flood prevention plan completed in 1920.

had concluded that such a conduit would be inadequate during hundred-year floods and, in any event, was not cost effective.[11]

Rather than eliminating the Great Bend, Metcalf & Eddy recommended simply deepening the entire channel, including the bend. The channel was to be a standard width of seventy feet, flanked by steep masonry walls and grassy banks. Although engineers acknowledged the appeal of landscaping, they recommended eliminating all shrubs and trees, which "not only tend to arrest the current but also, by catching sand and gravel, to make barriers and shoals in the stream."[12]

The cost of the entire project was estimated at $4 million, today's equivalent of $46.5 million. City officials swallowed hard. But they adopted the report, making clear that raising such an amount immediately "would be impossible in the light of other urgent needs of the city." It could, however, be stretched over ten or twenty years.[13]

City officials began working on the proposals even before the plan was formally adopted. In November 1920 they began negotiating with C. H. Guenther & Son's Pioneer Flour Mills on the report's top priority, eliminating Guenther's picturesque upper mill and dam that narrowed and blocked the river across from the U.S. Arsenal south of downtown. In March the city advertised for bids on another high priority, eliminating the horseshoe bend on the future site of Municipal Auditorium.[14]

By then it was spring, and fiesta was approaching. The Fiesta de San Jacinto Association made its annual request for a permit to decorate trees along the river. This time the city replied that, since all trees along the banks were going to be cut down to clear the channel, there would be "nothing to decorate but the walls." The permit was denied.[15]

The sudden realization that the river park's carefully planted trees and shrubs were about to be cleared away hit San Antonians like a bombshell.

On March 31, 1921, a wave of protest swept the city, from "men and women in all walks of life." Mayor Sam Bell and Parks Commissioner Ray Lambert were besieged with irate visitors and indignant phone calls. "It would be a disaster to take away the trees from the banks of the San Antonio River," one protester told the *Express*. "Nothing short of a calamity," said another. Declared a third: "I think that the man who would lift an ax to remove the beautiful old trees and landmarks along the San Antonio River should be ostracized from the community."

When Lambert was summoned to address a public meeting on the subject at the Woman's Club the next afternoon, the mayor and the parks commissioner hastily announced that they had decided not to remove the trees after all.[16]

The Boston engineers had emphasized that a flood control project should start at once: "We doubt if the citizens realize the ruinous loss which would result to-day, with the present condition of the river channels, from such a flood as that of a century ago. When such a flood will recur, no man can say." But since such floods generally occur on an average of once every hundred years, and since it had already been a hundred years since the last such flood in San Antonio, "a very great flood ought to be expected in the near future," they warned. "This disastrous flood is just as likely to occur next year as at any other time."[17]

Nine months after that report was issued, the remains of the season's second hurricane zeroed in on San Antonio.

Advance showers on the night of Thursday, September 8, 1921, broke a dry spell of two months. San Antonio's parched earth absorbed most of the first rainfall. Occasional hard showers followed early the next day.[18]

The main body of the storm hit Friday afternoon. Severe thunderstorms broke out at 6 p.m. "Lightning flashed almost continuously, and the thunder boomed and reverberated throughout the heavens," reported the *Light*. After three hours the thunderstorms ended and the rain's intensity began to ebb. The river was four feet from the top of the plank retaining wall near Pecan Street, and residents went to bed thinking all was well. Those who stayed awake expected to see at most a flood like those in 1913.[19]

Rain over Olmos Creek's watershed, however, had been twice as heavy as that over San Antonio. At 9 p.m. Olmos Creek began to overflow its banks. As its waters surged into the San Antonio River, the river began rising one foot every five minutes in Brackenridge Park. More than 100 tourist campers scurried for higher ground.

At 11:30 p.m., waters from the Olmos reached the Fourth Street/Lexington Avenue Bridge at the northern edge of downtown, where the river was already two feet above its banks. An hour later, water there was up nearly three feet more.[20]

At midnight Saturday, September 10, the river swelled over its banks at the sharp switchback north of downtown and onto St. Mary's Street. Within twelve minutes water was swirling more than six feet deep at the Travis Street intersection and spreading outward, turning six other north-south streets into auxiliary flood channels. At. St. Mary's and Pecan streets, water rushed through a frame building used by Travis Park Methodist Church while its sanctuary was being renovated, carrying away the pastor's desk and church records. Up on Travis Park at St. Mark's Episcopal Church, a block south of a river bend, water rose to four feet in the parish

As rainfall intensified on September 9, 1921, by 9 p.m. streams were overflowing their banks, and crested some five hours later. The extent of floodwaters within city limits was mapped in green by the U.S. Geological Survey. Along the San Antonio River, right, inundated areas extended six miles from the northern tip of Brackenridge Park, top right, through downtown and past Mission Concepción, where the river met San Pedro Creek. Flooding is also shown along four creeks—from left, Apache, Alazan, Martinez and San Pedro.

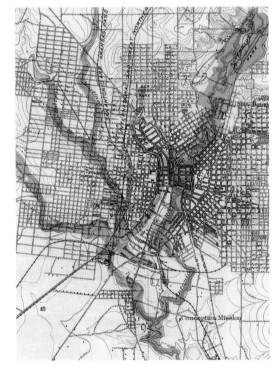

Water flowed peacefully through the river park north of the Houston Street Bridge until a deluge on the night of September 9, 1921 sent a torrent over its banks, right, as high as the oil smear below the "Driverless" sign above the railing at right of center in this photo, taken at 6:30 the next morning.

hall's basement auditorium and to six feet in the choir room, soaking vestments and sheet music. At St. Mary's and Houston streets, water in the Gunter Hotel lobby reached nearly to the mezzanine.[21]

At half past midnight floodwaters drowned boiler fires at the Market Street waterworks, shutting off most of the city's water supply. An hour later, water topped the walls of the power plant two blocks away, beside the river on Villita Street. Workers threw the switches, shutting off the city's electricity. Then the telephone system went down. Telegraph lines were out. The *Light*'s Associated Press wire still functioned, allowing news to come in and be sent out. Otherwise, San Antonio was cut off from the rest of the world. As word about the *Light*'s connection got out, residents lined up to plead with the newspaper to send messages to their relatives on the AP wire.[22]

Quantities of oil—most stored in open vats and tanks by the waterworks and two breweries up the river—were flushed downstream, smearing high water marks on walls. Floodwaters carried a mass of debris—bedsprings, automobiles, furniture, splintered lumber, washtubs, pianos. As water rushed well above the street level of bridges, refuse wedged behind trusses, creating dams that backed up water even higher.[23]

Basement floors buckled from water seeping up through the ground. High water burst through storefront plate glass windows. A stack of rugs and furniture was swept across Main Avenue from Stowers Furniture Company. Lunch counters and food supplies were pushed into soggy, oil-stained jumbles at the backs of the Saratoga and Metropolitan restaurants.[24]

Screams and cries echoed in the darkness. Police and firemen attempted rescues. City officials put in a distress call to Maj. Gen. John M. Hines, commander

Bridges became barriers for flood-carried debris, acting as dams and raising the level of water upstream. Shown are the bridges clockwise from above, at South St. Mary's, Commerce, St.Mary's and Romana streets.

of the U.S. Army's Second Division at Fort Sam Houston's Camp Travis. By midnight, hundreds of khaki-clad soldiers of the Second Engineers, First and Twentieth Infantry regiments and Twelfth and Fifteenth Field Artillery units were arriving. Army trucks rumbled to a stop and troops leapt out, formed in columns of twos and headed for flooded areas. Cavalrymen plunged into the water on horseback to reach victims.[25]

With the help of flashlights, smoky kerosene lanterns and automobile headlights, at least 500 rescues were made. In a backyard on King William Street, one woman made it to the roof of an outbuilding and shouted for help for three hours until rescuers arrived. A twelve-year-old boy clung to a tree on South Flores Street with a five-year-old on his shoulders until both were rescued. Strong swimmers pulled out struggling victims as best they could.

The howling of their fox terrier awakened the Harry Liecks, who found their two-year-old in a bed floating on a rear sleeping porch. The family got upstairs. On Fourth Street, a man barely escaped from his apartment as part of the house was swept into the river. His wife and child were nowhere to be seen. Searching downstream, an hour later he heard cries from remains of a house lodged against a railing of the Navarro Street Bridge. He broke through the roof to find his missing wife and child safe on a mattress floating within one foot of the ceiling.[26]

Residential areas hardest hit were the poor neighborhoods beside San Pedro Creek and Alazan Creek and its tributary Apache and Martinez creeks in western San Antonio. Alazan Creek went down a relatively steep grade, making its flow all the more forceful as the Alazan and its tributaries flooded simultaneously and rushed into San Pedro Creek. The scene became especially chaotic around the South Flores Street bridge, where San Pedro Creek nears its confluence with the San Antonio River two miles south of downtown. Dozens of homes were carried away. One family in the 1000 block of Nogalitos Street believed the safest place was inside their small home. Would-be rescuers scattered as a wall of water came crashing down, sweeping two small boys and a young girl outside the house, never to be seen again. Casualty estimates ranged as high as 250.[27]

The river crested at about 2 a.m., some three hours after the storm moved on to end twenty-three hours of steady rainfall. A three-quarter-square-mile area of downtown was submerged under two to twelve feet of water. Nearly seven inches of rain had fallen on the city. The Olmos Creek drainage area got as many as fourteen inches. Military engineers estimated the velocity of floodwaters at 22,000 cubic feet per second, the precise flow engineers nine months earlier had predicted for such a flood.[28]

As the storm headed northeast past Austin it met a high-pressure area backing in from East Texas, causing the storm to intensify and abruptly dissipate near Taylor. That town reeled beneath 23.11 inches of rain, the largest twenty-four-hour rainfall yet recorded in the United States. Unofficial reports indicated thirty-six inches fell during the same period at nearby Thrall.[29]

As dawn broke over San Antonio, receding waters revealed a frightful scene. Pictures snapped after the 1913 floods show smiling residents wading or dunking themselves in floodwaters and wagons with cheerful drivers surging onward. This time, few smiled for the camera. Stunned San Antonians seen through the

Devastation from floodwaters on Alazan, Apache and Martinez creeks in western San Antonio included houses swept away or wrenched off their foundations or, bottom left, caught by the International & Great Northern Railroad tracks.

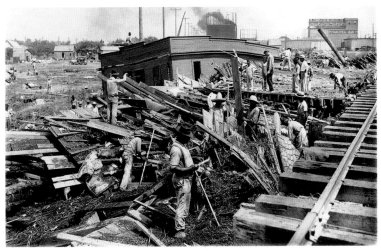

La Tragedia de la Inundacion

José Quiroga, owner of the Librería de Quiroga on Dolorosa Street and publisher of the Spanish language newspaper La Época, *also published a series of booklets of Spanish literature. To these he added* La Tragedia de la Inundacion de San Antonio, Un Recuerdo de la Terrible Catástrofe. *The 64-page anonymous work may have been written by Quiroga himself.*

The "souvenir of the terrible catastrophe" describes the flood and focuses on experiences of families in near western and southwestern San Antonio, where loss of life was greatest. This translated excerpt reports the fate of a family living in "a substantial house" swept away as easily as were homes more poorly constructed.

El Niño Francisco

We begin the drama at nine in the evening. At that hour the Gutierrez family was gathered at its residence at 2425 South Flores Street. Mrs. Anita Gutierrez arose with alarm from her crocheting. When she stood at the door she realized there

La Tragedia de la Inundacion de San Antonio

El arroyo del Alazán enfurecido destruyó todo lo que se interponía a su paso

was danger imminent. A danger that she never would have dreamed. The rear wall of the house came swimming toward them in current that they first thought was simply rainwater but soon realized was from the overflowing Alazan Creek. . . .

They all managed to escape through one of the windows, already in danger of being ripped out of its frame by the waters—Mrs. Gutierrez, the boys Francisco and Eduardo Harms and Mrs. Gutierrez's young daughter, Mrs. Esther Draeger, carrying her nine-month-old child. A house that had been ripped up from God-knows-where foundered in the current; by divine providence each person managed to reach that lifesaver which destiny had brought them.

Suddenly, things took a turn for the worse. The implacable waters did not leave that poor family together for long. An overwhelming wave furiously separated them. Mrs. Anita and her daughter kept fighting against the elements until they reached a tree, where, thanks to the assistance of Mr. Jesus

Cardenas (who was drowning and yelling for his wife) who pulled them up on his shoulders. Thus, forming a ladder, they reached the highest branches of the tree, where they awaited further help.

"Mother," Esther said, "we are safe but my little daughter has drowned. While I was swimming, a house or a piece of a house hit us and pulled away her little body."

"Perhaps my sons have also drowned," the unhappy Mrs. Gutierrez murmured hoarsely, praying to God that she was wrong and that her poor sons had managed to escape the furious torrent as had they.

Doubtless God heard her prayer. Eleven-year-old Francisco felt the waters part his little nephew from his side, and he yelled, "Eduardo, Eduardo, what's happened to you?" The sobbing voice of the small child answered, "I don't know where I am, Francisco, but I do know I'm going to drown."

"Wait," Francisco said. "I'm coming."

Guided through the dense darkness only by voice, the valiant and intrepid Francisco swam until he grabbed onto his nephew's overalls and pulled him onto his back, and transported him to a tree that had been revealed by a lightning bolt. The tree was barely a bush. Even so, Francisco, securing his nephew to his shoulders, held on to it from ten at night (the hour of the catastrophe) until four in the morning, when a rescue brigade passed by. Focusing the light of an electric lantern on the mass that was asking for help, they could perfectly distinguish that on the child's neck was a small human figure.

After these two unfortunate creatures were saved through a thousand difficulties, Francisco's first words were these: "Thank you very much. . . . Could you please save my sister and my mother, who stayed at the house?"

And thus, thanks to the integrity of that child, the same pious rescuer went to the place where the Gutierrez residence had been swallowed by that sea of mud and water. It was just a little further on, at the first light of a foggy dawn, where we found the two weeping women clutching each other. They were lowered from the tree, that refuge where they suffered the most frightening anguish that unfolded throughout that tragic and unforgettable night.

Floodwaters from flood-swollen tributaries in western San Antonio sent San Pedro Creek far over its banks at the South Flores Street Bridge, near where the creek joins the San Antonio River two miles south of downtown. One man drowned when his car was swept off the bridge.

lens after daybreak were making their way carefully along debris-strewn streets, stripped of mesquite paving blocks. They gazed soberly at the destruction. Others stood in food lines awaiting breakfast. As morning wore on, streets were cleared by pushing detritus into piles along curbs. Little could be saved, though there were occasional salvages like the children's chairs belonging to Travis Park Methodist Church found on the awning of the Gunter Hotel.[30]

As many as 1,500 soldiers were at first dismissed to return to their posts. Then looters were discovered picking through department stores and office buildings, the doors torn off by the flood and windows shattered. Called back to duty, the soldiers moved through flooded areas, stood guard, made arrests and kept looting from becoming widespread. One civilian was shot by a soldier guarding a store on South Santa Rosa Street, and later died of his wounds.[31]

Newspapers eventually provided San Antonians with their first general accounts of the tragedy. At the *Express*, beside the river at Navarro and Crockett streets, water flooded the basement pressroom and reached the first floor just past midnight, causing the paper to miss its Saturday morning edition. The *Light* was on higher ground on Travis Street near Broadway, but its basement pressroom was also flooded. Down the street at the St. Anthony Hotel, the *Light* commandeered a press used for printing menus and put out a makeshift extra edition. The paper managed to get out its regular edition that afternoon.[32]

Early damage estimates ran as high as $10 million. A more sober later estimate by the U.S. Army Corps of Engineers put the total at $3.7 million, today's equivalent of $48.2 million. The official death toll reached fifty-one, all but four along the San Pedro and Alazan creek systems. One grave at San Fernando Cemetery was

Two men are framed by the St. Mary's Street Bridge as they walk north at 7 a.m. on Saturday, September 10, as the last floodwaters receded. Nearby, the northern leg of the Great Bend was still overflowing into Crockett Street. Debris blocked the Navarro Street Bridge, where a scale model of an Alamo monument designed by Alfred Giles but never funded stood sentinel until removed during the bridge's replacement.

dug large enough to hold a family of six. In addition to the known dead, another twenty-three were listed as missing. More did not make the count, like the family of Mariano Escobedo.[33]

Escobedo, a laborer, left his small home on the banks of Alazan Creek near El Paso Street a few days before the flood in search of work. He had reached West Texas when he heard of the disaster. Without steady employment he did not have enough money to return immediately, and those whom he asked for help did not believe his story of wanting to check on his family. But Escobedo gradually made his way back. He arrived in San Antonio the first week in October to find his home gone and no sign of his wife or their two young children. The Red Cross had no record of them among the dead or missing. Escobedo searched for days, without results. Police suspected they had not learned of many others also washed away.[34]

Rescues over, workers on Saturday morning began helping the homeless and displaced. As in 1913, relief efforts were headquartered in San Antonio's largest civic gathering place, the second-floor auditorium of the Market House on Milam Park. From there the American Red Cross under Albert Steves Jr. helped more than 2,000 persons on the first day. Six hundred volunteers canvassed the city for clothing donations. Hannah Hirschberg directed women volunteers in 100 automobiles delivering Red Cross food and clothing to those who could not get to shelters. By the second day, Red Cross workers had made nearly 25,000 sandwiches—"all containing meat of some kind"—and dispensed them to shelters throughout the city. Cash was given out once aid applicants were verified, "principally by women's clubs, pastors and priests."[35]

By 8 a.m. Saturday a relief center was open near South Laredo and El Paso streets in the heart of the most devastated residential area, directed by Marta M.

After floodwaters receded, waterlogged furniture and goods were moved off the street or carried outdoors to line St. Mary's Street north Houston Street past the Hertzberg Jewelry Co., its weight-driven landmark clock still keeping time. At top right, sightseers paddled a canoe through the intersection of Travis and St. Mary's streets past an Army guard while three hotel guests watched from their perch atop an awning. On Travis Street, the Citizens Auto Company showroom was flooded when floodwaters burst plate glass windows, while a tree had blocked a Ford delivery truck from being carried downstream after being swept off Dwyer Avenue near the Bexar County Courthouse.

de Acosta, local president of the Mexican Blue Cross—La Cruz Azul Mexicana. From across the Rio Grande in Juarez, the Blue Cross sent a representative to help. Neighborhood volunteers located victims, took survivors to hospitals, assisted stricken families and found homes for orphans. Joaquin Martinez of the local Masonic lodge supervised distribution of clothing and shoes sent up by the Great Lodge of the State of Nuevo Leon in Monterrey.[36]

Military efforts, directed by Col. B. A. Poore, were based near the Alamo at the YMCA on Avenue E, where soldiers bunked. There 10,000 sandwiches and a like number of cups of coffee were made and given out by women from San Antonio's Protestant churches. Meals were served at field kitchens in a vacant lot across the street. Soldiers strung makeshift telephone lines so relief efforts could be coordinated and served meals from mobile field kitchens throughout the Alazan Creek area. Tents and cots were distributed to the homeless.[37]

A Chamber of Commerce businessmen's relief committee took charge of checking reports of those dead, injured and missing. Its chairman, Sylvan Lang, was confident that a $25,000 fund drive would be completed by noon Monday, September 12. Other groups—the Salvation Army, Elks, Shriners—were also assisting. New

Soldiers guarding the flood-devastated city included, clockwise from top left, one keeping watch at Navarro and Crockett streets; two guarding Commerce Street's San Antonio National Bank; those in a pontoon boat outside the Gunter Hotel; one standing on remaining pavement blocks on Travis Street at its intersection with St. Mary's Street; and a troop forming on Crockett Street to the right of the *Express* building.

A Goldbeck of the Flood

Among professional photographers on the scene to record the flood of 1921 was Eugene O. Goldbeck, 28, newly returned to San Antonio to establish his National Photo Service, the only Texas-based independent international supplier of news photos. Goldbeck had been traveling the world developing techniques in panoramic photography, a field in which he would practice with distinction for the next six decades.

To portray the flood, Goldbeck turned on end his panoramic single-photo horizontal format—43 inches wide by 10 inches deep—to be displayed vertically. At the top he placed an image of the upper half of the front page of an *Express* edition of September 11, followed below by a sequence of six images ranging from a drowned horse to a large dollhouse wedged beneath the Fourth Street Bridge.

Goldbeck's other flood photos include one of the water-soaked interior of the Walk-Over Boot Shop on Houston Street.

66 • American Venice

Braunfels textile magnate Harry Landa sent down two trucks with 450 loaves of bread.[38]

But help from outsiders was not generally welcome.

"San Antonio is able to take care of herself," declared Mayor O. B. Black, as he declined offers of aid from cities throughout Texas. He rejected a group of doctors and nurses offered by the state health officer. The mayor was particularly definite about not wanting unemployed workers, who were beginning to arrive from elsewhere in search of cleanup work. The city's first duty, he declared, was to offer work to the city's own unemployed.[39]

Within two days of the flood, a semblance of order was returning. Electricity was restored to most non-flooded areas, telephone service to a fourth of the city. Two dozen streetcar crewmen were driving their own automobiles to carry passengers—free of charge—along streetcar lines still without power, being reimbursed for their gasoline by the Public Service Company. Even though municipal water pumps were not functioning, the force of newly energized artesian wells and springs had maintained a low water pressure through much of the city. By Monday, September 12, pumping had resumed to parts of town where mains were undamaged. Everywhere were sounds of chugging engines pumping out basements and the clattering of debris as it was swept up and dumped into trucks.[40]

The main downtown business district remained closed for more than a week. Debris was cleared with the aid of more than 120 trucks, half of them compliments of the U.S. Army and others rented by the city from the Texas Highway Department. Contractors put workers on three eight-hour shifts daily until the Houston, Travis and St. Mary's street arteries were repaved. Nine days after the flood, on September 19, the last soldiers guarding the main business district headed back to Camp Travis. Except for two blocks hard to access because of damaged bridges, the district reopened that night. "Immense crowds" thronged in to view the progress and to shop.[41]

When emergency food distribution ended two days later, relief workers had filled 6,770 grocery orders and served more than 20,600 hot meals, 57,200 sandwiches and countless cups of coffee.[42]

A crowd gathered as searchers checked the river near South Flores Street for victims.

Some returning residents had to deal with damage from floodwaters like those that collapsed part of this home at 230 East Pecan Street.

The American Red Cross based its
relief efforts from the second floor of
the Market House on Milam Park,
while the Mexican Blue Cross had
relief units and helped set up tents
for the homeless near Alazan Creek.
The U.S. Army coordinated mobile
field kitchens from its headquarters
at the YMCA on Avenue E. At far
right, soldiers dispatched from Fort
Sam Houston's Camp Travis restrung
telephone wires near the courthouse
to help restore communications.

Cleanup efforts, clockwise from top left, began to restore the city's transportation infrastructure as trucks dumped dislodged mesquite street paving blocks in a vacant lot and International & Great Northern crews restored rail trestles over San Pedro Creek. It would take more than a year to replace the wrenched Navarro Street/ Mill Bridge that had spanned the widest part of the river downtown since the 1870s. Also needing to be rebuilt were a rail siding bridge over the river at Pioneer Flour Mills and the nearby concrete South Alamo Street Bridge.

EVERY DOG HAS HIS DAY

SAINT MIHIEL
·
CHATEAU THIERRY
·
SAN ANTONIO FLOOD

PUBLISHED IN THE INTEREST OF THE SECOND DIVISION

After nine days of helping the city recover, Army troops returned to Fort Sam Houston and Camp Travis with the last of their pontoon boats and supplies. The Camp Travis weekly newsmagazine cover ranked the flood with two of the Second Division's victories in World War I. A newsweekly cartoonist offered another perspective, a psychological boost their guard duty offered soldiers previously scorned by local girls.

Salvaged lumber and building materials were distributed among the homeless, who set about rebuilding. Businessmen rushed to recover by selling damaged goods. On the sidewalk in front of his store at Houston Street and Main Avenue, Nathan Sinkin spread out boxes of flood-soaked clothing for sale at 20 to 25 cents. Winerich Motor Sales offered soldiers "slightly flood damaged" Overlands for $625, accompanied by ninety-day guarantees. San Fernando Cathedral dedicated its new main altar of Carrera marble and gold mosaic inlay to the memory of San Antonio victims of both World War I and the recent flood.[43]

There was awareness that things could have been much worse. Had the rainfall been as heavy as it had become soon after over Bell, Milam, and Williamson counties, engineers believed that the increased level of destruction in San Antonio would have been so great as to make what actually occurred "seem insignificant."[44]

Flood events were examined by engineers. They were able to answer the question of why the river had overflowed its banks only slightly in far southern San Antonio. Engineers determined that Alazan and Apache creeks crested at different times before they joined San Pedro Creek, which could thereby maintain an even flow as it joined the San Antonio River two miles south of downtown. Through downtown, floodwaters at that time were being slowed as buildings acted as barriers, diverting some water into basements and giving time for more to be absorbed into the ground. Thus the highest waters from San Pedro Creek had already passed their juncture with the San Antonio River when they were replaced by the highest floodwaters arriving belatedly from the north.[45]

Mayor Black's pride in declaring that San Antonio did not need much outside help reflected not just a wish to believe things weren't so bad but also the pre–New Deal sense of self-reliance that made federal aid programs rare. Yet though San Antonio may have recovered from the flood without any direct help from state or federal governments, locally based and federally funded Army troops and trucks did provide critical aid in cleaning up the aftermath at no cost to the city. That aspect was ignored by U.S. Secretary of Commerce Herbert Hoover, whose mid-October letter apparently substituted for a hoped-for message from President Warren Harding. Hoover wrote San Antonio Chamber of Commerce President Morris Stern, the *Express* reported, that the city's achievement "without accepting one dollar of aid from outside was one of the finest examples of cooperation and civic spirit of which he knew." He congratulated the city and wished to assure its residents that "they had won the admiration of the nation."[46]

There was an element of denial also at work at the Chamber of Commerce's celebration luncheon in the Gunter Hotel ballroom on October 18. San Antonio may have been swept by a flood on the tenth of September, but by the tenth of October, celebration invitations declared, the city was already "completely rehabilitated." The lights in fact were on again, drinking water was flowing through the pipes and essential businesses were functioning once more. But many neighborhoods still needed serious repairs, and downtown traffic would be snarled for at least two more years while critical bridges were rebuilt.

A month after the devastating flood, the Chamber of Commerce sent out postcard invitations to a celebration of the city being "completely rehabilitated." Though the event would boost morale, much reconstruction, in fact, remained to be done.

```
SEPT. 10th - SAN ANTONIO SWEPT BY FLOOD.
OCT. 10th  - SAN ANTONIO COMPLETELY REHABILITATED.
OCT. 18th  - Lieut. Governor and Mayors of five
Texas leading Cities will unite with our people
in celebrating recovery.
            President Harding, also, will have a
message for the people of San Antonio.
            You cannot afford to miss it. Capacity
of Gunter Ball Room is limited.
            Play safe and sign attached return
postal card today.
            12:15 o'clock Tuesday, October 18th.
MEMBERS' COUNCIL-SAN ANTONIO CHAMBER OF COMMERCE.
```

As businesses recovered from the flood, City National Bank at Houston and Travis streets, top left, pumped out water from its basement. Carl D. Newton's Fox Company explained delays by enclosing a photo postcard of the wrecked Navarro Street/Mill Bridge, top right, with overdue photo finishing orders. At center, Ben M. Hammond's Bell Jewelry Company had to deal with a flood-strewn alley and a soggy interior, while at Commerce and Soledad streets, right, the National Bank of Commerce worked on its flooded basement.

At St. Mary's Catholic Church, its facade smeared with oil stains marking the level of floodwaters, windows were opened to ventilate and dry the sanctuary while, at the rear, pews and furniture were carried outside and vestments hung on a line to dry.

Dynamiting the dam of the upper Guenther Mill across from the U.S. Arsenal in 1926 cleared one obstruction in the river channel south of downtown San Antonio.

· 4 ·
Taming the River and the Great Bend

After the catastrophic flood of 1921, no longer would there be talk of stretching out flood prevention over ten or twenty years "in the light of other urgent needs of the city." Now, at last, there was universal agreement that flood control *was* the most urgent need.[1]

But it was going to have to be a homegrown undertaking, paid for by local taxes. In 1921 there were few funding options for public works projects, however essential to saving lives. It would take a national cataclysm six years later—flooding along the Mississippi River that left one million people homeless—before there was the political will to begin setting up a framework for federal funding and firm oversight for such work.

In San Antonio, the halting process became a case study in how far astray things could go without strong guidance by seasoned experts. Downtown businessmen pressured the mayor to require the flood control engineer to make changes against his better judgment. Then the engineer was forced out, others were hired, then fired. The city had to tear off the rear fifteen feet of its just completed police department building after plans for the flood channel suddenly changed. When a public restroom was planned atop a flood conduit, up came the idea of adding a barbershop and a Turkish bath.

Yet somehow the process worked, clearing the way for a world-class river channel already imagined, but hardly expected.

At the outset, a world still thinking of San Antonio as a disaster zone to be avoided got messages from boosters like the San Antonio Real Estate Board, which told those attending a mid-October 1921 real estate convention luncheon in Fort Worth: "The flood is over and San Antonio is at work." Contractors had indeed resumed construction on the latest additions to the skyline—the Maverick Building on Houston Street and Frost National Bank on Main Plaza.[2]

Negotiating downtown streets, however, would be a long-term challenge. In a city of bridges, thirteen of the twenty-seven spans were rendered unusable by the flood.

Most vexing was the loss of two key bridges on Navarro Street, which snarled traffic in the southwestern central business district. The Navarro Street Bridge near Crockett Street was short enough to replace temporarily with a wooden bridge, but any replacement for the double iron span known as the Mill Bridge had to be a permanent fix. A bond issue two years before the flood funded

A gently arching concrete bridge, above, sometimes compared with the Pont Neuf in Paris, was completed in 1923, replacing the flood-wrecked Navarro Street/Mill Bridge. Upstream, a concrete span, right, replaced the iron Fourth Street/Lexington Avenue Bridge, reassembled in 1926 as a narrow pedestrian bridge across the river in Brackenridge Park. At far right was the old First Baptist Church, on the site of the present structure.

both for eventual replacement as bridges of arched concrete. But now requested bids came back too high. The shorter bridge was successfully rebid using less expensive steel, though wet weather and slow shipments delayed its completion until December 1922. Six months earlier, the wrecked 1870s Mill Bridge had been finally taken down. Its wider replacement was completed in early 1923. For this the city had held out for an elegant concrete bridge, and got one. Its three graceful arches, sometimes said to resemble those of the Pont Neuf in Paris, have made it a favorite with photographers ever since.[3]

Two landmark iron bridges were taken down and reassembled across the river in Brackenridge Park, the 1890 "Letters of Gold" Bridge on St. Mary's Street as a vehicular bridge and the Fourth Street/Lexington Avenue Bridge made narrower for pedestrians. The city's first iron bridge, erected at Houston Street in 1871 and moved to Grand/Jones Avenue in 1885, was replaced in its second location with one of concrete, one of a series of concrete bridges constructed through 1930.[4]

Once San Antonians got their most pressing affairs back in order, they made known their concerns over flood control. Residents of western San Antonio were suspicious that Alazan Creek would be ignored in favor of channel improvements in the business district. Southern San Antonians feared their channel would not get widened after all, causing floodwaters to rush through a straightened channel upstream and be dumped upon them. Some businessmen believed that advocates of beautification were more concerned with landscaping than with the danger of floods and had no appreciation of the cash value of riverbed land. Women's organizations suspected businessmen of being in cahoots with politicians to make a few dollars. But all agreed there should be a dam on Olmos Creek.[5]

The chief of the U.S. Army Corps of Engineers unit at Fort Sam Houston, Col. Edgar Jadwin, made a survey at the direction of his superiors in Washington. Jadwin's engineers mapped the Olmos Creek valley and found Metcalf & Eddy engineers' test borings for a dam to be in an ideal location. Jadwin recommended an earthen dam, but a local civilian engineer, Clinton Kearney, dispatched by Mayor O. B. Black on a visual reconnaissance, thought the dam should be of concrete. Whatever the ultimate material, Jadwin made clear to the city that Washington would have no part in financing a dam.[6]

Mayor Black came down strongly against seeking state aid. To accept it "would be in violation of the self-help so far evinced by the city," he declared. "It would never do." After the chest thumping, Black admitted that state aid could not even be requested for a year or more, since the legislature was not in session. Even then it would require a two-thirds majority vote, and there were other limitations. City funding was the obvious route, though the process would be long. Reports had to be made and approved and a bond issue vote had to authorize funding before contractors could be selected and actual work could begin.[7]

It took nearly three years to work out plans and for citizens to approve $2.8 million in bonds to pay for them. Then came the question of who would supervise the work. Boston's Metcalf & Eddy had done a thorough study of the problem, but

Workmen paused in 1925 during their reconstruction of the landmark 1890 St. Mary's Street "Letters of Gold Bridge," rebuilt across the river in Brackenridge Park.

San Antonio's flood engineer Samuel F. Crecelius, in civilian dress, gave visiting members of the U.S. Army Corps of Engineers a tour of the Olmos Dam construction site in October 1925.

its engineers' insistence that riverbank trees and shrubbery be removed had displeased those who had worked so many years for an attractive river. Some businessmen, too, were irked at those engineers' rejection of their plan for an underground conduit bypassing the Great Bend so it could be filled in for development. They could hope for more influence with local engineers. Edwin P. Arneson, speaking on behalf of the San Antonio chapter of the American Association of Engineers, appealed "for the employment of San Antonio engineers exclusively on the project."[8]

So it was no surprise when a San Antonio–based engineer, Samuel F. Crecelius, 52, was picked to plan the $1.5 million Olmos Dam. Crecelius, a retired colonel in the U.S. Army Corps of Engineers, had designed two dams near Laredo and directed dam and navigation projects in Missouri, Indiana, West Virginia and Kentucky. He went to work at once.[9]

In two years Olmos Dam was finished, a concrete wonder 80 feet high and 1,925 feet long. Behind it stretched an 1,100-acre retaining basin, where a park and golf course were planned. A roadway across the top was lighted by electricity in a series of cast iron lanterns spaced across the top of concrete railings. The two-lane thoroughfare linked the San Antonio neighborhood of Laurel Heights to the west with the suburb of Alamo Heights, incorporated five years before. At dedication ceremonies on December 11, 1926, a cavalcade of automobiles led by San Antonio Mayor John W. Tobin drove from the San Antonio side to meet cars from Alamo Heights midway. Tobin shook hands with Alamo Heights Mayor Pro Tem W. H. Hume, substituting for the crusty Mayor Robert O'Grady, who had gone deer hunting.[10]

As dam construction was getting underway, in fall 1924 a crew began to clear, straighten and widen Alazan Creek where it joined San Pedro Creek. Two miles south of downtown, the junction of San Pedro Creek and the river near Mission Concepción was improved. In January 1926 a steam shovel moved into place nearby and in six months dug a 445-foot cutoff channel to eliminate a bend that meandered 2,100 feet. The old riverbed was added to the new Concepción Park.[11]

Next to go were two smaller bends in the southern river channel, one above the new park and the other at Pioneer Flour Mills, where a 300-foot-wide cut replaced a sharp narrow switchback at the tip of a 1,200-foot bend. Across from the U.S.

A roadway between San Antonio and Alamo Heights crossed the long-discussed Olmos Dam when it was completed in December 1926. The neighborhood at upper center later became the suburb of Olmos Park. Most of the dam's arches were removed a half century later when a spillway was built over the top. The road was redirected below the dam at left.

As a short-term solution to removing a sharp bend around Pioneer Flour Mills, a crew cut off the tip of the bend. The view is south to South Alamo Street, with the old Wagner Hotel at left.

Arsenal upstream, the old Guenther Upper Mill—last rented as a garage—and its unused dam were removed to straighten and widen the channel.[12]

Large bends were taken out at opposite edges of downtown. One straightened what remained of the Bowen's Island S-shaped bend, where the Great Bend had flowed west almost to the Bexar County courthouse before doubling back east and then heading south. To the north, straightening a twisting double bend cleared the site for Municipal Auditorium. Then a proposal came up to beautify the segment of the river between the northern end of the river park and the new auditorium.[13]

Property owners suggested there be a fountain ten feet in diameter in the middle of the new channel west of the auditorium. An operator could make spray from five concentric rings rise twenty-five feet. Six colored searchlights below the water line could evoke anything from "a waving field of ripening wheat to a crimson pyramid many feet high that looks like a huge bonfire." Mayor Tobin liked the idea so

In 1926 the city strung lights across the river between Navarro Street and St. Mary's Street's new concrete bridge to replace lights lost during the flood.

much he thought there should be five more fountains downstream, all visible from key intersections. None were installed. But as the city prepared to replace strings of lights washed away by the flood and pay for the electricity, Tobin declared: "The river is one of San Antonio's real assets, and we are to develop plans that will make it a thing of real beauty and something visitors will remember and comment on long after they leave."[14]

By this time the San Antonio Conservation Society, newly organized in a futile effort to save the city's 1859 Market House, was stressing the importance of preserving the city's unique features and its natural beauty. In November 1924 members thought of giving city officials a two-hour boat ride through the river park from Ninth Street to Market Street to show how the preservation of the river's beauty merited changing the next spring's Battle of Flowers Parade into a river parade. Volunteers were recruited to station themselves on bridges along the route and cheer as the boats passed beneath.[15]

Only two council members showed up, Mayor Tobin and Parks Commissioner Ray Lambert. Riding with Tobin was society member Lucretia Van Horn. With Lambert was Margaret Lewis, society stalwart and president of the Battle of Flowers Association, sponsor of the spring parade. Conservation Society president Emily Edwards rode with the new flood control engineer, Samuel Crecelius.

As the flotilla neared a large cottonwood tree near the Houston Street bridge, Crecelius remarked to Miss Edwards that anything blocking the river channel would be taken out. She asked if the tree they were passing was too near the channel. Crecelius replied, "Oh, yes, that would have to go." She called to Margaret Lewis in the next boat, "Mrs. Lewis, that has to go." Mrs. Lewis, who was "very excitable," called back, "That does NOT have to go!" Her boat began to rock. Her fellow passenger, portly Parks Commissioner Ray Lambert, no doubt clutching the sides of the boat, replied quickly, "No, no, no!" Emily Edwards believed saving that cottonwood tree was the first victory of the San Antonio Conservation Society.[16]

Six months before the flood, the city had agreed that trees around the Great Bend would not be removed nor would the channel be paved to accommodate floodwaters, as engineers with Metcalf & Eddy recommended. The engineers had made those recommendations in the belief that leaving the bend alone and instead building an open cutoff channel through three prime blocks of downtown from one end of the bend to the other would be too expensive. Now, however, the city's new flood engineer recommended two adjacent 650-foot-long underground box culverts to carry overflow past the bend. When floodwaters came, gates at both ends of the bend could be closed to keep floodwaters out and divert them into the new channel. At other times water would continue as usual around the bend.[17]

By this time, however, most of the 1924 flood prevention bond funds had been spent, and another $1 million would have to be approved. At Mayor Tobin's insistence, Crecelius cut right-of-way costs by narrowing the culverts' combined width from seventy feet to fifty. If the walls were made strong enough, they could support eight-story buildings having valuable frontage on Commerce, Market, and Dolorosa streets. Rent from the buildings could bring the city a quick $200,000 to put back into flood control.[18]

At that point the ailing Mayor Tobin left for an extended convalescence in San Diego, California—he was elected to a second term in absentia—and Crecelius's plans ran into trouble. One faction thought a new street should go above the culverts, not new buildings. Crecelius replied that such an idea had been "definitely abandoned" but he was countermanded by Acting Mayor Phil Wright, who announced that the street would indeed be built. Wright added that a public restroom building would go up in the new space north of Commerce Street for the benefit of shoppers. From San Diego, Mayor Tobin sent a sketch showing how the restroom structure could include a barbershop and a Turkish bath.[19]

Mayor John W. Tobin sat in the prow of a rowboat during a tour of the river given in 1924 by members of the newly formed San Antonio Conservation Society.

Construction began on the culverts' southern section as acquisition proceedings continued for the northern section when the off-again, on-again street was suddenly off again. This time, businessmen rebelled against the culverts' channel being narrowed, and petitioned to return the width to seventy feet. Water from a cloudburst north of the new dam might indeed be held back, they thought, but a cloudburst south of the dam might prove a fifty-foot channel too narrow.[20]

By then Mayor Tobin was back in town. Widening the channel would be "a useless waste of money," he said. There were only funds to finish a fifty-foot-wide channel, and that was wide enough. Besides, taxpayers would not stand for another bond issue, he added, declaring flatly: "We shall build it regardless of the protest filed."[21]

Undeterred, businessmen presented city commissioners a petition with forty-five signatures requesting a seventy-foot channel. Petitioners also sought early completion of the southern channel project to prevent "dumping floodwaters" on South Side residents.[22]

But soon Mayor Tobin died, and Crecelius was on his own to defend the fifty-foot channel. Questioned, Crecelius claimed he couldn't recollect the width of the downtown river recommended by Metcalf & Eddy—it was seventy feet, not fifty—but in defense of fifty feet he cited numerous statistics, including reduced costs. Commissioners went along with their engineer, and construction continued.[23]

Then everything came unglued.

The new mayor, C. M. Chambers, challenged complaining businessmen to come up with "expert advice" to support their opinion. The businessmen produced Dallas engineer O. N. Floyd. Floyd determined that the narrower conduit could carry the estimated amount of water, given its slope and assuming debris did not block its entrance. But he found a mistake in Crecelius's calculations. Corrected, they showed the velocity of water originally projected to enter the smaller channel was slower than it would be in reality. Floyd concluded that not only would a seventy-foot channel be required, it needed to be an uncovered channel, and that the modified project would cost less than Crecelius and the late Mayor Tobin had estimated.[24]

Crecelius admitted the error. Two days later the wider channel was approved, even though some concrete had already been poured for narrower conduits. Amid reports that the mayor would fire him, Crecelius submitted his resignation. But businessmen persuaded the mayor not to hold Crecelius responsible "for the turn things had taken." Chambers, believing that Crecelius's contract was legally binding for the duration of the project, did not accept the resignation but cut the flood engineer's salary by 40 percent. Six months later the mayor closed the flood prevention office and put the program under the city engineer. This time, Crecelius resigned for good.[25]

With Crecelius gone, the mayor reopened the flood prevention office and hired the Fort Worth firm of Hawley & Freese, in association with O. N. Floyd, to figure things out. Hawley & Freese picked former city engineer Hans Helland as its resident engineer. For a year work on the cutoff channel remained at a near standstill, while right-of-way for the wider channel was acquired and another $500,000 in bonds was approved. During the lull, a group of downtown businessmen saw their chance.[26]

The Great Bend's cutoff channel would be as wide as the Great Bend itself. Why should an expensive bypass sit empty waiting for a flood when it could just as easily be carrying the regular flow of the Great Bend? The regular flow would be dried up "within ten years" anyway, unless "scores" of artesian wells were drilled to augment the declining flow. Why not just fill in the bend now?[27]

A cutoff channel was planned to keep floodwaters from backing up as they rounded the convoluted Great Bend. Main Plaza is at far left center, the county courthouse below it.

Reported one newspaper in mid-February 1928: "Prominent businessmen are said to be meeting in closed conferences, outlining a process by which they can press city commissioners to reclaim this portion of the river when the psychological time arrives—upon the completion of the 'Big Bend' cutoff." The unnamed businessmen had statistics. The bend took up 294,000 square feet—nearly seven acres—of prime downtown real estate. The old riverbed could be sold for between $2 million and $14.7 million, and the city would get the funds. "At least three real estate promoters" went to work.[28]

The promoters, however, did not get far. "Numerous civic clubs" met to oppose the plan, which faced a "well-defined countermovement . . . particularly among women's clubs of the city." Fire and Police Commissioner Phil Wright said

In 1928 a group of businessmen proposed extending Losoya Street across Commerce Street to open up development property in La Villita. When it became apparent that the new street would overhang the river park, the idea was soundly rejected.

facing page During the city's Big Dig in 1929–30, clockwise from upper right, a construction truck descended an access ramp from Villita Street at the south end of the new cutoff channel. New bridges crossing the channel had attached beneath them the utility pipes propped up during excavations.

city officials had discussed the matter among themselves, and that "every one of them is unalterably opposed to any plan to reclaim the old river bed in the big bend."[29] Council members vied with each other for the strongest condemnation of the idea.

"As long as I am in this office the Big Bend channel will never be filled up," thundered Mayor Chambers. "I am absolutely against abandoning the river. In my opinion the San Antonio River is one of the biggest assets of this city." Tax Commissioner Frank Bushick said he "would never vote for it under any circumstances." Street Commissioner Paul Steffler believed that "to abandon the river would be a crime." He thought rerouting storm sewers emptying into the bend alone would cost almost as much as the value of the reclaimed land.[30]

The bend would remain. But the businessmen had one last card to play.

One of the choicest undeveloped areas adjacent to downtown was along the southern bank of the Great Bend's southern leg—the rundown neighborhood of antique structures in La Villita, settled in Spanish times. The noose had been tightening around La Villita as surrounding streets were widened, improving access and business opportunities. All that was missing was a direct north-south street to downtown to justify clearing La Villita for development. Filling the bend would have made that easy. But even with the bend still in place, such a street was not impossible. Developers quietly laid their plans.[31]

Businessmen in the eastern part of downtown organized as the Eastside Improvement League, headed by John H. Kirkpatrick, the "conquering hero" who had arrived in the river parade as fiesta king twenty-one years before. At the end of 1928, city commissioners promised the Improvement League that they would spend $100,000 to extend Losoya Street southeast to meet South Alamo Street at Market Street. But when funding was approved three months later, Losoya Street was suddenly to extend not southeast but southwest, crossing Market Street to reach Villita Street. To get there, the new forty-five-foot-wide street would pass over a parallel section of the Great Bend. At some points the entire street would be cantilevered over the river, leaving only twenty-five feet of the river and its banks visible from above. The future location of the as-yet unplanned Arneson River Theater would have been in the shadow of the bridge.[32]

Eighteen days after unanimously approving the project, city commissioners were swearing it would never happen. For when residents comprehended the impact of the overhang, it "met with a storm of protests from all sections of the city." Assistant City Engineer T. H. Coghill confessed that his staff had drawn up the new plan with help from the Eastside Improvement League, and a few days later said that only just now had it dawned on them that much of the street would have to be built over the river.[33]

Armed with those revelations, Mayor Chambers branded the attempt to take space above the river "grand larceny." He made it clear that his administration would "not tolerate any such plans." The mayor refused to let a four-member delegation from the Eastside Improvement League even present arguments. He said that for him to take a tour of the site to see where the street would cross City Water Board property would be a waste of time. The businessmen felt betrayed. Their meeting with Street Commissioner Paul Steffler was marked by "heated verbal tilts." Real estate broker Ernest Altgelt complained that he had already spent $11,000 for options "on trashy shacks and dives" to line up property "under the impression that the city was ready to proceed."[34]

After the commotion died down, the $100,000 for the Losoya Street project was approved as first intended, to extend the street southeast to connect with South Alamo Street.[35] The still-isolated pocket of La Villita was left to molder for another ten years, when it was rescued in a pioneering historic preservation project.

One denizen of the muddy riverbed that engineers hoped to cover with concrete south of downtown was this one-and-a-half-pound crawfish, displayed by Mrs. Rush Goodspeed after it was caught near Pioneer Flour Mills in June 1927.

The cutoff project got moving again in March 1929 with the decision to build a single wider, open channel. During the delay, east of the courthouse the city tore down the 1855 French Building, its rear having extended over the path of the entire new channel. The landmark's limestone blocks were used to line the river channel from Travis Street north to the new auditorium. In its place the city built a Police and Health Department Building, its back wall aligned with the expected edge of the narrow conduit. When the channel was widened, embarrassed city officials had to make room by tearing off the rear fifteen feet of their new building.[36]

While a swath of buildings was cleared through the heart of the city and steam shovels went to work, utility lines once in the ground beneath streets were propped up over the channel cut until they could be attached to the undersides of new bridges. One workman died in the cave-in of an excavation beneath Commerce Street as concrete laid for the narrower channel was being broken up. When residents saw the finished channel, new controversy erupted. Stark concrete walls plunging twenty-six feet down either side of an empty channel did not offer the ambience many thought appropriate for their city. Mayor Chambers grumped that it was "one of the biggest eyesores of the city and should be filled up."[37]

Then bids came in to line the channel south of downtown with concrete, as recommended by Hawley & Freese despite the mayor's preference for an earthen channel. Chambers, increasingly frustrated by the slow progress and by the steady stream of delegations at his door with complaints, returned escrow checks to all four bidders, fired Hawley & Freese and ordered the city engineer to build a wider channel of dirt. This would look better than concrete and be much less expensive: "We are not going to line the gutters with gold." When reminded that not building a concrete channel and leaving the trees would require the channel to be dug deeper, the mayor retorted: "Dig to Hades! I had rather spend a half million dollars beautifying this river than a million dollars making it a concrete-lined sewer." The earthen channel was made deeper, to await changes decades later.[38]

The mayor was reluctant to go back to voters for more money yet again. Since 1924, three bond issues had provided a total of $3.9 million. But by the fall of 1929 only $150,000 was left, and two major twisting sections were still unfinished—a block north of the new auditorium and the one only slightly shortened three years earlier below Pioneer Flour Mills.

Beyond the auditorium, the river stretched northward for nearly three miles to its headwaters. Metcalf & Eddy had wanted the entire channel straightened and widened, leaving only "substantial well-rooted trees not too close together." Samuel Crecelius, the city's flood engineer, thought it should also be lined with concrete. Those recommendations were ultimately rejected by city hall. There was, however, wisdom seen in straightening three bends as advised. The farthest, below Josephine Street, was straightened without incident early in 1929. Straightening the second and largest of the three, between Eighth and Tenth streets as far west as Central Catholic High School, began quietly in the fall of 1928 with condemnation proceedings against recalcitrant property owners.[39]

The third offending bend was so close to the fast-expanding downtown that fixing it got caught up in crossfire between developers and conservationists. Straightening that channel, southeast of the intersection of Trenton Street—present-day McCullough Avenue—and North St. Mary's Street, a block north of the new auditorium, would create a prime twelve-acre building site. In mid-1929 the Swiss Plaza Company proposed to loan the city $200,000 to straighten the bend and clear trees so it could begin construction of twin sixteen-story towers on the site. Women's clubs, however, were watching.[40]

Excavation of a channel to eliminate the longest of three bends targeted north of downtown began with land acquisition in 1928. Through a break in the trees left of center can be glimpsed a tower of the Lone Star Brewery, later the San Antonio Museum of Art.

The Woman's Club, the Conservation Society and a Federation of Women's Clubs committee all filed formal protests with City Hall. The federation pledged "united opposition" to any further change in the river's course upstream and to removal of any vegetation at all, and declared that the river was "being constantly menaced by the selfishness and greed of promoters and politicians."[41]

Upping its ante, Swiss Plaza agreed to donate the land for the shorter channel and also to pay for its construction in exchange for the old riverbed. Swiss Plaza promotional materials show a sudden endorsement by the Federation of Women's Clubs, which would now be having elegant clubrooms in one of the towers. The federation dropped its opposition in return for the city's guarantee not to pave the channel with concrete. Major opposition gone, the city accepted Swiss Plaza's offer. But in the worsening Depression Swiss Plaza's plans disintegrated. The bend was not straightened for thirty more years—and then without a concrete channel.[42]

As the 1920s passed and flood control elements took final form, public attention was shifting from "Where should the river go?" back to "How should it look?" The first river beautification drive since the 1921 flood came in 1928. Five thousand women were due in town for the national convention of the General Federation of Women's Clubs. The San Antonio branch was determined to show its guests a tidy city, and doled out assignments to its member clubs. The Old Spanish Trail Association got the task of river cleanup.[43]

Thanks to lobbying by ladies of that group, the river park gained a flagstone walkway along the west and south sides of the river, the same route businessmen twelve years earlier had targeted for a river walk. The walk extended for three blocks, south from Houston Street and around the start of the Great Bend

One new advocate for beautifying the San Antonio River was sculptor Gutzon Borglum, in town to do a monument to Texas trail drivers and prepare his designs for Mount Rushmore.

to Navarro Street. Banks were sodded and flowers and shrubs planted, with a ligustrum hedge added to screen unsightly backs of buildings.[44]

The Conservation Society got the job of tending to ornamental river lighting. Members persuaded the city to replace strings of red, white and blue lights with permanent floodlights, artistically placed. Speaking for the society on the matter was a new honorary member— newly arrived sculptor Gutzon Borglum. Borglum had set up a studio in the abandoned 1885 waterworks pump house in Brackenridge Park to work on a memorial to

Texas trail drivers and to design his mock-ups for Mount Rushmore. He believed the river could be worth "millions" to the city and urged the purchase of gondolas and canoes for tourists.[45]

Still, in 1930, as the cutoff channel was completed, no one seemed happy with how it looked. To soften the starkness, along the bottom of its channel the city planted grass, flowers and low shrubs on sod laid on either side of an open sixteen-foot median strip, which carried a small flow of water piped in to give the appearance of a natural stream.[46]

The city also had to make reassurances that water headed for the Great Bend would not be diverted into the new channel. Costly gates to seal the Great Bend during floods had not been built as planned. Instead, across the head of the cutoff channel a dam was built to the height of water's natural flow from upstream. Although some floodwaters could still find their way into the bend, most would pour over the cutoff channel dam and straight downstream as intended. A low dam was also built at the far end of the bend to back up a consistent level of water.[47]

There was still concern about the river going dry. After a summer 1927 drought threatened the river, installing a pump at a well near the headwaters to replenish water was approved without debate. The next summer a new underground sprinkler system kept downtown banks green. A visiting Southern States Art League official urged local artists to paint along the river, assuring them it was "the most beautiful thing you have; it has anything New York has got beaten a thousand blocks."[48]

The completed bypass channel, far left, connects the ends of the meandering Great Bend to divert floodwaters straight south. The stark appearance of the newly dug channel, center, was softened by landscaping on either side of a narrow channel at the base that ended where flow from the southern end of the bend entered the flood channel at lower right. Directing the normal flow into the bend was a bulkhead at the head of the flood channel, above right, over which floodwaters could flow. In the background are the Witte Building and the Nix Hospital.

In 1929, Robert Hugman's initial plans for the River Walk had a cobblestone lane descending from Houston Street, upper left center, passing the Shops of Aragon and crossing the river into Romula. Most of the last leg of the bend would feature a divided channel through sunken gardens.

·5·
Debating the River Park

A dam was built, the river straightened. In 1929 the Great Bend still had its trees and there was a bypass channel ready to divert high waters headed its way. The peaceful riverside park seemed destined to continue in perpetuity.

But seeds of change were taking root.

The latest conflict flared up at a time when San Antonio's rapid, helter-skelter growth brought awareness that there should be some kind of comprehensive outline for development, the sort of plan proposed during the reforms of 1912. Downtown by 1929 had four skyscrapers higher than twenty stories, compared with five in Houston and two each in Dallas and Fort Worth. More were expected. City officials recognized the need for some way to order future growth, but, tight-fisted as ever after enduring the high cost of flood control, many believed such a plan could be done on the cheap.[1]

At the end of 1928, Mayor C. M. Chambers appointed a fifty-six member City Plan Committee to pick a planner. A top candidate for the job was Harland Bartholomew and Associates of St. Louis, the nation's top urban planning firm. Bartholomew's hiring was especially favored by members of the San Antonio Conservation Society and its cofounder, Rena Maverick (Mrs. Robert B.) Green.[2]

At this point, onto the scene wandered a young architect, Robert H. H. Hugman, 27, freshly returned from New Orleans. Hugman was aghast at the severity of the flood cutoff channel's appearance, and thought the entire river held vast unrealized potential for San Antonio. If New Orleans could capitalize on its French heritage, why shouldn't San Antonio benefit along the river by drawing on its Spanish heritage? Its popularity was already proven by the appeal of Spanish Colonial Revival architecture, the dominant style for new construction in San Antonio and throughout the Southwest.[3]

Other San Antonio architects who had envisioned change for the San Antonio River—distinguished practitioners like Harvey Page, Alfred Giles, Atlee Ayres—came from elsewhere, bringing sterling credentials from the northeast and even Europe. Hugman was homegrown, from a modest background that left travel to his vivid imagination. In urban landscape design, his perspective came from books.

Upstart Architect vs. Seasoned Planner

Opposing concepts for the San Antonio River were advocated by two men whose backgrounds differed widely.

Proposing a radical departure from tradition was Robert Harvey Harold Hugman, 27. His close-cropped dark hair rimmed a high forehead, a sporty moustache tapered across his upper lip. He looked out through youthful dark eyes with the detached gaze of a dreamer.

Born to a working class family on San Antonio's south side, Hugman graduated from Brackenridge High School in 1920 and went on to study architecture at the University of Texas in Austin, leaving in 1924 without graduating. After a stint as a draftsman in New Orleans, he returned to practice architecture in San Antonio, and he needed work.

Robert Hugman saw the San Antonio River as offering a rare opportunity to exploit the city's Spanish heritage with a whimsical mix of landscaping, shops, restaurants, water features and open space.

In the other corner was Harland Bartholomew, 40 and clean-shaven, his graying hair combed straight back. His aquiline nose supported a pair of round, thin-rimmed glasses that accented the steady, appraising look of a professional long accustomed to sizing up a situation and moving forward.

Bartholomew was born in Stoneham, Massachusetts, and went to Erasmus High School in Brooklyn. Due to a lack of funds he was unable to study civil engineering for more than two years at Rutgers University, which awarded him an honorary degree in the subject in 1921. The first full-time planner hired by an American city, he was director of city planning for St. Louis. Harland Bartholomew and Associates, the consulting firm he ran on the side, did twenty of the nation's eighty-seven comprehensive city plans completed during the first six years of the 1920s, nearly twice as many as the closest competitor. When he died in 1989 at 100, the *New York Times* termed him "the dean of comprehensive city planning in the United States."

In 1929 Harland Bartholomew saw the San Antonio River as a rare refuge of calm in a busy metropolis, best kept landscaped traditionally and viewed not from along its banks but only, reflectively, from above.

Architect Robert H. H. Hugman, above, and urban planner Harland Bartholomew had opposing ideas for the Great Bend.

"We read descriptions of the old cities of Spain," Hugman said, "of a narrow, winding street barred to vehicular traffic yet holding the best shops, clubs, banks and cafes; prosperous, yet alluring, with its shadowed doorways and quaint atmosphere. . . . It occurred to me that such a street in the very heart of our growing city would do much to enhance its interest and naught to impair its progress." That street should be by the San Antonio River.[4]

One inspiration Hugman cited was Xochimilco, Mexico City's colorful water gardens, shallow enough so boats could be poled along as he realized they could be on San Antonio's river. In his hometown Hugman could see fanciful rockwork in San Pedro Park and more in the Japanese Sunken Gardens, a rock quarry transformed with curving waterside walks and narrow, arching pedestrian bridges of native limestone. He may also have known of development in old Spanish territory at Coral Gables, Florida, the new Miami suburb where Mediterranean architecture abounded along a new system of canals, a former quarry became the Venetian Pool and where developer Charles Merrick dreamed of "castles in Spain made real."[5]

Hugman was convinced that the banks of the San Antonio River should be enlivened with a sort of Spanish flavor. He came up with a proposal called the Shops of Aragon and Romula, names picked from his imagination. Late in 1928 he tried his ideas out on Amanda Cartwright (Mrs. Lane) Taylor, chairman of the Conservation Society's river committee. She liked them.[6]

Encouraged, Hugman called on city officials and engineers with some plans in a leather-covered brochure. He took one to Mayor C. M. Chambers, who was

Robert Hugman grew up in a San Antonio proud of the sort of ornamental pre-River Walk stonework in San Pedro Park, below, and in the Japanese Sunken Gardens, bottom right. He also drew inspiration from Mexico City's water gardens of Xochimilco, bottom left.

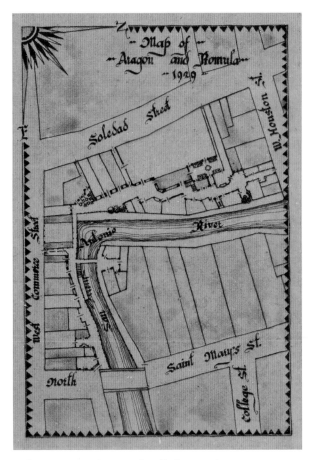

Robert Hugman's more detailed map of the Shops of Aragon and Romula shows Aragon's shop-lined lane beginning through Houston Street's Book Building at upper right center and winding down to the river level, then crossing to the Shops of Romula, on opposite sides of the river.

sufficiently impressed to endorse them with a "To Whom It May Concern" memo dated May 29, 1929. Chambers attested that the Shops of Aragon and Romula would be "a municipal improvement that will do much to preserve and enhance the distinctiveness of San Antonio, and as such it deserves the enthusiastic support of our loyal citizenship." While Chambers noted that it had not been officially accepted, he stated that the city "heartily endorses same, and if Mr. Hugman receives proper cooperation from owners along [the] route, we feel reasonably sure that the City will adopt same and begin work without delay."[7]

Armed with that endorsement, a month later Hugman took his drawings to a presentation at a Chamber of Commerce meeting of thirty business, civic and political leaders, including the mayor and two commissioners. He was introduced by Amanda Taylor, his early supporter who chaired the Conservation Society's river committee. Hugman stressed that his plan was of commercial value and must not be separated into parts. "Like a stage setting designed and directed by one mind to produce the proper unity of thought and feeling," it needed to be carried out as a unit, "shops, lighting effects, advertising—everything."[8]

Robert Hugman explained how his vision began with a romantic street near the Houston Street bridge, then the busiest span over the river. It would start at the street level with a passage leading through the three-story, red brick Book Building and opening into the Court of Roses, a "typical old Spanish patio" with flowers and flowing water overlooking the river. Hugman had been befriended by the 1906 landmark's builder, Dwight D. Book, a retired civil engineer who held out little hope for Hugman's goals but did allow him to be the "architect of the Book Building."[9]

Hugman described descent from the patio to "a quaint, old cobblestone street rambling lazily along the river, a "little street of my imagination," and the Shops of Aragon. The street would end at the start of the new cutoff channel with "a Plazita" and small café. From there, "leaving Aragon with its shaded charm," a stone footbridge would cross the river. Flagstone walkways would lead into the Great Bend and Romula. There would be a row of small shops along the bank immediately to the right and a bridge leading across to wider shops around a courtyard on the far side. Romula offered "unlimited opportunities for development in beautiful and interesting surroundings."

Near the far end of the bend, where the river was widest, Hugman would divide the channel "into two smaller streams to wind through a sunken garden, comparable in beauty to the famous gardens of Alcazar, or of the Alhambra." Hugman described how tourists could ride the length of Romula in brightly colored boats "fashioned after the gondolas of Venice, only with Spanish design. . . . It is a balmy night, fanned by gentle breezes fragrant with honeysuckle and sweet olive. Old-fashioned lamps cast fantastic shadows on the crystal surface of the water, and strains of soft music fill the night air.

"Who, if any," Hugman asked his listeners, "could resist such a unique and inviting atmosphere of romance and entertainment?"[10]

Most of those present pledged support. Two days later, the text of Hugman's proposal was published in the *Light*.[11]

But Robert Hugman found himself a pawn in a confrontation between the mayor and cost-cutters on one side and advocates of a professional city plan backed by the Conservation Society on the other.

The City Plan Committee came back with the recommendation to hire Harland Bartholomew and Associates to do San Antonio's long-awaited master plan. The firm's work, however would cost $40,000, today's equivalent of $545,000. Mayor Chambers, in the midst of an economy drive, was horrified at the fee. With a decision imminent, the mayor made a counter-proposal: use Hugman's plan for the river and get a master plan for the rest of the city through a nationwide competition. Prizes would total $7,000, a significant saving.

Leaders of the City Plan Committee, their hard-sought goal threatened at the last minute, would have none of it. Robert Hugman, once lauded for his plan, was hung out to dry. Hugman's plan was blasted as no more than an "idle dream" by City Plan Committee Chairman Newton H. White, who also headed the Chamber of Commerce. His committee had already studied the river, White told the mayor

In the 1920s, San Antonio's skyline was transformed by a burst of high-rise construction. In this 1930 view looking northwest, city hall is at left center edge and the courthouse below it. Below and to its right is the new Plaza Hotel, to its right the thirty-one-story Smith-Young Tower/Tower Life Building. The Great Bend winds in the foreground. Site of the Arneson River Theater is at bottom center.

and commissioners, and to adopt Hugman's plan would set his group's work back six months. In any event, White added, Bartholomew himself recognized the need to preserve San Antonio's individuality and the river. Local city plan competitions had already failed to produce results. How could out-of-town entrants with little monetary incentive do any better? Hugman's early backers at the Conservation Society, not wanting to jeopardize hiring Bartholomew, said nothing more of Aragon and Romula.[12]

City commissioners heard three more forceful opponents of the mayor's suggestion, and postponed a decision for three days. Then chairman Newton White and three of his committee members returned to plead the case for Bartholomew. Two speakers in the audience suggested that local architects and engineers be hired to do the master plan, and mentioned two candidates. The two were present, but rose and objected to doing the work. Harland Bartholomew was hired.[13]

That fall, the City Federation of Women's Clubs passed a resolution pleading that Hugman at least be hired as the river's landscape architect. The mayor replied that the question of Hugman's employment would have to wait.[14]

Harland Bartholomew, whose firm emphasized working closely with municipal governments to build consensus, took an active personal role in the San Antonio project. He gave particular attention to river improvements, a subject that dominated his first official visit late in 1929. In three years his firm produced a 400-page comprehensive city plan, covering streets, transportation, transit, zoning, recreation and civic art. The last category included a section titled "Proposed Treatment of the San Antonio River in the Central Business District."[15]

Bartholomew agreed that the San Antonio River was "one of the most distinctive and commendable features in the character of San Antonio. . . . To the visitor this is a picture not easily forgotten." He recommended a parkway along the river from downtown north through Brackenridge Park, an idea proposed the year before by Parks Commissioner Ray Lambert, to help make up for the city's deficiency in parkways and boulevards. But the most detailed river analysis was reserved for the downtown section.[16]

The master planner's solution for the Great Bend was the reverse of Hugman's. Instead of adding shops and restaurants beside the river, Bartholomew recommended that commercial activity be kept at street level and that riverside landscaping below maintain a natural, contemplative linear park through the heart of the busy city. Groupings of water elm, sycamore, cypress and pecan trees were to

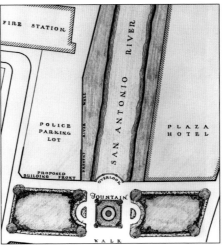

Harland Bartholomew's master plan would cover the cutoff channel as a pedestrian mall, with facing shops on either side, far left. The river bend would be inaccessible to pedestrians, who would view it from overlooks like the one proposed, left, where the end of the bend would disappear under the landscaped cover of the cutoff channel.

provide shade, screen backs of buildings, and overhang the water. Low flowers and reeds would line the channel. Flowering native shrubs would break up the straight vertical lines of retaining walls and produce masses of color, and vines would climb walls and lattices and provide ground cover. Beside bridges, tall evergreen cypresses would frame river views, with date and banana palms adding a tropical note. Riverside planting outside the bend, where tall landscaping would slow floodwaters, would be groups of low shrubs, flowers and vines to climb masonry walls. There would be only a few benches. General recreation was ruled out as too distracting.

He did find room in his plan for the sort of romantic shops Hugman had proposed for his Aragon and Romula. Engineers told Bartholomew that the "ugly and glaring" cutoff channel could handle major floodwaters even if it were covered with a top of reinforced concrete. Bartholomew proposed turning such a cover into a pedestrian mall, with walkways ten feet wide on either side of a fifty-foot-wide grassy median and landscaping of cacti and native plants able to thrive on just two feet of earth fill. At each end a fountain and overlook would offer vistas of the main river channel. Buildings facing or backing on the new mall could have doorways cut through to create shop facades with the sort of aging ambiance that eventually emerged as doorways were cut into existing basement walls along the River Walk. Additional colorful shops would be built on vacant lots, providing an overall total of 950 feet of new retail frontage that would generate tax revenues to pay for the project.[17]

Though Bartholomew's solution may have addressed beautification of both the river and the yawning cutoff channel, by the time the plan was finished and formally recommended to city commissioners it was March 1933. The full force of the Depression had plunged downtown San Antonio into a slump from which it would not recover for nearly forty years. San Antonio's building boom was at an abrupt end. City hall lost nearly twenty percent of a full year's operating funds in the city's worst bank failure, and there were massive layoffs of municipal workers. Civic morale wasn't helped by the fact that in 1930 Dallas had overtaken San Antonio as the largest city in Texas.

In the month that Bartholomew's plan was presented to the city, C. M. Chambers became San Antonio's fourth mayor in twenty-one years to die while in office. Some recommendations, including the city's first zoning ordinances and a street plan, had been implemented along the way, but other major recommendations went on hold.[18]

By this time, San Antonio's proud self-reliance of the previous decade was but a memory. There were federal funds for unemployed former city workers and for municipal projects, and city hall was now happy to share in the largesse. Robert Hugman found employment on the federal payroll with the Works Progress Administration as a planner under State Administrator Henry P. Drought and District Director Edwin P. Arneson, a civil engineer. Hugman helped redesign Woodlawn Lake, Elmendorf Lake and Concepción Park. In 1935 he supervised WPA design of a section along Walnut Creek in Seguin's Starke Park, thirty miles east of San Antonio. Its walkways and stone elements foreshadowed those of San Antonio's River Walk, though repeatedly damaged by unregulated flooding. Hugman continued to promote his plans for Aragon and Romula to all who would listen, hoping for some way to revive them.[19]

Despite the lack of action on so many of Bartholomew's recommendations, the city did not abandon river beautification. Renewed efforts focused on the old Tobin Terrace, the banks below Crockett Street between the St. Mary's and Navarro street bridges. In 1934, City Parks Commissioner Jacob Rubiola's Parks Department restored the riverside cascade built ten years earlier on the riverbank behind St. Mary's College to discharge air conditioning runoff piped underground from the Majestic Theater. The next spring, parks workers wrapped ten new flowerbeds nearby in low walls of native stone.[20]

Persistent hints of the commercial appeal of a beautified river continued. The occasional boat could still tie up beneath the Houston Street Bridge near the Book Building's basement, occupied in the 1920s by the Coffee House and the Riverside

In 1934–35, city parks workers restored the cascade discharging Majestic Theater air conditioning runoff into the river and also built a series of semicircular stone walls supporting flowerbeds.

Club and in the 1930s by Adolph Obadal's Riverside Gardens. Obadal counted on Olmos Dam to keep his restaurant dry, but the main river channel was still vulnerable. San Antonio's flood prevention system passed its first big test during a June 1935 downpour, when twenty feet of water were held behind Olmos Dam. But heavy rains a year later built up so much water behind the dam that its gates were opened to reduce the level. Water surging downstream below Houston Street—"where gondolas usually ply"— rose nearly to the ceiling of Riverside Gardens before reaching the cutoff channel.[21]

Safely at street level on the opposite bank was the longtime Riverside Restaurant/Cafe, with its balcony over the river park. Across the street past the Texas Theater, the Rio Vista Mexican Restaurant was among businesses on the block-long Riverside Walk, which extended to Travis Street along the upper edge of the river's retaining wall. Above the river elsewhere, other restaurants also advertised their river views. One was La Casa del Rio Café, in the historic Twohig house above the entrance to the Great Bend before it was disassembled and rebuilt on the riverbank behind the Witte Museum in Brackenridge Park. The move, in 1942, was the last project completed by WPA workers in Texas.[22]

The Riverside Gardens at the Houston Street Bridge hung out a sign in 1935 as the "Official San Juan Canteen," bottom left, to draw Spanish-American War veteran conventioneers down to the river. Four years later, as construction of the River Walk began, a visiting *Fortune* magazine artist imagined the bistro as a trendy Nite Spot, bottom right, of the sort hoped for along the river.

At the far end of the bend, the young manager of the swank Plaza Hotel, A. C. (Jack) White, knew that the river could help business, but as the city beautified the river upstream he thought the dreary stretch past the Plaza should be getting some attention, too. While bringing up the subject at City Hall, White spoke with long-time Building Inspector John L. Richter, who asked White why he was focusing on a small part of the river when the whole river downtown could be improved with Robert Hugman's plan. White had not heard of Hugman, and went to see him. "Being a hotel man and visualizing the importance of such a project to tourism," recalled Hugman, "he became very interested."[23]

Since Hugman was working for the WPA, he and Jack White met with the state and local directors, Henry Drought and Edwin Arneson, both San Antonians, to see if the WPA might be interested. They realized, Hugman remembered, "it could be turned into a marvelous . . . make-work project. It was strung out, it could work thousands of men and we had so many rock masons and artisans here that could do a good job." Discussions continued.[24]

Then came the enthusiasm of the Texas Centennial of 1936.

The Alamo Chapter of the Daughters of the American Revolution made "beautifying and conserving the natural charm of the San Antonio River" a centennial project. It was endorsed by the parks commissioner, who toured the river down from Brackenridge Park with two DAR members and promised the city would help clear away dead trees and refuse. Unable to get city funds to light the bend between Travis and Nueva streets at night, the Daughters got the money instead

TUCK THIS BLOTTER IN YOUR PURSE

Y. W. C. A. CAFETERIA
Cor. Presa and Crockett Streets (by the bridge)

(5 BLOCKS STRAIGH SOUTH FROM AUDITORIUM)

CENTRAL · MODERN · ATTRACTIVE
DELIGHTFULLY COOL

HOURS: 8 A. M. TO 7:15 P. M.
WAFFLE BREAKFAST

HAVE SUPPER ON THE BALCONY OVERLOOKING THE RIVER

Proximity to the river was a plus for restaurants at street level. La Casa del Rio Café occupied the historic Twohig House above the entrance to the Great Bend. The Rocking M Dude Ranch left diners with photos of their riverside evening.

Jack White, manager of the swank new Plaza Hotel, above, welcomed dedication near the hotel in 1936 of motorboats, upper right, planning to begin regular trips for passengers around the Great Bend.

from the city's independent Centennial Committee, which relied on state and federal funding.[25]

San Antonio's major centennial celebration began at the Alamo at sunup on March 5, 1936—one hundred years after the siege—and continued daylong with speeches, concerts, parades, presentations, a Pontifical High Mass and a flyover by nine bombers from Kelly Field. The ascendant city of Dallas may have out-hustled San Antonio to land the Centennial Exposition, complete with a reproduction of the Alamo, but the message was clear that San Antonio still had the real Alamo. And, unlike Dallas, San Antonio had a river to celebrate on as well.[26]

The next month came Fiesta, even more elaborate that anniversary year with the first Venetian carnival and gala river parade in twenty-nine years, now that a permanent low dam at the end of the bend backed up enough water to float boats.

On April 20, near the start of the Great Bend on the banks of the old Tobin Terrace, the DAR ceremoniously christened two flower-bedecked motorboats, complete with canvas awnings with scalloped fringes, in an effort to revive boating on the river as a fiesta activity each year. The next day more than 10,000 people

The first gala fiesta river parade in twenty-nine years passed the Plaza Hotel, left edge, during the Texas Centennial in April 1936, generating enthusiasm that would help lead to a WPA project and the River Walk.

crowded riverbanks near the Plaza Hotel to watch a parade of eighteen decorated boats. Co-chairing the parade were Plaza Manager Jack White and funeral director Andrew Morales, president of the Mexican Business Men's Association, who brought the boat decoration plans up from Mexico City, presumably used for boats in the water gardens of Xochimilco. Two bands played, a company of dancers performed and flower girls in Mexican costumes strolled the banks. The next day gondola rides began from a landing near the Plaza Hotel.[27]

If Jack White or any others needed solid testimony to the potential draw of an energized river, as Robert Hugman had proposed, this was it.

The River Walk, completed in 1941, transformed San Antonio's river park. At lower right, air conditioning runoff from the Majestic Theater becomes a waterfall flowing out between River Walk flagstones. Beyond a rustic cedar bench, a narrow arched bridge frames the arches of a flood control gate controlling water level inside the Great Bend. At far left center, a limestone block pillar supports a tree bending upward to Crockett Street.

· 6 ·
The Venice of America

Ten thousand enthusiastic spectators at the fiesta river parade in 1936 drove home a point to Jack White: there was great promise for a San Antonio River Walk.

The cheering around his Plaza Hotel still echoed in his ears as White got serious about how to get the River Walk done. He had seen Robert Hugman's plans. Hugman, conveniently, was now an architect with the WPA, the prime funding target for such a project. And Hugman's associates at the local WPA office thought it was a good idea, too.

Encouraged by the interest of a businessman of Jack White's caliber, WPA officials gave their blessing for Hugman and WPA engineer Edwin Arneson to do preliminary planning. Hugman did new sketches for a river walk, block by block, so cost estimates could be made. In January 1938 White organized a blue-ribbon committee as the San Antonio River Beautification Association. Members compensated Hugman and Arneson for their work. The plans were made public on the last Sunday in April. Drawings were displayed in the Plaza Hotel. A request for partial funding went to city council four days later.[1]

When Hugman's revised proposal was announced, the terms "Aragon" and "Romula" had disappeared, along with romantic phrases like "sunken garden of loveliness." Thanks to tips from advertising executive Tom McNamara, White could declare that this project would make San Antonio nothing less than the Venice of America.

Said White: "The committee believes that the river can be made the outstanding beauty spot of this country. Other cities can have beautiful parks, great zoos, magnificent stadiums and other attractions, but we know of no city that has a beauty spot such as we propose to make of the river. . . . It would attract unlimited publicity to the city from newspapers, magazines, newsreels and other mediums. A boat ride on the San Antonio River would attract tourists to this city as the gondolas do to Venice."

The full length of the river park would be transformed, as would additional blocks north past Municipal Auditorium to Fourth Street/Lexington Avenue. The idea of a grand entrance of shops descending a cobblestone street from Houston Street to the river was abandoned—the site was on private property anyway—in favor of broader access down more than two dozen new stairways

On the west bank of the Great Bend between Crockett and Commerce streets, top, a row of restaurants architect Robert Hugman dubbed Foods of All Nations would be anchored by the Clifford Building at far left left and the Casino Building at far right. Across on the east bank, above, he foresaw a row of shops in new and existing buildings.

from adjoining streets. An outdoor theater would have its stage on one side of the river and seating on the other. Along walkways beside newly terraced banks, doors would be cut into the backs of existing buildings as "beautiful front entrances of shops, cafes, etc., so that visitors and residents of the city could shop from a gondola." For the block between Commerce and Crockett streets, Hugman and illustrator Peyton Cooper prepared renderings to show how buildings on opposite banks could be redeveloped with newer structures into a promenade of shops and a row of restaurants known as Foods of All Nations.[2]

Understated design was paramount. Said Hugman: "I'll die if it looks like Hollywood."[3]

Initial cost estimates totaled $265,000, today's equivalent of $4.4 million. The city was asked for $50,000. Businessmen along the river from Municipal Auditorium to the Plaza Hotel would be asked to contribute $2.50 per foot of their river frontage to raise another $40,000. Once that $90,000 was raised locally, the Works Progress Administration would contribute the remaining two-thirds.

But city commissioners, Depression-era pressure making them even more frugal, declined to bring bond issue funding to a public vote. At least one commissioner, Frank Bushick, didn't get the big picture. Declaring his opposition to anything that would increase the city's tax burden, Bushick said: "This is a special

STEERING THE RIVER WALK TO REALITY

A. C. "Jack" White was just the person to take charge of Robert Hugman's plans for the River Walk, make the right friends and steer the project safely through a maze of bewildering obstacles. He was well tested in the ways of making up his mind and getting things done.

Born on a cotton farm near Weatherford and orphaned when he was six, he worked his way through grade school and high school. In 1907, at the age of 16, White came to San Antonio as night clerk at the Gunter Hotel and in six years became assistant manager. Ten years later he was manager of the new Robert E. Lee Hotel. After two years, he left in 1925 to manage the new Hilton Hotel in Dallas. Two years after that he was back in San Antonio as opening manager of the twelve-story Plaza Hotel, at the end of the Great Bend on part of the former Bowen's Island.

The Plaza and its restaurant overlooked a long neglected part of the San Antonio River, leading White in his search for change to find the architect Robert H. H. Hugman. The river parade White co-chaired in

1936 drew more than 10,000 people practically to the Plaza's doors, proving the potential of the enlivened River Walk Hugman had proposed. As chairman of the San Antonio River Beautification Board, White oversaw the project to completion in 1941.

When Hugman first discussed his project with White, Hugman remembered White saying, "This is marvelous. It's going to make me mayor."[1]

White next developed White-Plaza Hotels in San Antonio, Dallas and Corpus Christi, was elected president of the San Antonio Chamber of Commerce in 1948 and the next year was in fact elected mayor. He resigned in 1954, seven years before his death, after leading San Antonio through a stormy charter reform that permitted adoption of the current council-manager form of city government.

[1] Hugman, "Oral History," 5.

Jack White, center, engineered River Walk funding and oversaw the project to completion. At his left is Robert H. Turk, WPA construction superintendent, and at his right Robert McNamara, supervising engineer for the city.

issue which will benefit only a few people, the property owners along the river. The property owners are not small homeowners, but are big businessmen."[4]

A month later White announced that the $30,000 pledged so far by river property owners "has exceeded even our fondest expectations." But he was still far short of the $90,000 needed, and made a pass at replacing city funding with state funding through the Texas State Parks Board.[5]

When that ploy proved fruitless, White had a breakthrough. A once common technique to raise funds to improve a limited area was for residents to petition to form an improvement district. They then would vote to assess themselves to raise their own bond funds. White outlined an area approximately a block and a half wide down each side of the river from Municipal Auditorium to the Plaza Hotel. He got ninety property owners within that area to petition the city for permission to form an improvement district that would authorize the sale of $75,000 in bonds. That would make up for the lack of city funding and the shortfall in river property owners' pledges.[6]

City commissioners approved formation of the improvement zone, officially known as District No. 15. Within its boundaries were as many as 1,300 property owners, though only 107 lived there and were eligible to vote. Those few, however, owned $20 million—two-thirds—of its $32 million in assessed property value. A vote was set for October 25. The proposal passed 74 to 2. Mayor C. K. Quin and city commissioners appointed an eight-member San Antonio River Central Improvement Committee, later known as the River Beautification Board, to coordinate planning.[7]

Now that substantial local funding was assured, federal WPA funds could provide the remainder. The process was expedited by Congressman Maury Maverick, an ally of President Franklin D. Roosevelt. One story has it that the colorful Maverick was motivated to improve the river one night when he and his friend Louis Lipscomb went down to the banks of the river to relieve themselves. Maverick slipped and fell in. "Louis," he reportedly said as he pulled himself out, "we've got to do something about this river." Another story reports that funding was finalized when Roosevelt called his secretary of the interior, Harold Ickes, and, in his characteristic accent, ordered: "Harold, give Maury the money for his damn rivah so he will stop bothering me."[8]

As architectural and engineering plans were finalized, the project began to draw national attention, as Jack White had predicted. A February 1939 *New York*

Times travel story was headlined, "Gondolas For Texans: San Antonio to Convert City Stream Into an 'American Venice.' " The *Times* said the development would give "San Antonio a main street such as no other city will have and [make] it 'the city where you shop from gondolas.' "[9]

During an interview with the *Express*, Robert Hugman held his straight-stemmed pipe and spoke "rapidly for a native-born Texan" as he outlined his "colorful street in Mexico transplanted to downtown San Antonio. Here a potter will spin his wheel, shaping the simple pieces to delight visitors. A basket weaver may be next door. A few paces away, a Latin American florist will be tempting a visitor with exotic blooms. All the business that flourishes below the Rio Grande, lazily and charmingly conducted, will be found here." Adding to the ambience were to be swans and water pheasants, floating islands, adobe shops and brightly colored tile work.

Hugman predicted that within two years businessmen would spend as much as $5 million of their own money on retail development along the river. He noted, though, "The bonds and the WPA can only create the opportunity. That's as far as public agencies can go in developing the river street."[10]

On the morning of March 29, 1939, San Antonio's WPA-funded Tipica Orchestra played Mexican favorites as three hundred San Antonians gathered at Navarro Street's Mill Bridge to watch Jack White put his foot to a golden shovel and break ground for the River Walk. Construction got off to a quick start, despite a change in engineers. Robert Hugman had been hired to do the design and architectural work, Edwin P. Arneson to do the engineering and Robert H. Turk to be construction superintendent. Just after he signed his contract, however, Arneson, 50, was diagnosed with terminal cancer, and died a few months later. He was replaced by Walter H. Lilly, who began preparing WPA grant applications for various segments of the project.[11]

The greatest concentration of new features would occur along the three-quarter-mile course of the Great Bend. To the north, along the river park's mile-long stretch above the Great Bend, there would be newly configured channel walls, low rock features and low plantings, but more extensive work would interfere with flood control. Workers along a northern channel bend below Augusta Street came up

Edwin P. Arneson died soon after signing on as the River Walk's project engineer, and was remembered in the naming of the Arneson River Theater.

River Beautification Board Chairman Jack White broke ground for the WPA's River Walk project on March 29, 1939.

with thousands of crawfish in the mud, and dubbed the curve Crawfish Bend.[12]

To start, the Great Bend had to be drained. The bypass channel bulkhead built high enough to divert water into the bend was cut lower, so the entire flow of the river spilled directly into the cutoff channel. A bulkhead gate beneath the water level was also opened. At the bend's entrance, a cofferdam was built to block any additional flow, leaving the bend with only puddles from runoff and a muddy trickle from adjacent springs. Existing plants and shrubs were transplanted to a temporary nursery in Brackenridge Park. Remaining trees were kept watered and their roots protected. Decayed limbs were pruned, hollow trunks plugged with concrete and weak trees braced.[13]

The cofferdam was completed at the end of March 1939. Work could then begin on a permanent solution to keeping water in the bend at a level so precise that during heavy rains riverside shops would not have high water coming in the front door. Control by floodgates, promised long before, was the answer. Hugman designed one gatehouse for the entry to the bend at the north. At the south he designed a more complicated gate structure that could not only block rising waters but also raise the water level behind it back up the entire bend. Thus the bend's water, instead of falling seven feet from the start of the bend to the end, would fall only one foot, slowing the current so gondolas could be poled upstream.

Since gondoliers also needed an even riverbed to pole in, shallow places had to be cut down and deep ones filled. The consistent depth would be approximately three and a half feet, also shallow enough to guard against drowning. "After we drained the river, the bottom was full of muck in some cases five or six feet deep," remembered Hugman. "We had to build temporary platforms so that bulldozers and drag lines could get in there." Workmen with hand shovels, wheelbarrows, cranes dragging buckets at the end of a line and the occasional bulldozer removed thousands of truckloads of refuse—broken wagon wheels, wrecked bicycles, barbed wire, even sunken barrels that once kept bathhouses afloat.[14]

A plank footbridge, far left, crossed the drained bend south of the Commerce Street Bridge, as existing plants were temporarily transplanted to a nursery in Brackenridge Park. Tree roots were protected and leaning trees, left, gained custom-made supports.

At the northern terminus of the River Walk, workmen seen from the Fourth Street/Lexington Avenue Bridge cleared the riverbed and constructed walls below what became known as the Hugman Dam. El Tropicano Hotel was later built above the bank at left.

Workmen tore out the river park's two miles of concrete-covered rock walls, spaced apart so evenly they seemed to line a canal. Hugman believed the old walls extended too starkly above the water line and "confined the water to an extremely unnatural bank line." He designed new walls of native limestone not covered by concrete to bend gently and unevenly, almost imperceptibly in places, to give the impression that they followed natural contours. By subtly redirecting the water as it flowed, the new walls would also prevent buildup of the sandbars caused by the previous walls, which encouraged water to flow unchallenged on just one side of the channel while silt built up on the other side.[15]

Getting the Water Level Right

Key to Robert Hugman's plan for businesses at sidewalk level along the river bend was maintaining a stable level of water within the bend. When the bypass channel was completed in 1930, high water dropped over a bulkhead spillway below the northern end of the bend into the deeper bypass channel. Normal flow went around the bend and, at the southern end, over a low dam into the bypass channel and on south. But neither the spillway at the bend's beginning nor the low dam at its end could guarantee that the highest waters could not partly overflow into the bend.

Too, the top of the dam at the southern end was seven feet lower than the level of water entering the bend. An important feature of Hugman's plan was to have gondolas on the river. The seven-foot fall created a current too swift for gondoliers to be able to pole their boats upstream. Hugman's solution was an elaborate control structure at the southern end that not only sealed off possible high water but also dammed the level of water within the bend so the fall was not seven feet but one foot.

Hugman's elaborate southern control structure had two tiers. At the end was a dam for water to flow over into the bypass channel. Above it, an arch supported a street-level sidewalk. When viewed from upstream, the arch and its reflection joined to form a picturesque oval.

Inside the bend, a steel floodgate by the dam lay submerged in a pool, ready to swing upward and seal off the bend. The pool was created by a four-foot dam slightly upstream that curved gently in a forty-foot arc, allowing water to form a smooth, picturesque curtain as it flowed into the pool four feet below.

The northern control structure was a simpler matter. There, maintaining the water level did not complicate the design. A steel gate simply had to drop when high waters were coming.

The north gate, however, would have its own distinctive charm. Hugman broke up its lower level with a series of arches, through two of which gondolas could pass. Stairs allowed pedestrians to reach Commerce Street and also to cross to the other side, through a portico open on the side facing the bend. The portico was crossed above by cedar posts, which cast shadows on the rear wall that hid the floodgate. By requiring a wall to hide it, the floodgate served the dual purpose of blocking the view of buildings behind it, further screening the romantic River Walk from the world outside.

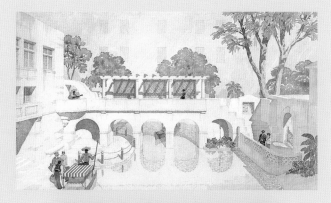

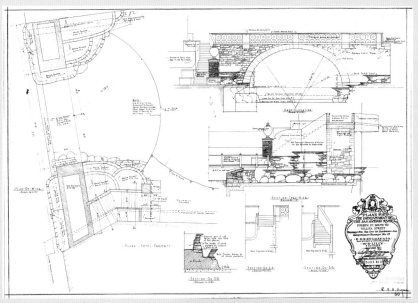

For the river bend's northern flood control gate, architect Robert Hugman designed a Spanish-style structure to screen the gate with a superstructure that also served as a shadowed walkway.

Where the end of the Great Bend emptied into the bypass channel, Hugman designed a low, curving upper dam that both raised the bend's water level behind it and created a pond, below, that hid a submerged flood control gate.

Beside the banks Hugman planned "simple gravel walks," but those were overruled as impractical. Instead would be solid walks of flagstones, cobblestone, brick and concrete inlaid with pebbles. Walkability was tested by women wearing shoes with different types of heels. The walks featured nearly a dozen geometric designs—some colored—to maintain a sense of ongoing discovery, enhancing the anticipation of new views framed beneath bridges. Where an abutment under the North Presa Street bridge left a sharp vertical corner with no space for a path, Hugman designed a walkway that swung widely around and over the water. Buttresses topped by railings held the walkway's thin slabs barely above the water, making it appear to float, while the glow of electric lights beneath the walk were to add drama to the scene. Linking opposite banks would be two narrow footbridges of limestone blocks, arched high enough so gondoliers could remain standing as they passed beneath.[16]

To emphasize the break with the modern city, waist-level gates of wrought iron would have to be opened at the street to descend the uniquely designed stairways. Down at the river was a new world of decorative rockwork, meandering walkways, semitropical landscaping, water features and benches and lampposts of rustic cedar. Since the Venice of America merited more than plain tie-up posts for gondolas, Hugman designed three types of wooden poles with distinctive turnings and stripes to be painted in colors he would choose. Descriptive plaques of brightly colored tiles made under the direction of Ethel Harris in another WPA project were to decorate retaining walls at two locations. A series of WPA tiles depicting the

Rigidly even walls of the 1914 river park encouraged water to flow toward one side of a curve, causing silt to build up on the other side into sandbars such as those near the center of the river in both 1932 photos below. The left view is upstream toward the northernmost Navarro Street Bridge, at right downstream toward the Augusta Street Bridge. The new River Walk's walls were slightly irregular, redirecting water flow and preventing the problem—and also giving the appearance of more natural banks.

history of Texas was to spread along a retaining wall known as Memory Lane below Crockett Street.[17]

Near the end of the bend, in the wide area once a millpond, Hugman planned three floating islands—two small wooden rafts chained to either side of a third and larger raft, all anchored to large concrete blocks by heavy chains fifteen feet long, allowing them to move with the current. Hugman designed huts on the rafts for waterfowl.

Eight switches hidden at intervals along the banks would control an electrical system of floodlights, wrought iron lanterns, lights below thick groupings of water plants and colored lights at strategic locations. There were to be special streetlights at the base of stairways and at gondola landings.[18]

As worked got underway, Hugman, recalled, "Mr. Turk and I soon realized that the men did not need much of an excuse to lean on their shovels. But at the same time, they were interested in the project itself." So Hugman and Turk "purposely talked loud enough for them to hear and understand." Then "all the workmen within earshot would stop and listen intently to our conversation [and] return to their work with added vigor and purpose." Thought Hugman: "That was one reason the project went so well. Each man knew what *he* was trying to create."[19]

Turk said the stonemasons "seemed to have a knack of knowing which rock to put where. When we would give a rock to a bricklayer, he would chip around on it and get nowhere. But the stonemasons got the job done."[20]

Two days before Christmas 1939, the cofferdam blocking water from the Great Bend was removed. Jack White ceremoniously turned the wheel to close the cutoff

New forms appearing with River Walk construction were, from left, a sidewalk supported over the river around a sharp corner below the North Presa Street Bridge; an arched bridge to be faced with limestone rocks; and varied patterns embedded in walkways.

A twisting pattern of bricks formed the supporting column of a stairway from Crockett Street facing the river and leading to a vista of backs of buildings that would depress visitors for more than two decades.

Widely varying stairway designs included, clockwise from upper left, a sweeping staircase to the Smith-Young/Tower Life Building at South St. Mary's Street; a limestone stairway past a stone bench softening the gloom beneath the Market Street Bridge; one partly of rustic cedar, later replaced, to the Crockett Street Bridge; and one of thick concrete being built at the Navarro Street/Mill Bridge.

A variety of lights were designed for stairways and gondola landings. Lighting descent from the St. Mary's Street Bridge near the head of the bend was a lamp hanging from a cedar post. At a landing below the Commerce Street Bridge was a fixture atop a pole with a cast iron base, with the iron Crockett Street Bridge in the background.

channel's bulkhead gate, raising the water level upstream and diverting it into the bend for the first time in nine months. Another two months remained for planting—or transplanting from the temporary nursery site—11,734 trees and shrubs, 1,500 banana trees and 1,489 square yards of grass. The project's final phase, lining and landscaping the channel of the bend north to Municipal Auditorium, would start in the new year.[21]

But among those closely watching the project unfold, all was not well. The specter of the beloved river bend stripped of its plantings and of the bend's muddy channel churned up for walls, walks, stairways and bridges in fanciful patterns of jarring, freshly cut limestone became too much for many San Antonians to bear, especially those who preferred the pastoral park favored by the distinguished Harland Bartholomew. What did this Robert Hugman think he was doing?

Three months into the project Hugman was already having to defend himself. His design would soon be in "as naturalistic [a] setting as possible," he explained. "Everything is being done to avoid a raw, new, garish effect." The look did not bother Ernie Pyle, who filed a syndicated newspaper column from San Antonio praising the project while noting, "Right now the new bare stonework seems harsh and cold. But age and shrubbery will soften that."[22]

Locally, however, Hugman was finding new critics in practically every direction. "There was too much walk work, the bridges were like Japanese bridges, and so on," he said. Emily Edwards, his former teacher at Brackenridge High School

From Junkyard to Theater

One inspired feature of River Walk design was an open-air theater past the Great Bend's last abrupt turn as it headed west to meet the cutoff channel. The stage would be on one side of the river, seating on the opposite bank.

At first it seemed a most unpromising site.

At street level behind the stage location loomed the City Water Board's industrial buildings and smokestacks. Near them, only a horizontal pipe kept parked cars from rolling over the bank and into the river. Across, seating would be below the dilapidated small homes of La Villita. Along the bank, auto repair and machine shop workers had dumped "many tons of machine parts, grease and car frames." On one side of that mess abruptly rose the intimidating electrical conduits and steel superstructure of the City Public Service power plant.

Robert Hugman saw beyond. He built the stage in a crescent outward from the north bank. He backed it with narrow stone arches beside a compact white stucco stage house with a red tile roof and decorative dovecote. Cast and crew would cross a narrow, arched bridge.

Across, once debris was hauled off, came excavations for a curved tier of concrete bleachers cut into the bank for 1,000 spectators. Pockmarks were pounded into the concrete risers to make them appear carved from natural rock. Sod was laid over the concrete seating to complete a natural appearance. Above was a white stucco, tile-roofed enclosure whose use as a movie projection and broadcast room did not develop. Nor was plumbing installed in the river bottom as first planned to produce a screen of water spraying upward between acts.

Next to the erstwhile broadcast room, an archway led into the National Youth Administration's La Villita restoration, a favorite project of Maury Maverick, the former River Walk-backing congressman and newly elected mayor.

As years passed, the smokestacks and buildings that overwhelmed the stage came down. Landscaping screened the rest. The power plant was replaced with Villita Assembly Hall. When completed in 1941, the theater was named in memory of Edwin Arneson, the project engineer who died just as River Walk work was beginning.

Plans for a new theater, top left on facing page, showed how a bridge across the narrow river could link a stage on one side and seating on the other. Tons of machine and auto parts had to be cleared to pour concrete for the seating, lower left, that could follow the contour of the bank. A rare snowfall in January 1940 provided the opportunity, top right, for perhaps the first drama in the still-unfinished theater.

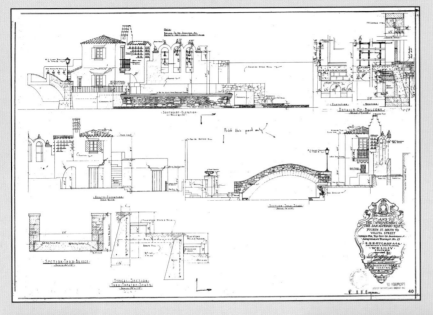

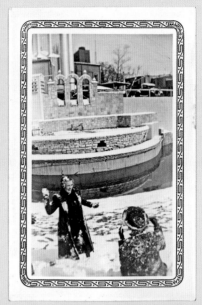

The view south from the Houston Street Bridge, left, leads in the distance to where the newly planted River Walk turned left into the Great Bend, avoiding the cutoff channel. The turn appears at right, with the Houston Street Bridge in the background. A flagstone walk in foreground crosses the top of the cutoff channel's bulkhead, permitting the regular flow to continue around the sharp bend while floodwater could flow straight and over the bulkhead into the channel below.

and cofounder of the San Antonio Conservation Society, didn't like the project, and asked to meet with her former student. A group of artists including the Conservation Society's other founder, Rena Maverick Green, a member of the City Plan Committee that endorsed Bartholomew's plan, resolved "that the stone work is much overdone, and looks so fantastic." Worse, Mrs. Green began complaining to her cousin Maury Maverick, the mayor. Even more ominously, Ruth White, the wife of Jack White, who oversaw the River Walk project, didn't like the way it was looking either.[23]

As work began in the upper channel past Houston Street to Municipal Auditorium, it was obvious that Hugman's pleas for patience—everything would mellow and look better with time—were not working. In January 1940 the Conservation Society passed a resolution condemning the project's "desecration of the beauties of San Antonio." The society endorsed Rena Green's letter to the *Light* entitled "A plea for simplicity in further landscaping of the river." Observed the letter: "San Antonio is surrounded by rock quarries and our last two park commissioners were stone masons, so the temptation to excessive stone work was great." At the urging of Ruth White, a critique on the "excessive stone work" was sent to Hugman.[24]

Rena Green sent one copy of the Conservation Society's resolution to the eminent architect Atlee B. Ayres, who as chairman of a committee nearly three decades earlier had backed a more conservative river project. Ayres replied that Hugman's work "was not done in a simple manner." He declared flatly: "With few exceptions, it is a most unwise expenditure and will be a source of ridicule to our tourist friends and others. I do hope that we won't have any more of this misnamed river beautification."[25]

Mrs. Green sent another copy of the resolution to Hugman, who could only respond with his familiar refrain that "given a little time, the softening effect of the planting that is just now getting under way will remove at least most of these objections." Through landscaping, "practically all of the new walls will be concealed and the result will be much more pleasing. However, I know that this is hard to visualize at the present time."[26]

Hugman found it difficult to compromise. When Mayor Maverick recommended he hire one of the mayor's cousins who was a landscape architect, Hugman refused on the grounds that it would be a political hiring, plus that the newcomer would be paid "$35 a day out of the meager fee I was getting."[27]

Since Hugman would not shift his emphasis from rockwork on his own, Mayor Maverick, who was catching much of the criticism, decided to force the issue by simply cutting Hugman's supply of the offending material. Agreeing with his cousin Rena Green that too much stone may have been used, Maverick wrote her, "In line with your ideas, I have eliminated a large amount that they originally planned to use."[28]

Maverick made good on his statement and Hugman, tipped off by a WPA bookkeeper, found his materials going instead to another project—La Villita—and was furious. Lacking the political instincts and close personal connections that would have helped him deal with the reality of what he was up against, Hugman collected copies of vouchers for the diverted materials and presented them with a protest directly to Judge Claude Birkhead, one of his original backers and a member of the project's oversight board. To Hugman's dismay, rather than being outraged at the revelation Birkhead was annoyed at him. Birkhead asked the oversight committee chairman, Jack White, to call a board meeting to discuss the situation. In March 1940 Robert Hugman was unanimously fired.[29]

A higher risk of flooding north of the bend limited riverside improvements to minimal landscaping, low rock features and these high cantilevered and scalloped riverside walks between Houston and Travis streets and the Milam building, in background. A double entrance visible across the river from the tree at center opened for a stairway up to an alley to Soledad Street.

HOW TO HIDE AN UGLY DRAINPIPE

Drainpipes protruding from banks above the river could become design opportunities.

River Walk architect Robert Hugman's most-photographed solution is near the buildings of the old St. Mary's College, where an underground pipe sent air conditioning runoff from the Majestic Theater rushing into the river. The spot had already been improved as a low cascade. Hugman rebuilt it with honeycomb rocks, hid the end of the pipe with banana trees and shrubs and captured the runoff in a pond. Flowing more slowly from the pond, the runoff fanned into the river between stepping stones in an arc rimming the pond's edge as part of the River Walk.

Another solution was found for the pipe on the west bank of the upper River Walk north of Travis Street, where the Milam Building's air conditioning system drained. A fanciful rock bridge attached to the retaining wall arched the pipe's mouth, further screened by lush planting in a new pond studded with boulders to reduce the force of

the water discharging into the river. The steps crossed to nowhere, for there was then no walkway along that bank.

On the opposite bank, runoff from a storm drain was made to appear as emerging from a newly built small cave.

But sometimes less could be done. Under a wall supporting the Commerce Street Bridge, a wide drainpipe discharged runoff from air conditioning at Joske's Department Store. Screens of honeycomb rock, ferns and an outflow under the narrow sidewalk were tried, but "there was not space enough there to build anything attractive," Hugman found, and he thought the effort "not very successful."[1]

[1] Hugman, "Oral History," 17.

Near the old St. Mary's College, a hidden drainage pipe's discharge cascaded over rocks, above, forming mini-waterfalls as it flowed between steppingstones into the river. Near the Travis Street Bridge, another pipe was screened by a fanciful bridge and plantings, its discharge slowed by small boulders in a pond before reaching the river.

A WPA mural of 154 tiles supervised by designer Ethel Harris was installed near the Navarro Street/Mill Bridge, the historic location of a river ford. The Nat Lewis Mill once above the site shows at upper right. The WPA logo is at the scene's lower left. Corner tiles feature four cattle brands. A smaller mural was installed at the bend's north floodgate.

OLD MILL CROSSING–LAST KNOWN PLACE WHERE HORSES DRANK AND FORDED THE RIVER. DEDICATED TO THE MEMORY OF OUR FATHERS ERECTED BY THE DAUGHTERS OF TEXAS TRAIL DRIVERS.

Hugman charged that he was the victim of "machine politics" for not hiring the mayor's landscape architect cousin. He first threatened legal action against the city, but finally decided "a poor boy does not fight city hall." Construction Superintendent Robert Turk said later that "Hugman never really got over being fired. We would fish together after we both retired, and he talked about it many times." Observed Hugman years after: "I think this was the greatest disappointment of my life—not because I expected any more from Maverick, but that the prominent citizens of San Antonio, who knew all that I had done, didn't say a word in my behalf."[30]

For his part, Mayor Maverick explained to the press merely that "work on the project has reached a point where less formal rock architecture and more landscaping with shrubs, trees and flowers is needed." The mayor endorsed Jack White's recommendation of replacing Hugman with the young architect J. Fred Buenz, a member of the city's park advisory and planning board. Hugman took some satisfaction in noting that for all the posturing about how the only expertise needed from that point was for landscaping, the mayor in truth recognized the need for

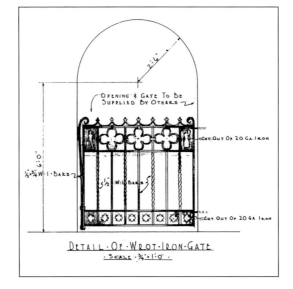

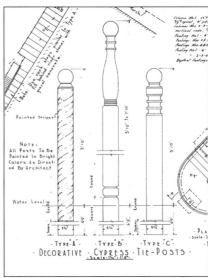

Among features originally planned but dropped after Robert Hugman's dismissal as project architect were wrought iron entry gates for the tops of stairways, decorative wooden tie-up posts for gondolas and a variety of wrought iron lanterns.

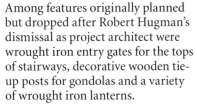

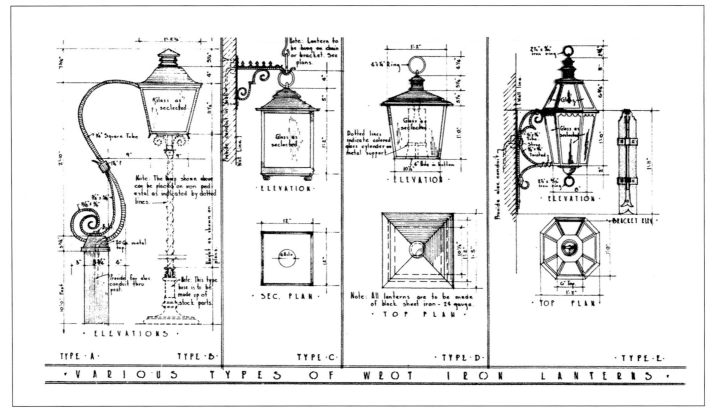

more complex skills, for he "appointed another architect, not a landscape architect."[31]

Hugman could also say that most of his work was already done—"all control structures, stairways, bridges, walks and the Arneson River Theater, plus about half of the work between the north end of the Big Bend and the Fourth Street Bridge." Attempts to change or remove features already completed were denied by the WPA, which had paid for them.[32]

Among accent features left undone were the color-tiled Memory Lane wall below Crockett Street, the floating islands near the end of the bend, the network of iron lanterns and lighting under the "floating" bridge beneath North Presa Street. For tie-up poles, rather than enjoying specially carved posts with bright colors, gondoliers would have to make do with plain cedar posts.[33]

Thereafter, work proceeded quietly. The Conservation Society, mollified, swung in to make the best of the project by relocating its October festival from Mission San José to become a River Jubilee. Food stands drew several hundred people to the river's newly landscaped banks around Navarro and Crockett streets, and there was a small river parade.[34]

On March 13, 1941, the Work Projects Administration signed over the completed River Walk to the City of San Antonio. The 21-block effort included 8,500 feet of riverbanks with 17,000 feet of new sidewalks, 11,000 cubic yards of masonry, 31 stairways and 3 dams, plus some 4,000 trees, shrubs, and plants and benches of stone, cedar and cement. The final cost was $442,900—today's equivalent of $7 million—of which $82,700 came from Improvement District bonds and contributions and the rest from the WPA. As many as 1,000 unemployed workers gained jobs. From its berth beneath one of the Navarro Street/Mill Bridge's gentle arches, a 16-foot motorboat with pump and hoses began its daily trek to water and maintain the new River Walk's landscaping.[35]

Wrote Mayor Maverick in his final report: "We believe that in all the United States there is no city in which a river has been made a more attractive resort for all people."

An estimated 50,000 people lined the River Walk on the evening of Monday, April 21, 1941, to launch Fiesta Week and dedicate the river project. The main event was the first of what became Fiesta's annual parade of boats sponsored by the Texas Cavaliers, a local men's social group established in 1926 to "preserve the Texas

A River Jubilee and night parade in October 1940 celebrated the near completion of the River Walk project. As the growing war in Europe spread fear of the loss of freedom, Ruth White, wife of River Beautification Board Chairman Jack White, posed defiantly on a float as the Statue of Liberty.

The completed River Walk was dedicated with a Fiesta river parade sponsored by the Texas Cavaliers on April 21, 1941. Addressing the crowd were the Cavaliers' King Antonio XXIII, right, next to Cavalier member Jack White and Mayor Maury Maverick.

tradition of horsemanship in this age of automobiles." The procession left from the Ursuline Academy landing and headed south.[36]

The group's king that year, Antonio XXIII, was George Friederich, whose Friederich Company machine shops produced a king's barge of galvanized iron to join the flotilla of sixty-one plywood boats, most of them built by WPA workers. Festooned on the day of the parade with fresh flowers, the boats had no motors but were poled or rowed. A visible link to the Cavaliers' equestrian origins came in the next-to-last boat, just before the king's: the king's white horse, which gave the crowd a thrill by tilting the boat when frightened by applause.[37]

Whether the king's horse would fall overboard was not the only concern that night. Another fear was that a light drizzle would turn into heavy rain. It didn't, but there were plenty of umbrellas in sight as the procession left the Ursuline Academy landing below Municipal Auditorium about 8 p.m., led by a police canoe followed by paddleboats with masked pilots. A floral American flag adorned the craft of Fort Sam Houston's Third U.S. Army commander, Maj. Gen. H. J. Brees. Sides of one boat were covered with balloons, occupants of another waved lighted sparklers and, farther along, hula girls moved only their hands and arms to avoid rocking their boat.[38]

The light rain caused trouble for Victor Braunig's float. Since Braunig headed the power company, his boat was decorated with strings of electric lights, lit by a small generator rigged up on board. But rain seeped into the light sockets, short-circuiting the strings and knocking out the generator. In the confusion of trying to fix it, the system's operator fell overboard. The boat remained dark for the rest of the trip.[39]

Past the St. Mary's Street Bridge the parade reached the reviewing stand, on the steep bank below Crockett Street, the old Tobin Terrace where a similar stand stood for the first festival river parades, in 1905 and 1907. Mayor Maury Maverick, wearing a raincoat, announced descriptions of each craft as it passed. After the boats' hour-and-a-quarter voyages they tied up by the Arneson River Theater. Participants disembarked for a reception above, in the newly restored La Villita.[40]

So did Robert Hugman's River Walk end its initial phase, buffeted by unexpected events and left with an appearance slightly different from original plans. Hugman was no longer on board, his guiding inspiration short-circuited by disagreements with initial supporters. War was ahead, and the outlook for the River Walk and for the nation were about to change. Yet downtown San Antonio's river was now transformed with a uniform design executed with uncommon flair. And that, as time would prove, was good reason to celebrate.

At left, a rustic cedar bench offered a contemplative view toward the newly completed Arneson River Theater, still overlooked by a power plant at left center and by chain-link fencing around a parking lot, center right. The postcard above showed a view upstream and boosted San Antonio as the "Venice of America."

A sailor and his girlfriend have the newly completed River Walk to themselves.

·7·

Disuse and Rescue

As city and nation turned to fight World War II, San Antonio's River Walk, dedicated so gloriously in April 1941, became an afterthought. Hardly a dollar materialized of the $5 million once predicted that businessmen would quickly invest. A steak house did open below the Houston Street Bridge, but around the Great Bend there were no rows of restaurants serving international cuisine, no potters at their wheels, no basket weavers, no colorful adobe shops. San Antonio had not become, as the *New York Times* expected, "the city where you shop from gondolas."

Part of the problem was a leadership vacuum. Maury Maverick's defeat for re-election as mayor ended his involvement in the River Walk. He left for Washington to run the War Production Board's Smaller War Plants Corporation. Architect Robert Hugman, fired halfway through the project and his input gone, did bear witness to his faith in the River Walk by opening an office along the Great Bend, in the basement of the turreted Clifford Building below the Commerce Street Bridge. Project sparkplug Jack White left management of the Plaza Hotel to open his own White-Plaza Hotels in Dallas, Corpus Christi and in San Antonio, in the former Lanier Hotel on North St. Mary's Street, off the river. His successor at the Plaza on the River Walk, Tom Powell, still promoted the hotel's riverside location, but lowered San Antonio's sights as the Venice of America to being the Venice of Texas.

The Texas Cavaliers suspended wartime Fiesta river parades, though the Conservation Society did hold three river jubilees during the war years. Celebrants descended from Navarro Street to nine themed food sections and boarded decorated boats to the Arneson River Theater, where they disembarked and formed a mummers' parade to a Carnival of Nations.[1]

Otherwise, it was a casual scene. Some San Antonians strolled down on weekends. Soldiers training at San Antonio bases paddled girlfriends around the bend in canoes. Actress Rita Hayworth, in town for three USO shows at Fort Sam Houston, entertained wives of Army pilots away on assignment with a boat ride in spring 1942. A year later, Treasury Secretary Henry Morgenthau Jr. used the River Walk during the "greatest publicity and advertising campaign" in the nation's history to help kick off a $13 billion war bonds drive. Crowds gathered around the Houston Street Bridge to watch workers representing five divisions of the war bond "army" race on the river in amphibious jeeps.[2]

THE PLAZA HOTEL IN SAN ANTONIO, "THE VENICE OF TEXAS"
Beautification of the river in downtown San Antonio has created a unique "River Street" through the heart of the business district. The Plaza Hotel overlooks this fascinating outdoor playground.

Jack White's successor as manager of the Plaza Hotel, Tom Powell, promoted San Antonio as the Venice of Texas on, clockwise from above, menu fronts, luggage labels, guest identification cards, postcards and matchbooks

Boatmen used poles to propel floats in a patriotic river parade in 1942, left. Boats were stored in an outdoor marina by the Navarro Street Bridge, top left. The marina also shows at bottom left of above photo. Beyond are the Villita Street Bridge and, near top, the new Arneson River Theater.

During World War II, a soldier sat with his girlfriends on a bridge, top left, while others were poled on a riverboat. At top right, a boat trip was hosted in 1942 by actress Rita Hayworth, facing fourth from left in the lead boat, for wives of Army pilots away on assignment. The next year, above, amphibious jeeps performed an exercise below the Houston Street Bridge to promote war bond sales. In 1945, above right, veterans were welcomed home in a victory parade.

Jack White did keep his River Walk boat concession, renting canoes and boats moored in a marina area beside the Navarro Street/Mill Bridge. He planned adding a fleet of sixteen motorboats, with names like the General Eisenhower and the Lieutenant [Audie] Murphy. In mid-1942 the city ordered ten more flat-bottomed wooden boats to be poled, but had to be prodded to keep up things up as the maintenance motorboat with its pump and hoses fell out of use. Six civic groups complained that lights had gone out and that oil and refuse were being dumped in the river.[3]

In July 1945, as the war was ending, San Antonio was no doubt the nation's only city to welcome its soldiers home on a boat parade through its downtown.

Things perked up for a while after war's end. Five newly assigned parks workers began watering the banks with hand-held hoses. Cavaliers resumed Fiesta river

J. B. Wicks, far left, got a city contract for building ten new boats in 1942. Boats were poled until 1948, when most switched to battery-powered motors. One is tested by boat concessionaire Jack White, center. In 1942 White gave his first boatmen their own badges, above.

parades. In 1947 the River Art Group launched an annual River Art Show. For the top award, noted San Antonio sculptor Pompeo Coppini designed a model of "King River" to be cast in bronze.[4]

But the national energy released by returning veterans and a booming economy was not reaching down to the River Walk. No matter how hard city promoters tried, tourists were not drawn in sufficient numbers to attract many businesses. In 1942, George Dabalis and Evangelos Sarantakes opened the first restaurant on Hugman's River Walk, the Riverside Sea Food & Steak House, in the Book Building basement space of the 1930s Riverside Gardens. A neon sign at its stairway from the Houston Street Bridge announced dining and dancing, canoes, boats, even pointed the way to La Villita, long though the walk may have been. But by 1951 the restaurant was gone.

It remained for another entrepreneur beside another bridge to open a longer-lasting restaurant on the River Walk. This, the first on the Great Bend, opened in October 1946, due less to optimism over the River Walk's future than to the competitive nature of the appliance business. Alfred Beyer owned an appliance store at the southwest corner of Commerce Street and the river, but kept being undersold by the appliance section of Joske's Department Store a block away. Anxious to find additional revenue, he built stairs down to the river, dug silt from countless floods out of the basement—the remains of a Spanish-era home—and opened it as Casa Rio Mexican Foods.[5]

Soon the inventive Beyer got the idea of having boats. He tried building a gondola, but it "sank like a stone." A swan adorning another—modeled on boats in

A stairway from the Houston Street Bridge led to the first business on Robert Hugman's River Walk, the Riverside Sea Food & Steak House, its sign shown above a pedestrian snapped on a cold February day in 1944. A stairway was built from the Commerce Street Bridge to the venerable Casa Rio, first restaurant on the river bend, opened in 1946 by Alfred Beyer in the basement of his appliance store.

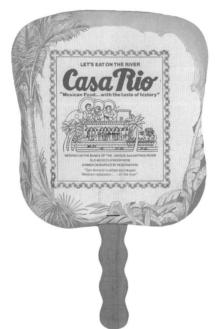

BOOSTING THE RIVER WALK

No other city had a River Walk like San Antonio's. Once tourism restarted at the end of World War II, San Antonio's Chamber of Commerce was quick to make that point, under the guise of a Municipal Information Bureau.

"Plan your vacation now!" Mayor Alfred Callaghan urged recipients in one late 1940s brochure. "You will thrill when you see our city's age-old charms. Parks, missions, the beautiful river walks, the quaint and colorful customs of this land of Inter-Americas." On covers of tourist brochures, gondoliers frequently poled barges past colorful impressions of the Arneson

River Theater. Scenes were improved by drawing in an extra bridge or by adding bells in belfries where they would not hang for another thirty years.

River Walk scenes fronted a host of other promotional materials, and touted San Antonio in national magazine ads as well. But picturing only the River Walk's finest features and alluding to beauty and romance did not overcome its down-at-the-ears setting, and few visitors spent much time along it. Noble though the effort may have been, it would take more than advertising, however enhanced, to make the River Walk a success.

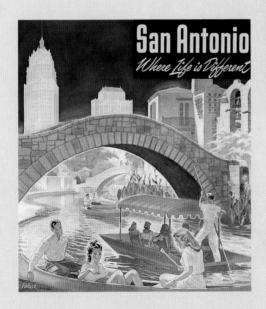

Enjoy a happy winter holiday in sunny San Antonio, with its fascinating contrast of historic old and dynamic new. You'll find a multitude of sights including the storied Alamo . . . four other ancient Missions . . . the Spanish Governors' Palace. Stroll along the Venetian-like San Antonio River. Take interesting side trips or follow the Pan-American Highway to Old Mexico. Write for FREE illustrated book of things to see and do in

San Antonio
WHERE LIFE IS DIFFERENT
MUNICIPAL INFORMATION BUREAU
734 INSURANCE BLDG. • SAN ANTONIO, TEXAS

Boston's Public Gardens—was decapitated by the river theater's bridge. A dining barge—the S.S. Enchilada—capsized, with diners aboard. But he finally got it right. In 1949 Beyer took over Jack White's old boat concession, and replaced rental canoes with two-passenger pontoon paddleboats. He got out of the appliance business. Family ownership of Casa Rio, much enlarged, is in the fourth generation.[6]

Meanwhile, public attention suddenly regressed to flood control. During the night of September 27, 1946, a cloudburst centered ten miles southeast of downtown dropped rain over parts of San Antonio with greater intensity than rainfall a quarter century before during the flood of 1921, though this storm was of shorter duration. Had it been directly over the city, damage would have been much greater. As it was, four lives were lost.[7]

There was some flooding in downtown San Antonio—water was nearly knee-deep in the lobby of the Plaza Hotel—but that was due more to overloaded storm

A heavy storm in 1946 flooded southern San Antonio neighborhoods, including, right, the one at the intersection of Frio City Road and South Zarzamora Street. The deluge led to extensive flood control efforts, including a concrete channel through the King William Street neighborhood, seen at top left looking north through the 1928 Arsenal Street Bridge.

sewers than to any cascade from Olmos Basin, where the dam held back the rush. The only major impact this time was in western San Antonio, along San Pedro Creek and its tributary Alazan, Martinez and Apache creeks. Floodwaters there were lower than in 1921, but damage was intensified by overbuilding in the floodplains.[8]

Some unfinished business obviously remained. This time public funding mechanisms were in place.

The U.S. Army Corps of Engineers spent five years studying and designing a flood control plan along thirty-one miles of the San Antonio River watershed. It would be more than a decade before most work was completed. San Pedro Creek's tributaries at last had their channels widened and deepened. The convoluted bends at McCullough Avenue and at Ninth Street were finally straightened—as recommended in 1920—as was another to the south near Roosevelt Avenue. Operation of the floodgate at the upper end of the Great Bend was improved. The bulkhead and its spillway beside it at the head of the cutoff channel were replaced by a tainter gate halfway down the channel.

The bend around Pioneer Flour Mills, shortened in the 1920s, was eliminated altogether in 1968 by a shorter channel. Riverbanks through the King William Street area that Mayor C. M. Chambers in the 1920s fought to keep from being paved were not only paved but also straightened and made much deeper, with high concrete walls, over protests from many residents. Riverside sidewalks and landscaping were extended a mile south from the end of the bend to South Alamo Street, around the curve known as Sauerkraut Bend for the neighborhood's original families of German origin. Beyond, the twisting course of the river was

Two stairways from the Commerce Street Bridge balanced a bucolic setting along the new River Walk. At the foot of the stairway at right, River Walk architect Robert Hugman put his name on the balcony over his office, above. A program, below, of the annual River Art Show, begun after World War II, promised the top winner a trophy designed by Pompeo Coppini.

straightened into a broad new channel, much of it lined with concrete, reaching the Spanish missions downstream.[9]

When he landed $15 million in federal funding to launch a key part of the project, Congressman Paul Kilday was so excited that he proclaimed the work would end flood damage in San Antonio "for all time."[10]

There was little such enthusiasm for the future of the River Walk. There were still river parades and art shows, and in 1958 Alamo Kiwanis Club began a long annual run of Fiesta Noche del Rio on summer weekends in the Arneson River Theater. There were paddleboats and dining barges, but walkways were mostly deserted. Fine semitropical plantings may have adorned the lonely ribbon of the River Walk, but the unkempt backs of commercial buildings loomed uncomfortably close.

Danger was a constant concern. At the end of 1945 the entire River Walk, from Municipal Auditorium to the Plaza Hotel, was put off limits for military personnel from midnight to 6 a.m. Fears were still being validated in 1962, when a visiting Air Force colonel was stabbed one evening and robbed of $150 on a deserted section near Pecan Street. A policeman was assigned to patrol the river on a paddleboat, though "his shoes and pants legs got all wet after one trip." The police department bought a twelve-foot flat-bottom boat that sank on its first cruise. It was raised and

Influence of the design of boats in Mexico City's water gardens of Xochimilco persisted on the early River Walk. The style was used on the studio set for San Antonio's first television broadcast on December 11, 1949, on WOAI-TV. It featured the young singer Rosita Fernandez with her children Diana and Raul, who remembered, "They kept mopping the floor with very wet mops so it would look like we were floating in the water." Raul appeared later on the Xochimilco-style *Lupita*, moored below the Arneson River Theater for a Lone Star Beer calendar photo.

a drainage plug fixed, but the boat wouldn't move; its electric motor wasn't strong enough. Police put in a five-horsepower motor, and a patrol program finally got under way. "We feel like we've prevented a lot of disturbances and obnoxious incidents," said Police Chief George Bichsel.[11]

Neglect was encouraging owners to encroach on the city's River Walk property. That drew the attention of some new landladies, members of the San Antonio Conservation Society, which had purchased two historic La Villita properties backing on the River Walk. Mayor Alfred Callaghan promised the group he would keep an eye on the situation. In 1950, however, on the northern leg of the Great Bend, came an encroachment so blatant that the Conservation Society rose up as a body. The proposal slipped in from an investment group innocuously named Endowment, Inc. It was all about education, banker Walter McAllister explained to the Conservation Society, apparently with a straight face, when they found out about it.[12]

St. Mary's University Law School students, it seemed, were having trouble finding places to park downtown. The school, which occupied the old riverside St. Mary's College buildings, needed to keep those students in order to justify an appeal to increase endowment. The school had sufficient space to build a parking garage in the rear—overlooking the River Walk—but the garage needed an exit. That, unavoidably, must be a new bridge, only twelve feet wide, over the river to Crockett Street. Of course, customers of nearby businesses could use the garage, too. Yes, the bridge would cross between one of the River Walk's two distinctive pedestrian bridges and a picturesque cascade, but the new bridge would be high enough so that any pedestrians or boats wanting to pass could still do so.[13]

Conservation Society members a decade before may have disapproved of Hugman's project, but times had changed, and there were new members as well. Sixty-eight members petitioned Endowment, Inc. to abandon the project. Petitioners declared that "the San Antonio Conservation Society was formed twenty-seven years ago to save the downtown river from being covered over and made into parking lots," an assertion apparently being made for the first time. Also, co-founder Emily Edwards rewrote her 1924 puppet show script to portray not the importance not of saving all of the city's unique features, but to emphasize the

Rosita Fernandez, "San Antonio's First Lady of Song," was a longtime performer at Fiesta Noche del Rio, begun on summer weekends in 1958 at the Arneson River Theater.

importance of saving the river, and awareness of the scripts was soon conflated. Legends of the society having a founding relationship to the river grew, leading to decades of confusion on the subject.[14]

Conservation Society members marched on city hall. They funded a lawsuit against the city for granting a construction permit. They asserted the garage would serve a private rather than a public purpose, thereby violating "the public park and recreation area" along the river. A district judge, however, ruled the plaintiffs had no standing to file because they would suffer no personal damages from the construction. The decision was upheld on appeal.[15]

By its high profile if unsuccessful assault on the intrusion, the San Antonio Conservation Society may well have saved the River Walk. The flat bridge did slice

Canoes and poled barges offered scenic trips through the Arneson River Theater, below, but unsightly backs of buildings overshadowed the River Walk for blocks elsewhere and caused tourism to languish.

across a favorite River Walk view, and concrete bays of the new parking garage gaped from above. But the noisy debate returned the River Walk to public consciousness and, with awareness that a formidable advocate was on watch, suddenly offered hope for its future. Things would not get better right away. But they would not get worse.

What the River Walk needed was another Jack White. In 1959 one emerged in the person of David J. Straus. Like White, the well-connected Straus had the clout to get things done, got along well with others and was committed to long-term involvement. "I was on the chamber's tourist committee," Straus recalled, "but none of the members focused on the River Walk. I knew the River Walk had tourist potential, was aware of how a lot of people were embarrassed about it and thought I should see what I could do."[16]

Outrage over construction of a St. Mary's University Law School parking garage and its flat bridge through a scenic area renewed public interest in the River Walk's fate.

Straus got himself appointed chairman of a new Chamber of Commerce committee to focus on the River Walk, but found little support from owners of River Walk property. As Jack White got behind Robert Hugman's existing plans to achieve reform, Straus decided to seek a tangible plan to better demonstrate what could be done. In 1960 he helped persuade the chamber and the city to jointly finance a $15,000 study by California's Marco Engineering Company, a theme park designer noted for its recent work on Disneyland. A good contact was a former Chamber of Commerce official, James V. McGoodwin, who had gone to work for Marco.

Marco engineers, not surprisingly, found the River Walk "run down and in need of repainting, improved lighting, better housekeeping, police protection and additional park benches." Their solution was "intensive application of creative design to the selection and arrangement of props and dressings." Translation: Add bling.

The sixty-page Marco plan recommended incorporating La Villita as the grand entrance to a River Bend Park. Since only two river-level pedestrian bridges then linked opposite shores, planners recommended adding two pontoon bridges that could open to let through barges vending food and souvenirs. The city should construct and own shops and restaurants along the river, though these "probably

David J. Straus took on the case of the derelict River Walk in 1959. An infantry officer in World War II and the Korean War, Straus was 37 and president of the family's Straus-Frank Company, a wholesale appliance firm founded in 1870 as L. Frank Saddlery. He was at a party when the subject of the condition of the River Walk came up. The inevitable question was asked: "Why doesn't someone do something?"

"And so I got to thinking about it that night," recalled Straus. "The next morning I went down and called on [Chamber of Commerce president] Walter Corrigan at the chamber office and said, 'Walter, do you remember the conversation last night about the River Walk and why doesn't somebody do something about it? Why don't you appoint me as chairman of a committee . . . and let's see if under the auspices of the chamber we can't do something?' And so he said, 'Okay, you're chairman of the new committee.' "

Straus and Harold Robbins, the chamber's manager of tourist advertising and promotion, tried identifying property owners through deed records and called on them in hopes they would fix up their properties. They also called on prospective tenants to put them in touch with property owners. But, said Straus, "we just couldn't get anybody to do anything."[1]

When the California planners Straus supported did not produce an acceptable master plan, he and Robbins studied protective zoning ordinances in New Orleans and in Carmel, California and returned to persuade city council in 1962 to establish an advisory River Walk Commission to oversee property issues. He organized the Paseo del Rio Association as a chamber committee supporting River Walk businesses.

Straus continued to lead efforts behind the scenes, finding an architect to design the type of river barges still in use and getting the city to build them, lobbying building owners to improve their properties and involving community leaders in the River Walk. He gathered investors for what was termed a model for River Walk development, the three-building River Square complex near the Commerce Street Bridge. It opened four years after HemisFair '68 launched a new era for San Antonio and the River Walk.

As his interest continued, decades later Straus was a member of the Historic Civic Center Task Force and of the San Antonio River Commission, the River Walk oversight body formed in 2007 under Mayor Phil Hardberger.

[1] Holmesly, *HemisFair '68*, 60–62.

Always ready to get behind a new approach, David Straus stands between Casa Rio Restaurant founder Alfred Beyer, left, and restaurant manager Jonathan Smith at the inauguration of a Casa Rio dining barge. Its paddlewheel, however, splashed water on diners on board and could not be used.

DEVELOPMENT OF THE SAN ANTONIO RIVER BEND

MARCO ENGINEERING COMPANY
Wiard Ihnen: *Project Architect*

A garish River Walk plan by
designers of Disneyland was
rejected following a public outcry.

would not attract the maximum patronage." What would was "considerable show
and entertainment" in the form of a River of Fiestas, which within three years
should extend all the way upstream to Brackenridge Park. Events could range from
a Fiesta de Bellas Artes in January to a Fiesta of Parasols in August to a Fiesta de
Piñatas at Christmas.

Across South Presa Street from Villita Assembly Hall, a plaza for fiestas would
be divided by the river and anchored on one end by a replica of the facade of Mission
Espada beside a merry-go-round. A water tank near the Arneson River Theater was
to be encased in simulated stone for "an authentic ancient appearance."

The project could draw 700,000 persons to the River Walk in the first year
alone, planners projected, and would yield a sizable profit immediately. It should be
overseen by a new city agency, a River Development Board. The plan was forwarded
to city council in May 1961.[17]

Horrified San Antonio architects reacted as if all that was missing were Mickey
Mouse and Donald Duck. O'Neil Ford fired a four-page blast to the Chamber of
Commerce charging that "not one man on the city council is trained or able to
make a sound judgment on such designs as this holiday play park group of designers are submitting, and they should not have such a responsibility put upon
them." He was incensed that such a development would use public land, which he

In the early 1960s, offices of the Chamber of Commerce, which supported River Walk reform, overlooked the River Walk beside the Navarro Street/Mill Bridge, on part of the site later occupied by the Westin Riverwalk Hotel.

said should be preserved, rather than using only private property, where Hugman and others had intended developments to go. Were favorite public spots going to be covered with "plaster imitations of Hollywood Spanish architecture?" Ford demanded that a brochure incorrectly implying his participation in the planning be withdrawn from circulation at once.[18]

Disenchantment spread. The chamber's Tourist Attractions Committee, headed by David Straus, unanimously rejected the plan as out of keeping with the city.

The uproars over the St. Mary's Law School bridge and the Marco plan could have been softened had the public been better prepared to deal with what was coming. Recommendations would have helped from some intermediate group charged with studying and passing judgment on complex issues. Districts in other cities had such advisory bodies, and David Straus thought it time that San Antonio's River Walk had one, too.

Straus and the chamber's Harold Robbins visited Carmel, California and New Orleans, where they were impressed with how the Vieux Carré Commission maintained the French character of New Orleans, Straus remembered. "They kept a mix of local businesses with no outside chains, and there very few visible parking structures. We wanted the River Walk to maintain the Spanish character of San Antonio the same way."[19]

Straus took ordinances of both cities, excerpted the parts most appropriate to the River Walk, added a few of his own and had attorney Carlos Cadena check the language. The result, approved by San Antonio's city council on March 28, 1962, was City Ordinance 30238. Its purpose was to maintain "the charm and the atmosphere of old San Antonio" along the River Walk, promote "an integrated shopping, entertainment, and recreation area for visitors" and to create the River Walk Commission.

There were to be seven members of the commission, at least two of them "recognized practicing professionals in the field of design and applied arts." Though only an advisory body, it would be the first stop for permits for construction, modification or painting within the River Bend. All work was to be "in sympathy with early San Antonio architecture." The commission would also advise city council on property development issues not just within the bend but also along the rest of the River Walk and the two miles beyond to the headwaters, and in La Villita as well.[20]

The organizational meeting was held June 1, 1962, at the Chamber of Commerce office beside the Navarro Street/Mill Bridge, on the ground floor with a picture window overlooking the River Walk. Atlee B. Ayres, who in his 30s as City Plan Committee chairman made early river beautification a top priority and in his 60s scorned Robert Hugman's River Walk design, now was made, in his late 80s, a charter member of the River Walk Commission. Investments broker Walter Mathis was elected chairman.[21]

Planning began at once for additional entrances to the River Walk, for promotion, for rules and regulations governing concessions and for ways to get owners to fix up their properties. In six months the commission was working on a master plan. The pendulum swung back to local experts, and the San Antonio chapter of the American Institute of Architects was asked to form a committee for the project. The AIA named eight members, headed by Cyrus H. Wagner. As a project title, committee member Ignacio Torres suggested translating River Walk as Paseo del Rio. The term stuck.[22]

Under Wagner's leadership, the architects decided the public River Walk property should be left as it was, enhanced only by further plantings. The focus would be on style and building materials for commercial and retail development on private property up to street level, and for residential and hotel development above that.

Following rejection of a master plan by California engineers, San Antonio's chapter of the American Institute of America showed how dismal backs of buildings could be transformed into vibrant River Walk frontage. In 1963 architect Cyrus Wagner sketched the potential for change of a section on the west bank between Commerce and Crockett streets.

Development would be sorted into activity noise zones of quiet, on the bend's southern leg—antique shops, art galleries, and apartments; moderate, on the central leg—a mix of restaurants, shops, and apartments; and loud, on the northern leg—clubs and restaurants. To draw more tourists, a pedestrian link would extend from the Alamo down to the River Walk. The Marco plan's proposal for monthly fiestas was salvaged, and its attendance projections were cited.[23]

Photographs were taken along the river, a base map was developed, overlays made, drawings sketched, models constructed and a slide presentation assembled to show civic groups and gain further input. "In many planning circles during the early '60s," Wagner

recalled, "it was an accepted fact that people would not walk more than 500 feet to get from one place to another in an urban environment. In order to dispel that 'fact,' I made a cutout model of the North Star Mall at the same scale as the model and overlaid it on our model. [The mall] extended from the [eastern edge of the bend] to St. Mary's Street, a distance of about 1,400 feet. A slide was made, incorporated into the show, and in our presentations we made a point that people *would* walk well over 500 feet if the walking environment was interesting and pleasant. The slide was always a big hit with audiences."[24]

Unveiling came on April 15, 1963, in a presentation by Wagner and Allison Peery to a receptive crowd of civic leaders at Villita Assembly Hall. Two years later the Paseo del Rio plan received a national award from the American Institute of Architects. As others mulled its implementation, Wagner kept the show on the road to all who would hear him. Gradually, individual projects began to emerge. A proposal for shops and apartments overlooking the River Walk on South Alamo Street was drawn up by architects O'Neil Ford and Allison Peery with design by Mike Lance, and won a national award in *Progressive Architecture* competition in 1963.[25]

Insurance executive James L. Hayne, who played trombone in an off-hours jazz combo headed by wholesale grocer Jim Cullum Sr., put together a group of twenty-two investors to open a performance base for the musicians in a deserted section

River Walk tables were not overcrowded at Michelino's Italian Restaurant, formerly the Venice Restaurant, in the mid 1960s.

of the River Walk. They turned a 2,400 square foot room in the basement of the Nix Hospital's parking garage into a bistro dubbed The Landing. Two hundred people could sit at its small tables. The Happy Jazz Band moved in just in time for Fiesta 1963. It was the first business to open in the Chamber of Commerce's new drive to make the River Walk a serious tourist attraction.[26]

Already a few new restaurants were springing up. Burton Louie's Chinese restaurant Lung Jeu opened in 1959 near the Commerce Street bridge north of Casa Rio, but survived only a few years. A few doors upstream, in mid-1964 Victoria "Mama" Fontana opened her Venice Italian Restaurant in the Casino Club Building basement at the Crockett Street Bridge, in the former space of a barbecue restaurant tried by Casa Rio. She put up a red neon sign flashing "Pizza." The River Walk Commission, caught unawares, got a sign ordinance through city council. Commission members told Mrs. Fontana she could legally keep her sign since it went up before the new rules, but she agreed to take it down.[27]

Straus credited the upsurge in private property development beside the publicly owned River Walk to developers being able to have "most dealings with property owners rather than working through city government politics." To support them, he organized the Paseo del Rio Association as a Chamber of Commerce committee, soon chaired by James Hayne and run by chamber staff member Jimmy Gause.[28]

Boats poled by gondolas may have been a visual link with Venice, but, realized Straus, "Poling boats along the river was difficult enough with gondolas because of the mud on the bottom. What was needed to move larger groups were larger boats, with motors." For a design, he went to Reginald Roberts, an architect and boat enthusiast. City Council, however, dismissed the idea of advertising for bids. On his own, Straus built a boat half the size of those proposed. Next, "I asked Casa Rio to provide food, invited the mayor and council to lunch on board and said, 'This is what I had in mind.' That did the trick. The city advertised for bids, the boats were built and Casa Rio got the concession to operate them."[29]

The now familiar flat-bottomed, steel-hulled barges, seating up to forty people for sightseeing and twenty for dining, went into operation in 1967. At the same time

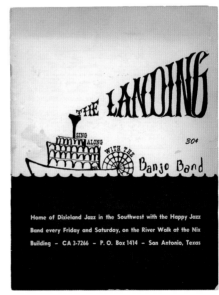

A 1940s gondola dramatized an arrival at The Landing, a pioneering basement bistro opened in 1963 by Jim Cullum Sr.'s Happy Jazz Band.

the downtown business establishment, suddenly awakening from a long post-Depression slumber, was jump-starting development with plans for nothing less than a world's fair, to open in 1968 and celebrate the two hundred fiftieth anniversary of the founding of San Antonio. It would key off the city's central location in the Western Hemisphere with the theme Confluence of Cultures in the Americas and the name HemisFair '68. The site, selected in July 1963, was ninety-two acres of a declining neighborhood southeast of downtown. The last high-rise hotel built in central downtown had been the Plaza, in 1927. New hotels would be needed, and quickly, not only for fairgoers but for future throngs at a new convention center going into a corner of the fairgrounds within sight of the River Walk.[30]

As if that were not good news enough for Paseo del Rio boosters, a new River Walk extension, planned by O'Neil Ford, would be dug a third of a mile east to a square lagoon surrounded on three sides by the convention center and its theater. The extension would be financed through part of the HemisFair bond issue overwhelmingly approved in January 1964. Fairgoers would ride on river barges. It took a very short leap for developers to realize that if the new hotels were built on the River Walk, pedestrian traffic generated by the fair and then the convention center could support many new shops and restaurants along the way.[31]

Two new major hotels—indeed on the River Walk—were built for the fair. The larger was the twenty-one-story, 481-room Hilton Palacio del Rio, facing the fairgrounds across South Alamo Street and opening directly onto the River Walk below. The hotel seemed hopelessly behind schedule when construction magnate H. B. Zachry took charge. He finished the Hilton in 202 days, barely on deadline, by having individual modular rooms built offsite and furnished down to towels on the racks and soap in the soap dishes, then trucked to the site and stacked in place with giant cranes.[32]

Location of the second hotel seemed coincidental. While in the Nix Hospital awaiting the birth of his youngest child, St. Mary's University alumnus Patrick

By 1967, traffic from paddleboats and new barges was picking up by the Commerce Street Bridge at Casa Rio, its gas lit tiki torches flaming on the far side of the river.

The Hilton Palacio del Rio met its HemisFair '68 construction deadline when furnished modular rooms were trucked to the site and lifted into place by cranes. Fair bonds funded a new bridge on the hotel's River Walk side.

Kennedy happened to gaze down on the original St. Mary's buildings, last used by the university for its law school and recently abandoned. They were on the River Walk, the historic section was attractive and there was room for more construction, once the parking garage—with its bridge across the river—was removed. The result was the 200-room La Posada: The Inn on the River Walk, soon renamed La Mansion del Rio and, in 2006, Omni La Mansion del Rio. Its four-story stone, mansard-roofed main building, built in 1852, was renovated and joined by new construction, all in white stucco and enclosing a Mediterranean-style central patio.[33]

By the end of 1967, with the fair only four months away, the number of businesses on the River Walk had jumped to ten. Twelve buildings were being renovated so more could open in time for the fair. The 1,650-foot River Walk extension, four feet deep, was dug from the central leg of the river bend just north of the Market Street Bridge. Its channel passed beneath a new pedestrian bridge and through a new cut twenty-six feet under South Alamo Street, then on eastward below the south side of Commerce Street until it turned south to form the lagoon. Two pedestrian bridges were added across the main River Walk, one behind the Hilton Hotel and the other, designed by Ayres & Ayres, north of the Commerce Street Bridge.

Opening of the fair on April 6, 1968, launched a new era for the city. The River Walk drew particular praise from visiting architectural critics. Ada Louise Huxtable of the *New York Times* wrote for most when she termed it "the city's outstanding amenity." Austin architect Sinclair Black, writing later in *AIA Journal*, thought La Mansion del Rio's new rear wall beside the River Walk, "neatly folded in response to the giant cypress trees, serves to define the river space and animate its edge. The scale of the magnificent trees becomes more evident by their proximity to

Jackhammers went to work removing a controversial bridge across the River Walk as the adjoining parking garage was being torn down for what is now the Omni La Mansion del Rio Hotel, far right. The hotel was completed in time to be ready for visitors to HemisFair '68.

the building." Black used the Palacio del Rio's "conquistador contemporary" design to make a backhanded but "very valuable point about the strength of the river as an urban design context. To have a measure of success, buildings need not be special or particularly well-designed when located on the river. . . . Even a self-conscious attempt inevitably and fortunately fails to dilute the power of the river space."[34]

At first the River Walk extension design did not pass muster. With a concrete-walled dark passage below South Alamo Street emerging to more concrete walls rising starkly above landscaped but inaccessible terraces, one writer thought that "boating through this extension of the Paseo del Rio seems like being under the ramparts of the Morro Castle."[35]

Morro Castle or not, the River Walk extension would be re-landscaped and extended and extended again, as San Antonians traded the consequences of neglect of the River Walk for the challenges of its success.

HemisFair '68, San Antonio's world's fair, vaulted the city into a new era. In the view at left, the new landmark Tower of the Americas rose on the fairgrounds near a circular arena, with a new performing arts theater to its right and a convention center above. Another legacy of the fair was an envigorated River Walk, extended past the convention center and also shown at below right. Filming her barge ride on the River Walk extension during the fair, below left, was Princess Grace of Monaco, who stood beside her husband, Prince Ranier.

Making a grand entrance into the Arneson River Theater during the 2006 Fiesta River Parade, sponsored by the Texas Caavaliers, is King Antonio LXXXIV, Rick Shaw.

$\cdot 8 \cdot$
Crown Jewel of Texas

Eighty years before HemisFair '68, an anonymous writer predicted that San Antonio's river could one day become the "crown jewel of Texas." Prevailing wisdom dismissed such predictions as "idle dreams."

And yet, some thirty years after the fair, that prophecy came true as San Antonio's River Walk first surpassed the Alamo as the top tourist destination in Texas, and became a key to the city's annual $12 billion tourism industry.[1]

The River Walk "provides an experience that has not been successfully duplicated anywhere else in America," concluded one writer. Another sensed it "a trip through a linear paradise of infinitely changing vistas." And that was long before the River Walk was extended from its traditional nearly three miles through the heart of town to fifteen miles, north nearly to the headwaters and south to the Spanish missions.[2]

Robert Hugman's tiny bridge at the Arneson River Theater has been ranked with the world's best-known bridges. In 1982 it was named Rosita's Bridge upon the retirement of Rosita Fernandez, star for twenty-six years of the summertime Fiesta Noche del Rio. At each performance she dramatically crossed the bridge to the stage to sing Latin American favorites. A Japanese documentary on bridges of the world termed Rosita's Bridge more significant than the London Bridge, Brooklyn Bridge or Venice's Bridge of Sighs. Those bridges, the documentary observed, simply let people pass from one side to the other. Rosita's Bridge, however, had united cultures.[3]

Another cosmopolitan moment for the theater came in 1984 when it was the setting for Bizet's opera *Carmen*, jointly produced by the Berlin Opera and the short-lived San Antonio Festival. During the performance, some singers stepped onto the stage from boats that rounded the river bend on cue. The San Antonio Symphony, aboard barges anchored in front, played the accompaniment.

From throughout the nation and the world—from China, Peru, Canada, Malaysia—planners began coming to decipher the River Walk's appeal. Singapore's Urban Redevelopment Authority examined two riverside developments "very different but both strongly tied into their communities"—the Seine in Paris and the River Walk in San Antonio. Planners remaking a usually dry river in Israel's Negev Desert into the Beersheeba River Park made several trips. In Mexico, Monterrey pumped water back into its long dry Rio Santa Lucía and planted cypresses beside sidewalks lined

Among river walks around the world inspired by San Antonio's is the one along the Rio Santa Lucía in Monterrey, Mexico.

with tiers of new buildings. "It's supposed to be just like San Antonio," said one Monterrey official. When residents organized to upgrade the noxious setting of New York City's Gowanus Canal, there was no question where they were headed. The goal was to become, the *New York Times* reported, "Brooklyn's version of the Riverwalk in San Antonio."[4]

When HemisFair closed in October 1968, promise of growing River Walk success generated such optimism that within five years a "river corridor" from Olmos Dam south to Roosevelt Park was being seen as a solution to problems ranging from a declining downtown to health and education ills. San Francisco's Skidmore, Owings & Merrill—urban designers and planners—and Marshall Kaplan, Gans & Khan—economic and social planners—were brought in to advise an eighteen-member River Corridor Committee of leaders from six government entities. Proposed solutions like fighting crime by providing searchlights to park rangers in boats proved to be far off the mark, but concepts like better flood control with underground tunnels and revitalizing neighborhoods by extending the River Walk beyond downtown were not. Results might take decades, but meaningful discussion of broader river development had begun.

In the meantime, River Walk tourism was boosted with a new campaign: "Forget the Alamo!" New committees, boards and commissions were formed to keep development on course and preserve the River Walk's distinctive character. Jurisdiction of the River Walk Commission was extended even to those parts of buildings "within a visual line from the River Walk area.[5]

With enough businesses along the River Walk to support it, the Paseo del Rio Association, formed as a Chamber of Commerce committee, was spun off as an independent organization under the direction of Claire Regnier. Its former director, chamber staff member Jimmy Gause, joined City Manager Tom Huebner on road trips to land more conventions and river-oriented hotels.

David Straus found it easier to assemble investors. They purchased three dilapidated properties in the heart of the bend near the Commerce Street Bridge and went searching for tenants. Straus contacted a friend at a Chicago consulting firm that worked for the Playboy Clubs. Would Hugh Hefner like to put a Playboy Club on the River Walk? The response came that Playboy was more interested in Houston and Dallas. Instead, River Square, designed by Cyrus Wagner, opened in 1972 with tenants far more prosaic—a Mexican folk art shop named La Sirena and two restaurants, The Stockman and Kangaroo Court, opened by Straus's assistant Arthur P. Veltman Jr. and Robert Buchanan. By combining historic preservation with new construction and linking the street with a riverside courtyard, River Square was considered a model for River Walk development.[6]

In 1979 Straus pioneered new residential development along the River Walk as a principal in construction of the Left Bank, a twenty-four condominium complex on the upper River Walk across from the historic Ursuline Academy campus, restored as the Southwest School of Art.

Now that things were looking up, more attention was paid to the River Walk's designer, Robert H. H. Hugman, so ignominiously dismissed by the city in 1940 while overseeing completion of the project he had conceived and nurtured. Hugman

Considered a model for River Walk development when completed in 1972 was River Square, which transformed one riverside scene, left and center, as completion of the complex neared, below.

Pioneering new residential developments along the River Walk in 1979 were the Left Bank condominiums beside the North St. Mary's Street Bridge, built in 1915.

never attempted another project of that scope, but quietly did residential and institutional design in San Antonio and South Texas, for a few years with Paul G. Silber in the firm of Hugman & Silber. In 1957 he went to Randolph Air Force Base as a project architect, and retired fifteen years later.[7]

Hugman's first public honor for the River Walk did not come until 1970, at a ceremony held by the San Antonio Chapter of the American Institute of Architects. After thirty years of being ignored, he was overwhelmed by the sudden recognition. "When we praised Mr. Hugman for his vision and design, he broke down and cried," remembered architect Boone Powell. "The rest of us stood and cheered."[8]

After that, Hugman made occasional public comments on directions the River Walk was taking. Was it becoming "the Venice of America or the Convention Center on a creek?" he asked in an address at a River Walk Commission luncheon in 1972. "Lasting good taste, beauty, quiet dignity, satisfying aesthetics and good food are the things which will perpetuate the river," Hugman wrote Commission Chairman David Straus a few years later. "Please do not allow these river assets to be eroded. Once they are gone it is too late." He urged Straus not to approve plans to replace sod with concrete along the tops of Arneson River Theater bleachers. The grass remained. When a parking garage was proposed on the riverside site later that of the Hyatt Regency Hotel, Hugman protested in person to city council. The parking garage was built at the corner of Commerce and Presa streets. "Very little he suggested I didn't think was sound," thought Straus.[9]

Hugman's standing with the city came full circle in 1978, two years before his death at the age of seventy-eight. Mayor Lila Cockrell dedicated five bells hung in Hugman's honor in the once empty arches behind the Arneson River Theater stage, where he had originally intended bells to be. Hugman did the first striking. After Hugman's death, the arching bridge he designed on the bend's northern leg was named in his honor. His onetime office sign—"R. H. H. Hugman AIA, Architect"—was duplicated in its original location, on the curving outdoor river balcony of the old Clifford Building beside the Commerce Street Bridge. The sign became, in effect, Robert Hugman's public signature on the River Walk project.[10]

Like a knot being untangled, progress along the River Walk accelerated as one strand, then another was freed by solution of a related problem. Promotions were working, planning regulations were in place and the hotels built just in time for HemisFair paired nicely with the new convention center and the improving infrastructure for a fast-growing tourism industry. Leading the new era off the drawing boards was San Antonio's first major post-fair hotel, the 500-room Marriott Riverwalk. Opened in 1979, its rectangular cube-like design formed a visual terminus at the eastern end of the fair's river extension. Ground was broken the same year for a 633-room Hyatt Regency Hotel  on the eastern bank of the Great Bend's central leg, its plain design making the six-teen-story hotel "surprisingly unobtrusive" in its historic setting.[11]

When the Hyatt opened in 1981, it incorporated a River Walk feature recommended by architects eighteen years before: a pedestrian link between the Alamo and the river named Paseo del Alamo. Its entrance was through newly excavated remains of the Alamo's Spanish mission wall along the west side of Alamo Plaza. Steps descended beside and passed beneath water cascading down a complex of concrete channels symbolizing the city's historic acequias. Water flowed into the hotel's river-level atrium to become a lagoon. Water appeared to flow along a narrow channel outside into the river, but a transparent pane kept Paseo del Alamo waters within the atrium, to be recycled up to Alamo Plaza. Outside the hotel, screened by shrubbery, a well pumped fresh water into the river to maintain water quality.[12]

Marriott was so pleased with its hotel on the extension south of Market Street that in 1988 it opened a new hotel north of Market Street—the 1,000-room Marriott Rivercenter, at forty-two stories the tallest building in San Antonio. It rose next to an urban phenomenon, a new downtown shopping center. Named Rivercenter Mall, it also opened in 1988. "Just add water" was the slogan for the $200 million, ten-acre, million-square-foot mall, which had 135 shops, restaurants and Imax theater on three levels wrapped in glass—in subtle, blue-based colors—around a lagoon formed by an extension of the River Walk extension. A bridge reached an island stage in the center. An adjoining garage could park 3,100 cars. The mall was credited with creating 3,000 new jobs. The River Walk's impact on San Antonio's economic growth could hardly have been dramatic. Nearby, a thirty-four story, one thousand room Grand Hyatt opened in 2008.[13]

Then came yet a third River Walk extension. As part of a $218 million Convention Center expansion, the convention center lagoon's south enclosure was

River Walk architect Robert H. H. Hugman regained standing once the River Walk became successful, and in 1978 did the first striking of new bells named in his honor at the Arneson River Theater.

Across its top, the Convention Center's Lila Cockrell Theater features a tile portrayal of the history of the world completed in 1968 by Mexican muralist Juan O'Gorman. The lagoon below disappeared when its sides were narrowed for new plazas and the river was extended to the right.

The atrium of the sixteen-story Hyatt Regency Hotel, center, designed to be unobtrusive in its setting, included an entry to the Paseo del Alamo, far right. The paseo, built in 1981, descends from Alamo Plaza past water features that symbolize San Antonio's Spanish acequia system.

removed so the River Walk's HemisFair extension could be cut through and extended south betweention convention halls. Through a setting designed to resemble the Texas Hill Country, it passed landscaped islets to end by encircling an island near a cascade flowing from HemisFair Plaza above. The old lagoon was narrowed to the width of the new channel and the rest filled for enlarged gathering space. The project was completed in June 2001, on deadline for the 25,000 Rotarians arriving for a Rotary International convention.[14]

While new development along the River Walk extensions benefited from availability of vacant or little-used acreage cleared years before for HemisFair '68, developers along the Great Bend were having to scramble for new space. Along the largely deserted stretch near the south end of the bend, two hotels took advantage of parking lots above opposite sides of Navarro Street: the 513-room Westin, opened in 2002, and the 265-room Contessa, opened in 2005.

Smaller new developments were also having to claw back into riverbanks. Developers of South Bank, a three-story cluster of new brick buildings in a late-nineteenth century style, dug away two street-level parking lots to build inside the sharp northeast corner of the bend. Tenants included a Hard Rock Cafe,

At top left, new landmarks seen over the umbrellas of Casa Rio Restaurant and past the River Walk stairway and elevator are, left from the former Joske's Department Store, the Torch of Friendship steel sculpture—symbolizing relations between the United States and Mexico—and three hotels, the Marriott Rivercenter, Marriott Riverwalk and Grand Hyatt. At top right, across from Casa Rio an arched bridge at right of photo leads along a River Walk extension to the 42-story Marriott Rivercenter Hotel, left, and a lagoon at Rivercenter Mall, above.

The quest to build a major hotel along the River Walk easily brings a collision with the past, raising the issue of how to maintain context in the cherished heart of a historic city.

Some developers haven't had to deal with the matter, for vestiges of history were already gone. The 1,000-room Grand Hyatt San Antonio rose in 2008 along a sliver of the Convention Center lagoon. The site was partly vacant and partly occupied by a parking garage, its removal un-mourned. Nor did anyone complain about the nondescript buildings cleared along the river in 1968 for the Hilton Palacio del Rio.

Developers of downtown's other major 1968 hotel, now the Omni La Mansion del Rio, found an advantage. Two historic St. Mary's College stone buildings could be renovated for rooms and provide a unique marketing angle while lesser buildings on the site—including a parking garage—could be replaced without fuss.

Across the river, the Mokara Hotel & Spa was to occupy the shell of the Frank Saddlery Company's 1901 building. But during hotel construction one of the original walls collapsed. The rest of the old building was removed as well, and the hotel opened in 2004 as the Watermark in a structure replicating its predecessor's style.

The landmark Nat Lewis Mill beside the Navarro Street/Mill Bridge had been flattened for a parking lot long before the thirteen-story Contessa was a gleam in any hotelier's eye. But one artistic concrete bench in the row of three designed by Robert Hugman for the original River Walk marina was right where a hotel entrance needed to go. San Antonio's Historic Design and Review Commission approved its removal. Hotel Contessa opened in 2005 with the missing bench enshrined indoors.

The 265-room Hotel Valencia's site had greater complications. At one corner—Houston and St. Mary's streets—was a two-story 1898 landmark designed by noted architect Alfred Giles. That was handled by preserving the building's exterior and erecting walls of the twelve-story hotel a short distance behind and within a far corner of the landmark's original footprint. At the other end of the Valencia's block was the onetime Riverside Restaurant's distinctive 1918 balcony overhanging the River Walk. When the Valencia opened in 2003, the balcony, removed from its doomed and undistinguished parent structure, had been reassembled and spruced up as a focal point in the hotel's outdoor River Walk restaurant.

Construction of Rivercenter Mall and its adjoining forty-two story Marriott Rivercenter Hotel sparked a major River Walk-related preservation achievement. The new hotel needed space occupied by an old hotel—the modest, three-story brick Fairmount, built in 1906 but suddenly a block from the planned mall's lagoon. An agreement hammered out with developers led to moving the hotel off the site, no matter that the Fairmount weighed 3.2 million pounds.

Under 280 tons of steel supports, the Fairmount was raised and beneath it were slipped thirty-six dollies, each with its own hydraulic lifts and disc brakes and set of eight fifteen-inch pneumatic tires. It took five days to roll the hotel six blocks, including a nine-minute crossing of the Market Street Bridge over the River Walk extension. The Fairmount was lowered onto new foundations at the southwest corner of South Alamo and Nueva streets, where it was renovated, joined by a new wing and opened in 1986. The Fairmount made the *Guinness Book of World Records* as the heaviest building ever moved on pneumatic wheels.[1]

[1] Fisher, *Saving San Antonio,* 469–85.

Artifacts rescued from major hotel construction along the River Walk include, above left, a 1918 restaurant balcony repositioned by Hotel Valencia and, above, a concrete bench designed by Robert Hugman and moved inside Hotel Contessa. At far left, Hotel Valencia incorporated a landmark façade designed by Alfred Giles. The old Fairmount Hotel, left, made the *Guinness Book of World Records* when it was moved to make way for the Hyatt Rivercenter.

An islet reached by a short bridge by the Hotel Contessa is a favorite wedding site. The iron altar commemorates the first local Mass and naming of the San Antonio River in 1691.

County Line barbecue restaurant and Starbucks. To the south, Rio Plaza, built as Presidio Plaza and anchored by Planet Hollywood, used a wide walkway between two buildings to fan out behind and replace a parking area with a five-story complex of office space and river level shops. Below Crockett Street, Robert Hugman had designed a wall of stone arches to shelter small shops, in the manner of stalls along the Seine. The wall was finally built in 1988. Arches were opened thirteen years later as underground entrances beneath Crockett Street to a complex of restaurants and shops in the Mokara Hotel & Spa and in the former 1926 Aztec Theater facing St. Mary's Street.[15]

By 2005 fully one-third of the restaurants on the central River Walk had become the sort of chain outlets common to strip malls throughout the country. Then Landry's, which already operated a Landry's Seafood House and a Joe's Crab Shack on the River Walk, gutted the 1895 Chandler Building at the Crockett Street Bridge for a Rainforest Cafe that opened in 2006. Justin Arrechi's ice cream company had been one of three locally owned businesses ousted from the Casino Club Building in 1981 to make room for a Landry's Saltgrass Steak House. Of Landry's new Rainforest Cafe Arrechi complained, "it's filled with fake rocks, fake trees and howling monkeys. It's just not right." Jazzman Jim Cullum Jr. gathered more than 6,500 signatures on a petition to limit chain outlets along the River Walk. Landry's chief Tilman Fertitta responded. "This is my business. I started it," he said of the company at that time having 38,000 employees at 311 restaurants in thirty-six states. "I don't think of myself as this big corporate chain."[16]

Mayor Phil Hardberger disagreed with Fertitta's self-assessment, and determined to keep the River Walk from looking like "a shopping mall in Minneapolis or New Jersey." He put the city attorney to work on an ordinance based on San Francisco's limiting of "formula restaurants"—those sharing such characteristics as names, signage, menus and staff uniforms with nine or more restaurants under the same ownership.[17]

Already there were nineteen pages of River Walk building codes and guidelines for signage, colors, maintenance and vendors' carts. In 2001 were added noise

control regulations, enforced by park rangers armed with sound meters. The Hyatt Regency Hotel constructed a soundproof wall for the latest incarnation of The Landing, where Jim Cullum's Jazz Band broadcast the public radio favorite "Live From The Landing" through 2011. General River Walk oversight changed in 1992, when the city merged the River Walk Commission and Fine Arts Commission into a citywide Historic Design and Review Commission. In 2007 Mayor Phil Hardberger sought to re-establish a finer focus with a seven-member San Antonio River Commission, but, lacking more than advisory authority, it disbanded three years later.[18]

Through it all, San Antonio was ending up with the sort of River of Fiestas envisioned by the Marco plan in the 1960s. The largest annual event—and the oldest—remained the river parade first sponsored by the Texas Cavaliers in 1941, drawing some 200,000 spectators each April. A dozen others, overseen by the Paseo del Rio Association, ranged from the St. Patrick's Day Parade on a river dyed green—with 35 pounds of "environmentally friendly green dye"— to a canoe race to a mariachi festival. More feted presidential candidates—Ronald Reagan in 1980, Bill Clinton in 1992; important guests—Queen Elizabeth II in 1991; and celebrated victories like the Spurs' fifth National Basketball Association championship in 2014. A Mud Festival with its own celebrity king and queen marked the channel's draining for

As River Walk frontage became increasingly scarce, Rio Plaza, left, added a water feature at the end of a path from the River Walk back into a new courtyard with shops. Arches of a wall along Crockett Street, right, were opened as entrances beneath the street to river-level restaurants and shops of the Mokara Hotel & Spa and the basement of the former Aztec Theater.

The Rainforest Café, "A Wild Place to Shop and Eat," offers an experience unintended by creators of the River Walk.

The river, above right, is dyed green for the annual St. Patrick's Day parade.

maintenance, a chore that's turned up everything from Timex watches—still ticking—to a wedding band—returned to its owner—to the occasional relic from the Battle of the Alamo.

Perhaps most dramatic has been the Holiday Parade the night after Thanksgiving, kicking off a month-long extravaganza of lights and caroling on boats by singers from dozens of school, church, business and civic groups. Some 2,000 sand-weighted bags held votive candles for the Fiesta de las Luminarias, inspired by Santa Fe's, during the first three weekends in December. Origin of the holiday lighting is attributed to department store president William W. McCormick of Joske's, who in 1975 sought to lure suburban shoppers back downtown by lighting the river bend's trees. The appeal of holiday lights, visible in treetops rising above street level, were to draw visitors down to the River Walk. The River Commission agreed, and approved $25,000—the current equivalent of $108,000—to hang some 30,000 white Christmas lights in trees along the bend.[19]

The holiday lighting caught on so well that three decades later a Bulb and Socket Party was held each August by Amigos del Rio volunteers, who aided city workers in readying light strings as long as ninety feet and holding 120,000 bulbs. Lights were hung by four professional tree climbers, two groundspeople and electricians. When an effort was made in 2011 to change to LED lights on wired nets wrapped

As the River Walk continued in the celebratory role of a Main Street, the San Antonio Spurs were hailed in 2014, above left, for yet another National Basketball Association championship. Queen Elizabeth II sat between Prince Philip and Mayor Lila Cockrell as she was honored with her own boat trip in 1991. Presidential campaign rides have featured Ronald Reagan in 1980 and, in 1992, left, Bill Clinton, with Texas Governor Ann Richards at his right and, at his left, vice presidential candidate Al Gore and his wife, Tipper, and U.S. Senator Lloyd Bentsen.

The Hilton Palacio del Rio shows in this Christmas view from the Commerce Street Bridge.

around tree trunks and limbs rather than on wires hanging from limbs, widespread complaints of the appearance and costly gnawing on LED wires by squirrels led two years later to lights—though LEDs—again hanging from limbs.[20]

As the annual number of River Walk visitors began to range past eleven million, traffic logistics became an issue of its own, causing occasional modification of Robert Hugman's design. In 2006 one project restored elements damaged by simple wear and tear. Access for those with disabilities had been improving since the first wheelchair ramps were built in 1979, but more needed to be done. Past a picturesque cascade, water first flowed between separated steppingstones into the river, requiring pedestrians to pay attention and not trip. To fill the gaps, decorative custom grates were inserted between the flagstones. Full compliance with the Americans with Disabilities Act was finally achieved in 2010, with completion of a $3 million project that constructed elevators, modified some stairways and walkways and leveled sidewalk sections becoming so tilted by underlying roots of trees and shrubbery that, thought one contractor, "This sidewalk is alive!"[21]

With a million tourists a year taking rides on the river, the boat concession the Beyer/Lyons family had held since 1949 became a significant prize. In 1995, a fiercely contested ten-year contract valued at $40 million was awarded to Yanaguana Cruises, a new concessionaire that promised to replace the fleet of gasoline-powered barges with thirty new barges run not on gasoline but on compressed natural gas, operating more quietly and not emitting strong fumes. After Yanaguana Cruises fell out with the city over commission payments, however, the contract was transferred to JoAnn Boone's Rio San Antonio Cruises. By the time Rio San Antonio won renewal, its fleet was up to forty boats, Rio Taxi service had expanded from nine stops to thirty-nine and the contract's value was estimated at $120 million.[22]

Whether the city had the authority to grant exclusive authority to operate boats was decided in 1998, when a court denied an independent company's attempt to operate its own boats by concluding that the River Walk was not a

An increasing volume of foot traffic has led to modifications of Robert Hugman's original River Walk. A picturesque cove seen north from the Commerce Street Bridge in 1951, above left, was later filled and straightened, above, to better accommodate pedestrians and restaurant frontage. At far left, water once flowed through uncovered gaps in the flagstone walk forced pedestrians to pay attention to their surroundings. It now flows beneath custom-made fillers, aiding persons with disabilities, who can also take advantage of elevators like the one to Crockett Street, left, which masquerades as a clock tower.

Only the landmark Clifford Building seems unchanged in the evolution pictured across to the facing page. At left, an iron bridge still crossed Commerce Street next to the Clifford Building in 1902, and riverbanks were overgrown. In the 1930s, right, the banks formed a park, lined by even channel walls. By the 1950s, the WPA had left a channel appearing more natural and with sidewalks, a scene still deserted but enlivened by the occasional gondola. Sixty years later, far right, the solitude was gone, a pedestrian bridge arched the river and in the distance rose the tower built for HemisFair '68, the world's fair that helped vault the River Walk into position as one of the nation's favorite travel destinations.

waterway under federal law. Therefore the city could limit boat traffic in the interest of public safety.[23]

Then the question flared up over who actually owned the River Walk. Four restaurant owners refused to pay the city more than $1 million in back rent charged for revenue-producing tables on what the city claimed was public right-of-way. The city sued. The restaurant owners pulled out Spanish land grants they said proved their property rights to the edge of the river. But to what edge? Did construction of the River Walk move the property edge to the water's new edge, or did the legal line remain where it was before the River Walk was built? And just where, by the way, was that? At some high water mark, or low? The city, for more than two centuries having had little impetus to define the issue, settled out of court in 2001. The restaurant owners surrendered their title claims in return for lower rent, lease options longer than those of others and for more say in how rental revenues would be spent.[24]

One way to deal with the crowds along the River Walk was to try to reduce the number of people. Only a few years before the problem had been getting pedestrians from then busy Houston Street down to the uncrowded River Walk. But the challenge seemed to become how to get pedestrians from the busy River Walk up to the now uncrowded Houston Street. The point was made none too subtlely beside a wide stairway at the North Presa Street Bridge, where an incongruous large arrow pointed upward "To Houston Street."

Another solution to reducing congestion was incorporating the cavernous bypass channel into the River Walk.

The tainter gate structure midway in the bypass channel had served as a movable dam to maintain a consistent level of water in the Great Bend, keeping water higher on its upstream side than on the other. But its manual adjustments were not always sufficiently precise. After taking a magazine writer on a tour in 1977, Paseo del Rio Association Director Claire Regnier complained that "water all but covers the sidewalks in some blocks, particularly in the south section of the bend. It is difficult to maintain our positive image while 'wading' a guest through a walking tour." She also had to be careful "to avoid walking near those staircases and footbridges which I know to be in a state of disrepair." Until things were fixed, she thought tours for writers and convention executives should be conducted by boat.[25]

Moreover, by blocking the channel the gate forced boat operators to double back at each end of the bend, creating two-way boat traffic increasingly hazardous in the narrow channel as the number of trips increased.[26]

Bond issue funding led to an overhaul of the downtown river's flood control system, completed in 1988. The tainter gate was removed, its function replaced by a dam a block south of the end of the Great Bend, below Nueva Street. Just above the dam at one side went a marina for the main armada of passenger and dining barges, park rangers' patrol boats and maintenance barges. At a new River Walk operations center upstairs, the upstream water level could be electronically monitored and maintained within a fraction of an inch. At San Antonio River Authority headquarters eight blocks south, a laboratory monitored quality of river water.[27]

The dam at Nueva Street, top, was built at the end of the Great Bend in 1988 to maintain the water level and permit removal upstream of the tainter gate that had blocked river barges from being able to continue back to the start of the bend. A half-mile south of the dam, at San Antonio River Authority Headquarters, below, water quality scientists Maru Garayar, left, and Yolanda Gutierrez tested wastewater and stormwater samples from the river.

Daily maintenance remained the charge of the city's Parks and Recreation Department, long accustomed to running early morning boats with workers who scooped out floating debris like dead leaves and foam cups with long-handled nets. Their job became easier in 2006 with the debut of Lady Eco, a maintenance barge five years in development. Its two arms extended to a combined span of thirty-five feet. Each arm had six detachable nets to skim the water and could retract to dump trash into a bin on board. A crew of three could sweep the River Walk from Lexington Avenue to the Nueva Street maintenance center in forty-five minutes.[28]

Opening the bypass channel to boats improved traffic flow around the bend, but treated passengers only to views of sheer concrete walls on either side. The solution was a byproduct of a project inconceivable during the flood control work of earlier eras. Completion of Olmos Dam in 1926 and straightening the river channel below may have been a strong defense against catastrophic flooding, but much of downtown San Antonio remained classified as within a flood plain. Building permits were sometimes difficult to obtain. Floodgates at both ends of the Great Bend were so secure that buildings could open directly on the River Walk. Outside the bend, construction was not permitted lower than eighteen feet above the River Walk, for the full depth of the bypass channel had to be kept clear for possible high waters.

In 1987, construction began on a flood tunnel twenty-four feet in diameter and some 140 feet deep beneath central San Antonio. High waters could enter at an inlet structure near Josephine Street below Brackenridge Park on the north, and exit into the river channel three miles south at Roosevelt Park. When completed eleven years later, the $111.4 million tunnel reduced the predicted level of heaviest flooding above by ten feet. The full depth of the cutoff channel was no longer needed to hold floodwaters. Improvements could be built within.

Soon walkways were being built along the channel walls so pedestrians, like boats, could make a single circuit around the main River Walk. In 2001 the river's long-recommended link with Main Plaza materialized in the form of Portal

San Fernando. Lake/Flato Architects used two hundred tons of limestone in designing a park with symbolic water features descending from Main Plaza. Removing a portion of the old channel wall created an opening to a cantilevered walkway that zig-zagged beside the channel's remaining west wall, then crossed newly-placed islets to meet the original River Walk at the start of the bend.[29]

A $3 million walkway along the eastern edge of the channel joined the historic River Walk at both ends. Near Portal San Fernando, a seventy-foot steel pedestrian bridge across the channel was designed by Davis Sprinkle & Co. Architects and featured copper embel-

lishments by Judith Maxwell. The span was donated in 2010 by owners of the adjacent 310-room Drury Plaza Hotel Riverwalk, based in the old Alamo National Bank Building at Commerce and St. Mary's streets but newly linked to the River Walk through the bank's old parking garage beside the channel.[30]

Upstream, the tunnel also freed the mile-long upper section of Robert Hugman's River Walk from heavy flood restrictions. Previously overshadowed by the more developed section within the Great Bend, the little traveled upper River Walk had suffered neglect and was beginning to have structural failures. In 1998, one section was closed when a channel wall began collapsing. With prodding from Mayor Howard Peak, a $12.5 million overhaul began in 2001. Water was drained from the upper channel for more than a year as the bottom was paved, providing a solid footing for channel walls rebuilt with matching stonework. Remaining walls were reinforced, a walkway was extended the length of the upper River Walk's left bank and a parking lot at Augusta and Convent streets was converted into a small park. A faux-wood trellis of concrete trees by artisan Carlos Cortés buttressed a retaining wall beside Municipal Auditorium, transformed in 2014 into the Tobin Center for the Performing Arts, its riverside plaza having a 600-seat event space.[31]

As happened along the Great Bend, increasing numbers of pedestrians led to new hotels. The 325-room Holiday Inn Riverwalk had been built just outside the bend in 1987, but as improvements sped up the 149-room Hotel Indigo opened

River Walk maintenance was made easier by a boat, top, that swept floating refuse into nets on arms that could swing out to a span of thirty-five feet. Below, the riverbed through downtown is periodically drained and cleared of debris.

The Flood Tunnel at Work

Sixty-seven years after a cataclysm hit San Antonio, the city's luck changed. In December 1920 the city finally adopted a long-delayed flood control plan and began work. Nine months later, the project hardly started, a disastrous flood caught the city unprepared. In December 1997 a long-delayed flood control tunnel beneath the city was finished. Ten months later, what would have been a disastrous flood was averted by the newly completed project.

Known as an inverted siphon tunnel, it extended three miles, beginning south of Brackenridge Park at Josephine Street and ending south of downtown at Roosevelt Park, an elevation 35 feet lower than the intake shaft. It was 24 feet in diameter and some 130 feet beneath downtown San Antonio. To the west, a similar tunnel finished in 1991 carried San Pedro Creek floodwaters for a mile, from Quincy to Guadalupe streets. Unlike the city's 1920s flood control projects, the river tunnel's delays, dramas and frustrations occurred mostly underground and out of sight as completion lengthened to ten years and costs tripled, to $111.4 million.

A 620-ton, laser-guided machine nicknamed the "Mole" bored a three-mile tunnel 24 feet in diameter and 140 feet beneath central San Antonio.

This flood control effort engendered very little controversy since, unlike the 1920s project, it did not have to be totally funded by the city. This time federal funding covered three-fourths of the cost, and the U.S. Army Corps of Engineers did the work. Construction began in 1987 using a 620-ton, laser-guided tunnel boring machine nicknamed the "Mole." As it ground through the earth, the Mole placed pre-cast concrete segments in rings one foot thick. But less than 500 feet from its start at the southern end, formations of fractured shale caved in, leaving fragments larger than the machine could grind. The Mole got stuck 150 feet below the Brackenridge High School girls' gym. Workers dug a vertical shaft 900 feet away and tunneled back to clear the fallen shale. It took a year to free the Mole.

When completed at the end of 1997, floodwaters could be diverted from the river channel into an inlet structure with a sloped apron that filtered out debris, letting water drop through a vertical shaft to the vertical shaft of the outlet structure and into the tunnel. Floodwaters emerged through a fanned grating 230 feet wide and flowed back into the main channel.

Ten months after the tunnel was finally completed, up to twenty inches of rain fell on October 17, 1998. Flooding claimed eleven lives in low-lying areas and caused more than $120 million in property damage, largely in the Salado Creek drainage area to the east. The tunnel carried as many as three million gallons a minute. Traffic on the expressway between downtown and the airport was cut off as floodwaters blocked by Olmos Dam backed up Olmos Basin and over US 281, but most of the city's 1.2 million residents were unscathed.

Another payoff came with realization that the tunnel could also be used to recycle water in the River Walk. Normal river water passing the tunnel's outlet structure could be diverted into the outlet shaft, pumped to the upstream intake and sent back down the river. Wastewater pumped from treatment plants to the tunnel's inlet was added. Previously, each day three pumps in Brackenridge Park sent five million gallons of drinking-quality water daily to fill the River Walk. The pumps were no longer needed.

During a torrential storm in 1998, water rose to nearly the top of Olmos Dam, left. Some water released from the dam, center, churned downstream past the sealed gatehouse entrance to the Great Bend, upper right, and on down the cutoff channel. More of the torrent, however, had already dropped into the flood tunnel, and boiled out at the tunnel's exit far south of downtown, lower right.

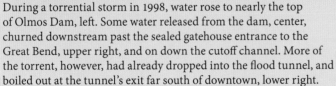

Portal San Antonio, right, linked the cutoff channel with Main Plaza in 2001, as a tunnel lowered the risk of flooding. Five years later, a walkway was built along the east side of the channel.

farther upstream in 2013. Apartments rose near the river south of the Nueva Street dam, which blocked boat service south toward the King William Street area.

As one engineering feat and then another kept escalating change, San Antonio's River Walk had become, as longtime San Antonio River Authority General Manger Fred Pfeiffer once pointed out, "less a product of nature enhanced by man than a product of man enhanced by nature." Nature's part would remain critical in an expansion of the River Walk more dramatic than even the most "idle dreams" of those who, more than a century before, had tried to imagine what San Antonio's river could become.

In 2001, the upper portion of Robert Hugman's River Walk was drained for reconstruction of channel walls, far left. A faux-wood concrete trellis, left, designed by Carlos Cortés, was built as a retaining wall near the Tobin Center for the Performing Arts. Other improvements in the section included a recycling cascade, below left, from Pecan Street's Weston Centre and, below, the transformation of a parking lot into a riverside park.

The first barge through the locks at the triumphal opening of the Museum Reach's first section on May 31, 2009—Mayor Phil Hardberger's last day in office—carried in front from left, Bexar County Judge Nelson Wolff, former mayor and River Oversight co-chair Lila Cockrell, Hardberger and San Antonio River Authority vice chair Sally Buchanan.

·9·
Reaching North and South

Quintupling the length of San Antonio's River Walk borrowed lessons from the Roman Empire.

During his successful campaign for mayor in 2004–05, Phil Hardberger recalled mentioning the river in each of his sixty-eight debates and working it into every speech. "Cato the Elder ended every single one of his speeches to the Roman senate with 'Carthage must be destroyed,'" said Hardberger, whose credentials included six years as chief justice of the state's Fourth Court of Appeals and four as secretary of the Peace Corps in the Kennedy administration. "It's persistence politics."[1]

The payoff a decade later was two vastly different new sections equal in quality to Robert Hugman's original River Walk, with the same emphasis on ever-changing vistas, unexpected flourishes, imaginative landscaping and unique bridges.

Since completion of a federally funded River Corridor Feasibility Study in 1973, a succession of committees had been proposing major changes along the river beyond Hugman's River Walk. "There were good planners who were hired to make plans and give ideas," said former mayor and longtime parks advocate Lila Cockrell. "However, we really didn't have any money." Planning came into focus in 1998 when Bexar County, the City of San Antonio and the San Antonio River Authority created the San Antonio River Oversight Committee, co-chaired by Cockrell and architect Irby Hightower. Members included twenty-two representatives of businesses and neighborhoods along the proposed route.[2]

With governmental bodies committed to the project and a committee of stakeholders in place, the San Antonio River Improvements Project began to take shape. The section north of the original River Walk, nearly four miles long, was named the Museum Reach after the two major museums along that part of the river. It was subdivided into the navigable Urban Segment, about a mile and a half in length and protected by the flood tunnel, and the more bucolic upper Park Segment, some two and a half miles long, with walking trails.

The nine-mile section to the south, named the Mission Reach after four Spanish missions along its path, would emphasize recreation and ecosystem restoration, to help that section function as it did prior to a flood control project a half century earlier. The first mile south of the end of the River Walk at South Alamo Street was designated as the Eagleland Segment, a transition

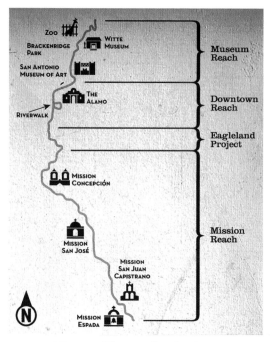

The new fifteen-mile-plus San Antonio River Walk extended in both directions from the original River Walk, shown as the Downtown Reach. The four miles northward were termed the Museum Reach. To the south was the one-mile Eagleland Segment Project and the nearly eight-mile Mission Reach.

zone between the manicured, urban original River Walk and the restored natural stretch of native growth of the Mission Reach.

No longer could a single architect like Robert Hugman be expected to plan such a project and carry it out through one or two public entities like the city and the WPA. Now federal funding required the project to be directed by the U.S. Army Corps of Engineers, which, noted River Oversight Committee co-chair Irby Hightower, "wanted a project that measurably functioned like a riparian habitat; the community wanted a linear park that looked like a river." The challenge for local officials was "how to persuade the Corps to adapt its criteria-based approach to the design-oriented goals of the community." They succeeded.[3]

Chosen in 2000 for concept design was SWA Group, Houston-based landscape architects, planners and urban designers, who would be aided by a team of civil and structural engineers, architects, economists and environmental scientists. Museum Reach architects were San Antonio's Ford, Powell & Carson—whose Boone Powell, like Hugman, drew most of his design not by computer but by hand. Mission Reach architects were the San Antonio office of Carter & Burgess, which before the project ended joined the Jacobs Engineering Group.

Initial coordinator would be engineer Steve Graham, the San Antonio River Authority's director of watershed management. When Graham was promoted to assistant general manager, he was replaced as project manager by Authority engineer Mark Sorenson. Preparing a master plan for sidewalks, artworks and other amenities would be Seattle's Lorna Jordan Studio in association with San Antonio's Bender Wells Clark Design.

A long series of public meetings and presentations began. As plans firmed up, the Oversight Committee managed to keep the direction in place through three mayors, four city managers, two county judges and three River Authority general managers. Then came Phil Hardberger.

Once elected, Mayor Hardberger took a direct approach. "It had been planned, and there was this committee and that committee. . . . I said, 'We're going to stop planning and start digging.' " He found ready support from Bexar County Judge Nelson Wolff—a critical ally, since counties in Texas collect the dedicated flood control tax and Bexar County would be the majority funder. As momentum swelled, the $384.1 million project drew joint funding from the City of San Antonio, Bexar County, the San Antonio River Authority and the U.S. Army Corps of Engineers. In addition, private funds were raised by the new San Antonio River Foundation.

The San Antonio Water System contributed funds when water and wastewater lines needed to be moved.[4]

"There was the usual hue and cry and people saying this is costing too much money," Hardberger recounted. "My answer to that was, 'Yes it's going to cost us millions, but it's going to bring back billions.' And so we are going to go forward and we are going to get it done."[5]

Hardberger's optimism, however, was challenged by federal deficits and harder times. Construction bids were higher than anticipated. Washington delayed full funding of the U.S. Army Corps of Engineers' share and the city, facing its own financial problems, would not increase its promised share as costs rose. "The city said to us essentially, 'This is it, make it work,' " said San Antonio River Authority General Manager Suzanne Scott.[6]

A creative funding solution resulted. It enabled construction on the Museum Reach's Urban Segment to begin on May 8, 2007, despite a construction bid that came in $18 million over budget.

Scott and City Manager Sheryl Sculley noted that while the River Authority's tax revenue could not be used for capital projects, it could be spent on operations and maintenance. City bond funds were originally to include long-term River Improvements Project operations and maintenance costs. The city agreed to use its funds originally earmarked for operations and maintenance to instead cover the $18 million shortfall. The Authority, in turn, agreed to use its annual tax revenue to assume the operations and maintenance responsibility. Bexar County, the segment's primary funding contributor, was satisfied that operations and maintenance assurances protected its investment, and a final agreement in April 2007 assured the funding.

In addition to the funding arrangement, a catalyst to begin the Museum Reach was acquisition of the abandoned Pearl Brewery by former picante sauce magnate Christopher "Kit" Goldsbury, according to the River Authority's Suzanne Scott. Its riverside site was near the key intersection of Interstate 35 with U.S. 281 and Broadway. The brewery had opened there on twenty-two acres in 1881 and by 1916 was the largest brewery in Texas. Its centerpiece was a seven-story brewhouse with arched windows and a mansard-roofed tower that was San Antonio's tallest building when built in 1894. Goldsbury planned an imaginative multi-use development

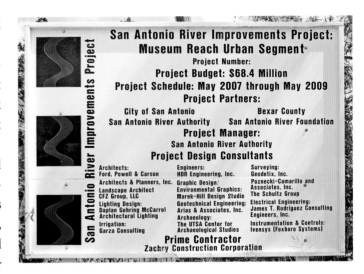

Completion of the first segment of the Museum Reach took a broad range of participants.

known as Pearl that fit well with plans for the extended River Walk. Its focal point would be the old brewhouse, renovated and enlarged to become Hotel Emma, a boutique hotel named for the widow of Pearl founder Otto Koehler. She kept the brewery open through Prohibition.

The Pearl was conveniently located a block south of the flood tunnel's intake facility on Josephine Street. It was thus within the tunnel's flood protection zone, and the river past it would be fed by an ample supply of water from the tunnel's recycling system, leaving that part of the river no longer, as Irby Hightower described it, little more than "a trapezoidal ditch with a trickle of water." Since the river plain upstream rose slightly, the Pearl was the logical site for a dam marking the northern end of navigation on the Museum Reach and thus the Urban Segment's northern boundary. Below the dam could be a turning basin for riverboats. Banks below the Pearl could be landscaped for a small amphitheater and walkways up to restaurants, shops and offices. But, first, the problem of the fall of the river had to be resolved.

Below the low dam at Lexington Avenue and on past the Great Bend to the higher dam at Nueva Street, the river was level enough for riverboats. But from Lexington Avenue up to the Pearl the elevation rose nine feet, too steep for boats. There was general agreement that the low dam at Lexington Avenue could be replaced with a higher one two blocks upstream at Brooklyn Avenue. But how to deal with navigation was another issue. One idea was having separate upstream and downstream boat services that passengers would transfer between. Another option was a dam

The Pearl Brewery's brewhouse, below, was the tallest building in San Antonio when completed in 1894. At lower right it remained on the skyline as Hotel Emma in the mixed-use Pearl complex, near the turning basin at the northernmost point for passenger barge navigation on the Museum Reach.

with a sloping face that boats fitted with wheels could crawl up. Others suggested a dam with a lock system that would raise and lower boats.

The ultimate solution was the simplest, if the most expensive: a dam with two locks. "Ours is just a recreational lock and dam," explained Mark Sorenson, the River Authority's manager for the River Improvements Project. "It's one-tenth the size of a commercial lock, but it operates in the same way." Locks would measure 13 by 30 feet to accommodate 11 by 27 foot boats, raised or lowered to the appropriate level in five minutes. Work was by the Museum Reach's prime contractor, San Antonio's Zachry Construction. Operators in quarters atop the structure would run the computerized operating system daily from 7 a.m. to 11 p.m. Nearby went an observation gazebo and a ticket office next to public restrooms. Of the dam structure's $6.5 million cost, $5 million was contributed by AT&T, which had a major building nearby.[7]

Two years after ground was broken in 2007, the Museum Reach's Urban Segment was completed on schedule. Opening ceremonies were held at the new locks on May 31, 2009, one day before Mayor Phil Hardberger was term-limited out of office. Already the master plan for the area had been chosen as one of the best urbanist projects in the world by the Congress for the New Urbanism.

In addition to historic buildings at the Pearl, the Urban Segment was anchored by another set downstream at the original 1884 Lone Star Brewery, its centerpiece a crenellated five-story landmark built in 1904 as the brewhouse. When renovated

Flexible pipes carried the river's reduced flow south to join the river where the original River Walk began at the Hugman Dam, below center in top left photo. Construction of a dam and two locks at Brooklyn Avenue, top, opened navigation upstream. North of the Pearl, channel construction continued through rundown neighborhoods, above, to link the Museum Reach's Urban Segment with the Park Segment past the Josephine Street Bridge, center.

At opening ceremonies for the first section of the Museum Reach were, from left, Irby Hightower, River Oversight Committee co-chair; Sally Buchanan, San Antonio River Authority vice chair; Mayor Phil Hardberger; Bexar County Judge Nelson Wolff; and Edward E. Collins, chair of the San Antonio River Foundation. Afterward, far right, Mrs. Cockrell and Hardberger took a hand at piloting the first barge through the lock. At top left sat the River Authority's project manager, Mark Sorenson.

in 1981 as the San Antonio Museum of Art, the iron bridge used for rolling barrels from one tower to another was replaced by a glass-enclosed walkway. The bridge was left to molder until donated to the San Antonio River Foundation to become a nearby pedestrian bridge across the revived river. A similar iron conveyor bridge between the Pearl Brewery's brewhouse and its full goods warehouse was relocated to become an eighty-six-foot pedestrian bridge across the river at the Pearl.

Years before, the Museum of Art had purchased land on the other side of West Jones Avenue, and now found that its 15 acres included 1,200 linear feet along the river that made it the largest owner of downtown riverfront property. For the river-banks behind its main complex, the museum raised $5 million to replace chain link fences and uproot overgrown banks for improvements centering on a 4,000 square-foot open pavilion with river views. The River Foundation installed in the River Walk wall across from the museum—which includes a noted collection of Asian art—a donated set of nine metal tiles with characteristic Shang Dynasty designs that were part of Taiwan's pavilion at HemisFair '68.[8]

Nine tiles with Shang Dynasty designs that were part of Taiwan's pavilion at HemisFair '68 were reinstalled along the River Walk across from the San Antonio Museum of Art.

A block down the river, at the end of Tenth Street, was Veterans of Foreign Wars Post 76, in a three-story columned Classical Revival home built by lumberman Van A. Petty in 1897. When riverside over-growth was removed, VFW members found themselves occupying one of the signal landmarks on the Museum Reach. Below the post, construction crews enlarging the riverbed uncovered remains of a stone dam built for the 1870s Alamo Mill/Crystal Ice Company, which

The San Antonio River was imagined as a broad, distant stream in an early drawing, left, of the Lone Star Brewing Company and its 1904 brew house, now the San Antonio Museum of Art. The museum replaced the iron conveyor bridge between the brew house's two towers with a glassed walkway, shown above left in the cold December of 2008 as construction continued in the riverbed and the museum's riverfront was being upgraded. The conveyor bridge was installed across the river, above, as a pedestrian bridge.

drilled the first artesian well into the Edwards Aquifer. Much of the dam was preserved and an interpretive marker was prepared.[9]

But nowhere was transformation more dramatic than in the once dilapidated blocks at street level on either side of the Museum Reach. Headlines termed the project "a developer's dream." Long before ground was broken, savvy developers were buying up dilapidated homes and bars and drug-infested motels within a 377-acre neighborhood designated River North, on either side of the river from

The neighborhood of VFW Post 76, at top in photos, improved dramatically from the dismal view in February of 1966, top left, as riverbanks along the Museum Reach were cleared in 2008, right, and finished, above, the next year.

downtown to Interstate 35. Its master plan integrated planned Museum Reach stairways with the neighborhood street grid above and recommended changes in the area's existing commercial and industrial zoning. When development was finished, neighborhood population was expected to grow from a few thousand to 50,000.

By the time Museum Reach ground was broken in 2007, land appraisals in the area had risen eighteen percent, from $260 million to $309 million. After AT&T and the San Antonio Museum of Art, the property owner with the highest valuation was developer Edward Cross II, who with his partners already owned 32 properties valued at a total of $16 million. City officials were delighted at the anticipated $1 billion economic "jolt" the River Walk extension was generating as new hotels and high-density housing projects got underway in an area once all but written off as having no potential.[10]

A year after the opening, Rio San Antonio Cruises reported overall riverboat ticket sales up fifty percent, riverside joggers caused a spike in sales of running shoes at a Pearl sports outlet and beer sales at VFW Post 76 had doubled. Dramatic works of art began adorning walkways and bridges. Benches were installed for spectators at an unexpectedly popular event, the nightly flight of Mexican free-tailed bats from beneath the Interstate 35 overpass. Five years after opening day, annual economic benefit of the Museum Reach was pegged at $139 million. The

As the view south from Brooklyn Avenue was being transformed by Museum Reach construction, above, a flurry of apartment construction was underway north of Jones Avenue, far left and center left. Two blocks south, a hotel was being built on one side of the Ninth Street Bridge while an office building, at bottom right, was going up on the other.

Long-Eared Sunfish, Sonic Passages and Rippling Shadows

Unsightly undersides of seven bridges posed a special challenge to Museum Reach planners. No one enjoyed walking through such dead spaces. Those, remarked artist Stuart Allen, "you think of as places where trolls live."

To the rescue came the San Antonio River Foundation.

Since its formation in 2005, the River Foundation has raised more than $20 million from private sources to enhance the extended River Walk with projects that could not qualify for public funding but would contribute significantly to its unique flair. There were opportunities for landscaping and recreational enhancements and for public art.

Perhaps the most difficult space gaped below the high overpass of Interstate 35. The solution of Philadelphia's Donald Lipski takes viewers' minds from the distraction of traffic noise above. His *F.I.S.H.* represents a school of twenty-five fiberglass long-eared sunfish of the type native to the river, though each of Lipski's is seven feet long, painted inside and out and lit from within. Unevenly hung from the bridge's underside, they sway in the breeze as if moving in an underwater current.

Under the Brooklyn and McCullough Avenue bridges, Stuart Allen suspended colored panels evoking sky, water plants and land and named for their coordinates—*29°26'00"N/98°29'07"W* and *29°25'57"N/98°29'13"W*—that appear to move with the viewer. Beneath the Ninth Street Bridge, forms of Mark Schlesinger's *Under the Over Bridge* use his custom colored cement for reflective effects by day and glow-in-the-dark colors by night.

Beneath the Lexington Avenue Bridge, London-based Martin Richmond installed *Shimmer Field*, hundreds of pieces of dichroic acrylic that filter some colors and reflect others. For the Jones Avenue underpass, San Francisco sound artist Bill Fontana's *Sonic Passages* plays recorded sounds of birds, crickets, bullfrogs, insects, rushing water and manmade noises.

At street level, above the railings of the McCullough Avenue Bridge Roland Briseño designed flowing red metal ribbons of hands—their cutout design inspired by lace gloves—entitled *Puente de Encuentros*, or *Bridge of the Encounters*. Above the Brooklyn Avenue Bridge railings he overlapped circles of galvanized steel and perforated metal sheets he titled *Puente de Rippling Shadows*.

For the sides of the Newell Street Bridge, metal sculptor George Schroeder designed *River Origins and Movements #1*, steel ribbon-like weavings of cuts, twists and curls. For *River Origins and Movements #2*, on the sides of the Camden Street Bridge, Schroeder's steel strips represent yuccas and other drought-resistant plants.

Between those two bridges rose *The Grotto*, a three-story creation by Carlos Cortés of *faux bois*—concrete false wood—that forms winding passageways with cave-like walls, ceilings hung with realistic stalagmites and stalactites and, deep within, the giant head of "Father Nature," a waterfall pouring from its mouth.

First along the Mission Reach were Mark Schlesinger's *Up On The On*, a footbridge southwest of Roosevelt Park lined with a repeating pattern of painted and textured rocks alongside natural river rocks, and Anne Wallace's *The Once and Future River*, etchings along a new sandstone pedestrian bridge near Concepción Park of freshwater prawns, bullhead minnows, log perch, pickerel weeds and other flora and fauna that once thrived along the river and are expected to rebound with the habitat restoration.

Art along the Museum Reach included, facing page, a stairway designed by Carlos Cortés. Mission Reach art included bridgework designed by Mark Schlesinger, below right. On the Museum Reach, clockwise from bottom right, were Donald Lipski's fiberglass fish, George Schroeder's shadow-producing poles and hand designs, the face of "Father Nature" by Carlos Cortés, acrylic strips shown being installed by Martin Richmond and panels by Stuart Allen.

area had gained 1,260 new housing units and fifty new companies.[11]

By Christmas 2010 the Museum Reach was aglow with holiday lighting not just at the locks but, upstream, with underwater lights, in green, pink, white and blue.

Beyond the Urban Segment, river channel restoration would be limited to erosion control and removing invasive plants. New pathways northward along the Museum Reach's Park Segment would skirt riverbanks through the Brackenridge Golf Course and Brackenridge Park and follow to their east a route along the formerly concrete-lined drainage channel to be restored as Catalpa-Pershing Creek. They would link with existing paths into 343-acre Brackenridge Park, where the river was already lined with rock walls, many built by the WPA at the time of River Walk construction downtown.

The extended River Walk's lock and dam structure was decked out with holiday lights at Christmas, while, upstream, dozens of colored lights glowed from beneath the water.

Some channels had been lined with rock since the World War I era, both in the park and in the adjoining San Antonio Zoo. In addition to a variety of low bridges spanning the river were the two nineteenth century iron bridges removed from downtown and reassembled in Brackenridge Park after the flood of 1921. Near the park's northeastern edge, the Witte Museum installed a small riverside theater below its new South Texas Heritage Center. Nearby, excavations turned up the 1719–20 channels where the Alamo Acequia drew its water from the river.

Across from the end of the Museum Reach at Hildebrand Avenue, on the campus of the University of the Incarnate Word, the Headwaters Coalition, directed by Helen Ballew, was at work on a 53-acre sanctuary to restore the sort of urban forest that once surrounded the originating springs of the river at the Blue Hole, usually dry.

Completion of the four-mile Museum Reach cost $84.8 million, $71.2 million for the Urban Segment and $13.6 million for the Park Segment. It produced immediate, tangible results. Extension to the north dovetailed with the older River Walk's ambience of a narrow passage between high banks. Width of the Museum Reach's public right-of-way averaged eighty feet, and was bordered

primarily by private property in neighborhoods continuously evolving since the city's founding. Banks on either side were ripe for private commercial and residential development.

The eight-mile Mission Reach, however, was a more long-range and complicated project, with cost estimates nearing three times higher. Its right-of-way sometimes neared four times the width of the Museum Reach and it carried three times more water, making the Mission Reach highly susceptible to periodic flooding. Most of it had been scraped in the 1950s into a broad, open flood channel that destroyed habitat and isolated the river from its surroundings. Recreating

The Park Segment of the Museum Reach would pass the Brackenridge Golf Course, shown at top in the 1920s when a suspension bridge reached the third tee. To the west, a natural section of the river, above left, would be reached by a side trail. Near the Park Segment's northern end, blocks lined in semicircles formed a riverside theater by the Witte Museum's South Texas Heritage Center, above.

Much riverside rockwork connected by trails to the Museum Reach's Park Segment predated the original River Walk. Above, a pond held sea lions in the early days of the San Antonio Zoo. At top right, the river was dammed in Brackenridge Park for swimming and boating near the early Koehler Pavilion. At right, the still-popular low water crossing bridge was partly straddled in March 1921 by Vaudeville actor Bob Carleton, in town to perform at the Majestic Theater. In 1940, far right, the WPA added sidewalks around the 1877 Water Works pumphouse, then in use as a bathhouse for swimmers.

that habitat and restoring the balance of nature would be the primary thrust of Mission Reach work.

Much of the Mission Reach right-of-way adjoined public land, meaning that private developers could not contribute as much to the ambience as they could along the Museum Reach. But the southern reach did adjoin lands of four of San Antonio's five Spanish missions, dating from the 1720s and 1730s and incorporated into San Antonio Missions National Historical Park. Portals to these missions would be major design elements.

Otherwise, since most new development did not extend far south until the turn of the twentieth century, there were few landmarks to restore. The only major mill along the southern stretch of the river had been the briefly prosperous four-story frame Mission Mill near Mission San Juan, built in 1879 by brothers Louis and Henry Berg to clean wool and manufacture fabric. Upstream, across from Mission San José, was the first movie studio in Texas, the 1911 Star Film Ranch, which took advantage of the missions and riverside brush lands as settings for a host of silent movies. It stood near the Hot Sulphur Wells Hotel, a spa complex built after an artesian well drilled near the river in the 1890s struck mineral water. For four decades the spa drew celebrities ranging from Will Rogers to Douglas Fairbanks to Cecil B. DeMille.

Mussels thriving in the warm mineral waters flowing into the river were found to contain freshwater pearls. This discovery led to a pearl rush "reminiscent of Klondike Days." Prospectors found up to three dozen pearls a day until the mussels were gone.[12]

Aside from periodic plans to revive ruins of the Hot Sulphur Wells Hotel and the ongoing restoration far upstream of the warehouse-district-turned-Blue Star

U.S. Senator Kay Bailey Hutchison in 2011 raised the gate to allow water back into Mission San Juan's acequia, severed by the 1950s flood control project. Behind her are Bexar County Judge Nelson Wolff, center, and San Antonio Mayor Julián Castro and his twin brother Joaquin, soon elected to Congress.

The Mission Reach was designed past four eighteenth-century missions and their churches and chapels near the river, including, clockwise from immediate left, Espada, San José, Concepción and San Juan.

Vanished landmarks along the Mission Reach included a woolen mill at Berg's Mill, top left, and the bathhouse of the Hot Sulphur Wells Hotel, top center. Remaining was the Lone Star Brewery complex, at center in above view, opened in 1933 and closed in 1996. The original convoluted course of the river was changed in 1954 by a straightened and greatly widened channel, top right.

Arts Complex, as the Mission Reach was completed the vacant Lone Star Brewery buildings were drawing the greatest interest from developers. The brewery had opened upstream from Mission Concepción as the Salinas Brewing Company when Prohibition ended in 1933, was renamed Lone Star Brewing Company in 1940 and closed in 1996. Hopes for Museum Reach-style development along the Mission Reach were buoyed with plans for the $50 million Big Tex Grain Company urban residential project south of the Blue Star Arts Complex.

The major challenge for Mission Reach work was overcoming a massive flood control project done sixty years earlier. While that may have succeeded in speeding floodwaters out of the city, straightening the winding river and bulldozing its banks destroyed much of the surrounding environment. Now 113 acres of aquatic habitat needed to be restored, with systems of riffles, runs and pool sequences and 13 acres of embayments or side channels to shelter aquatic plants and fish. Another 334 acres were designated for woodland habitat restoration, with plantings of more than 23,000 young trees and shrubs of 44 native varieties. More than 10,000 pounds of seeds of 60 species of native grasses and wildflowers would also be planted.[13]

Rather than re-digging the river's precise original convoluted path, the new, gently meandering channel was to reclaim the functioning of the river, reducing erosion, drawing back wildlife and restoring the balance of nature. The channel's base of concrete rubble would be returned to a soil base. Planners observed that the channel "is not currently a place where most people find recreational opportunity," adding dryly of the concrete rubble base, "the public has expressed a negative reaction to this application."[14]

Difficulties could be expected, given the newness of the science of fluvial geomorphology, which studies the evolution of rivers and watersheds. As the district commander of the U.S. Army Corps of Engineers, Col. John Minahan, said at the Eagleland Segment groundbreaking in 2004: "Twenty-two years ago, if you'd told me I'd be standing here in San Antonio taking a perfectly good flood-control project and putting it back the way we found it, I'd probably [have said], 'That's not possible.' "[15]

The $13.6 million Eagleland Segment bordered a former industrial area being converted to a mixed-use arts district. It was a mile long, from South Alamo Street past the Blue Star Arts Complex to the flood tunnel outlet on Lone Star Boulevard near Roosevelt Park. It was designated after nearby Eagleland Drive, named for the Eagles of adjacent Brackenridge High School. Ecosystem restoration techniques were tested along the Eagleland Segment for future use on the rest of the Mission Reach. Seventeen acres along the river's right-of-way were cleared of invasive plants and re-planted with natives. Its first hike-and-bike trails opened in 2007, with additional amenities completed in 2012.

The nine miles of the Mission Reach were divided into three phases. Groundbreaking for the first, on June 2, 2008, launched a $25.2 million mile-long construction project by Laughlin-Thyssen Inc. from Lone Star Boulevard to the confluence of the San Antonio River and San Pedro Creek. Some 360,000 cubic yards of soil were relocated during construction of a pedestrian trail, two footbridges across the river, picnic areas, a new channel, grass and wildflower seeding and restoration of 34 acres of native vegetation. Among speakers at its opening in June 2011 was U.S. Secretary of the Interior Ken Salazar.

Similar work on the second phase was begun by Zachry Construction in February 2010, south from the confluence of the San Antonio River and San Pedro Creek to Mission Drive. This $22.7 million, mile-long project involved moving 800,000 cubic yards of soil. It was opened along with the first phase in June 2011.

Down the mile-long Eagleland Segment, walkways wandered through surroundings broader than the River Walk downtown, and crossed the river on a new hike-and-bike bridge.

A Magnificent Urban Ecosystem

In a real sense, the fifteen-plus miles of riverbanks through the heart of San Antonio form a giant botanical garden masquerading as a River Walk, one lined with a vast range of plants and trees maintained by the city's Parks and Recreation Department and the San Antonio River Authority.

Even when the River Walk was limited to three miles in central downtown, it was named—in 2004—a Horticultural Landmark by the American Society for Horticultural Science. It was cited as "a magnificent urban ecosystem where man and nature embrace a great engineering work that supports the rich diversity of South Texas plants."

The downtown River Walk's protection between narrow banks twenty feet below street level keeps it five degrees warmer in winter and five degrees cooler in summer. Trees and plants usually safe from occasional South Texas freezes only indoors can thrive—banana, lime, avocado and ficus trees plus more than a hundred species of plants like caladiums, gingers and philodendrons. In addition, some 30,000 annuals are set out each year.

Adding to cypress trees and basic plantings already beside the river was landscape architect Stewart E. King, hired as "city forester" by Mayor Maury Maverick in 1939. Through 1951 King also headed the city's Parks and

Recreation Department. Considered ahead of his time in environmental consciousness, King pioneered the hardy native plantings that help form the foundation of today's River Walk landscape.

The semi-tropical sense was extended up the Museum Reach by landscape architect Cullen Coltrane. He oversaw replacement of the tangled understory with plantings resilient, colorful and fragrant, and added three marshy areas to attract fish and wildlife. Retaining walls were built in three-foot segments that could be spaced so large trees could remain in place.

Work on the Mission Reach was more long-term. Grasses and wildflowers planted beside its broader banks had to develop deep root systems in time to survive periodic flooding. It would take as many as fifty years for thousands of trees—planted in phases—to grow and more fully restore the original riparian woodland.

The ecosystem would always need touch-ups, though invasion by non-native plants would diminish with time, said Lee Marlowe, sustainable landscape superintendent for the San Antonio River Authority. When soil nutrients in one area turned out to be too low to support new plantings of native grasses, it took a work crew a week to hand-pull and dispose of more than three tons of newly invaded weeds.

Enhancing the River Walk's role as a botanical garden are, facing page from top, Texas Wild Olive/Anachuita, Texas Sage/Barometer Bush and Texas Star Hibiscus/ Scarlet Rose Mallow. Riffles added to the Eagleland Segment, top left, provide hiding places for fish from a Snowy egret, while Blue flag iris and other grasses in a new marsh on the Museum Reach hide prey from a Yellow-crowned night heron, lower left. A springtime riot of Coreopsis, top right, replaces the concrete rubble that once lined the river along the Mission Reach. Semi-tropical Mexican fan palms and Variegated ginger, lower right, flourish along the River Walk downtown.

The start of one stretch of Mission Reach channel restoration south of the old Lone Star Brewery, left, concluded with completion of a colorful bridge designed by Mark Schlesinger.

The largest and final phase, covering nearly six miles from Mission Road to just beyond Mission Espada and costing $99.3 million, was begun by Zachry Construction in October 2010. Within three years more than two million cubic yards of soil were relocated, 260 acres of native vegetation restored and more than 18,000 trees planted, in addition to new elements similar to those in other phases.

In the meantime, work continued on links with the major attractions along the Mission Reach, the four Spanish missions themselves. Hikers and bikers as well as nearby residents would be drawn to the mission complexes by four distinctive portals, designed by teams of artists, architects, landscape architects and historians, financed by Bexar County and the San Antonio River Foundation and overseen by River Authority engineer Robert Perez and Mike Addkison and Stuart Allen, project managers from the River Foundation. Already begun was the foundation's $10 million Confluence Park, managed by Stuart Allen. Its three acres at the confluence of the San Antonio River and San Pedro Creek were designed by Ball-Nogues Studio of Los Angeles—succeeded by Rialto Studios—and irrigated by water collected and stored in an underground cistern.

Reworking the river allowed restoration of the connection with the eighteenth-century San Juan acequia severed in the 1950s flood control project. Rewatering of the acequia in 2011 permitted development of a Spanish Colonial era demonstration farm using some of San Juan's old mission fields.

The Mission Reach project was not without setbacks. In early 2007, before construction started, it was clear that the U.S. Army Corps of Engineers would not get federal funding in a timely manner to do its part of the project. In May 2008, Bexar County voters approved a visitor tax providing $125 million to more than cover the federal shortfall. With sufficient local funding guaranteed, the next year U.S. Senator Kay Bailey Hutchison helped Congress authorize sufficient funding for the remainder of the Mission Reach project.[16]

By then, the original cost estimate had soared from $127 million to $233 million, which officials of the project manager, the U.S. Army Corps of Engineers, acknowledged "came about as engineers and designers realized just how complicated this project really is." Using authority included in the Congressional funding bill, in June 2010 Bexar County commissioners succeeded in having construction administration responsibility transferred from the Corps of Engineers to the San Antonio River Authority, which soon issued the construction contract for phase three, the largest. Estimates of savings by bringing the project under local control ranged as high as $24 million.[17]

Less than three years later, as the Mission Reach neared completion, effects of a massive storm were mitigated north of Lone Star Boulevard by the flood tunnel,

The three-acre Confluence Park, below left, marked the meeting of the San Antonio River and San Pedro Creek. Nearby, the Mission Concepción portal, below, was one of four designed to signal nearness to the nearby missions.

but effects to the south devastated some of the newly finished work. The May 2013 deluge, which dumped up to fifteen inches of rain on parts of the city, caused $3 million in damage to the Mission Reach. During more than two weeks of clean-up, 10,000 pounds of debris and 7,000 pounds of garbage were carried off. Newly planted vegetation was uprooted and rock piles and sandbars intended to improve aquatic habitat were swept away. Significant damage at the confluence of San Pedro Creek and the river resulted in a redesign to withstand future floods. The work would minimize erosion and slow floodwater with large rocks on the confluence's east bank and near an existing curved weir, a dam built across the confluence. In addition, boaters gained a paddling chute through the weir. The project's grand opening was held on schedule four months later, on October 5, 2013.[18]

Official completion of the $271.4 million Mission Reach left more than 16 miles of hike-and-bike trails, 12 of them paved along the river and the rest, along the San Juan acequia, left unpaved. There were also 89 benches, 137 picnic tables, 5 over-looks with shade structures, 9 water edge landings, 6 foot bridges and 4 pavilions. But there was more to come, as the San Antonio River Foundation raised funds for new amenities and enhancements to the four mission portals. Progress of habitat restoration would be measured not in years but in decades, as trees and unmowed vegetation matured and made the Mission Reach landscape appear more natural.

As the San Antonio River Improvements Project was completed, predictions made a decade earlier about the anticipated billion-dollar return on investment

A flood in May 2013 caused the curved weir at the confluence of the river and San Pedro Creek to be redesigned and filled with rocks, right, to better slow future floodwaters. A paddling chute was added.

proved prophetic. A River Walk Impact Study concluded that the River Walk—including the recently opened Museum Reach and Mission Reach—directly supported more than 21,000 jobs and indirectly nearly 10,000 more. It estimated that each year 11.5 million people made the River Walk a primary destination. Its annual economic impact was estimated at $3.1 billion annually, a number expected to grow substantially as the Museum Reach and Mission Reach change and mature.[19]

Indeed, the entire San Antonio River Walk remains a work in progress, one forever precarious and unfinished yet standing before the world as a triumph of enterprise and human imagination.

Recreation along the Mission Reach includes kayak races and springtime jogging past acres of bluebonnets and other wildflowers.

CREDITS

Associated Press, 151, below left; 165, above right; 165, below, by Steven Savoia; 171, below, by Eric Gay

John Carter Brown Library at Brown University, 5, top

Daughters of the Republic of Texas Library at the Alamo, 7, above right; 24, right; 132, below right

Mary M. Fisher, 164, left; 165, above left; 181; 182, above left; 183, above left; 185, above, below right; 189, below left

Ford, Powell & Carson, 158, far right

Fort Sam Houston Museum, 68, bottom right

Fortune Magazine, 100, below right

Frees & Nichols Inc., 85, below

C. H. Guenther & Son Inc., 10, below left; 79, below

Hall S. Hammond, 72, center right

Harry Ransom Center, The University of Texas at Austin, 44, right; 47, below left; 48

Patrick Kennedy, 150, left

Bill Lyons, 134, above right

Mike Menjivar, 186; 187, above left and center, three right below; 197, left; 198, left

Metcalf & Eddy, 53, 54, 97

National Park Service, 191, above right

Mike Osborne, 166; 147, right; 191, center and below

Paseo del Rio Association, 164, right

Roberto Perez, *La Prensa*, 152

Maria Watson Pfeiffer, 52

San Antonio Conservation Society Foundation, 5, below right; 30; 90; 94; 106; 113, top right; 117, left; 119, upper left; 124; 157, right

San Antonio *Express*, 26; 27, below; 33, left; 35, center and right; 83; 84

San Antonio *Light*, 35, left

San Antonio Museum of Art, Photography by Roger Fry, 183, below

San Antonio *News*, 81

San Antonio Parks & Recreation Dept., 171, above

San Antonio Public Library, 67, below

San Antonio's River, 110

San Antonio River Authority, 65, below right; 170, below; 172; 178; 183, above right; 187, below far left; 188; 194; 195, above right; 196; 197, right; 198, right; 199

San Antonio River Foundation, 187, above right

Robin Stanford, 2, lower left; 6; 7, above left, lower left and lower right; 9, right; 10, top and center right; 12; 13; 15, right; 18

David Straus, 145, below

University of Texas at San Antonio Libraries, Special Collections, 31; 73, bottom; 74; 78; 80; 85, above; 86; 87; 88; 89, far right; 92; 102; 103; 107; 111, top; 113, below right; 115, left and center; 116, center left and bottom; 119, below left; 125; 126; 132, below left; 133, left and center; 139; 140, below right; 142; 143; 149, center; 151, below right; 157, left; 184, above left; 190, below right; 192, upper right

Witte Museum, xii; 5, center left; 10, below right; 14, left; 25; 50; 68, center right

C. Thomas Wright, 161, below right

Unattributed images are from author's collection

NOTES

Chapter 1:
SAN ANTONIO'S RIVER

1. Olmsted, *A Journey Through Texas*, 150.
2. Olmsted, *A Journey Through Texas*, 149; Sidney Lanier, "San Antonio de Bexar," in Corner, *San Antonio de Bexar*, 91.
3. Harriet Prescott Spofford, "San Antonio de Bexar," *Harper's*, 835.
4. *Along the San Antonio River*, 21.
5. Newcomb, *The Alamo City*, 38–40.
6. *Light*, "When Boats dotted the River," 8; *Express*: "History of City Long Linked," Dec. 31, 1933, C-7.
7. Maria William James, *I Remember* (Charles Albert Sloane, comp., San Antonio: The Naylor Company, 1938), in Steinfeldt, *San Antonio Was*, 222; Crystal Sasse Ragsdale, *The Golden Free Land: The Reminiscences and Letters of Women on an American Frontier* (Austin, 1976), 169, in Steinfeldt, *San Antonio Was*, 222.
8. Ferdinand Roemer, *With Particular Reference to German Immigration and the Physical Appearance of the Country* (Oswald Mueller, trans., Waco: Texian Press, 1967), 124–25, in Steinfeldt, *San Antonio Was*, 216.
9. Knight, "The Cart War," 322; San Antonio City Council Minutes, OL-9, May 8, 1851, p. 20; "Nymphs at Natatoriums" in Donald Everett, *San Antonio: The Flavor of Its Past*, 57; Richard Everett, "Things In and About San Antonio," 102.
10. *San Antonio Ledger*, Jul. 28, 1853; Charles Merritt Barnes, *Express*: "Bathing in the San Antonio River," Jul. 30, 1911, 17; "History of City Long Linked to Winding River," Dec. 31, 1933, 7-C; "Two Are Here Who," Aug. 23, 1936; Bushick, *Glamorous Days*, 44.
11. Bowen's Island was defined as an island on a technicality. At the end of the Great Bend the westward-flowing river turned sharply south, then doubled back on itself to flow east before heading south again, creating a small peninsula, farmed by John Bowen, San Antonio's fourth postmaster. The Concepción Acequia first began at the river near the northern base of the peninsula. To drain high water backed up before it flowed around the peninsula, an overflow channel was dug from the acequia to join the river at the southern base of the peninsula. Thus when the overflow channel carried water, the peninsula was surrounded on all sides by water and became an island. Long after the source of the acequia was moved, the tip of the peninsula was cut off to straighten the river, and the site was no longer island or peninsula. The landmark now known as the Tower Life Building was built there.
12. *Express*, "Nymphs at Natatoriums," Aug. 15, 1895, in Everett, *San Antonio: The Flavor of Its Past*, 57; Barnes, *Express*, "Bathing in the San Antonio River," Jul. 30, 1911, 17.
13. Arda Talbot, "Beautiful Homes of Bexar County," *Bexar County Homes and Cookery* (San Antonio, 1937) in Steinfeldt, *San Antonio Was*, 222; *Express*, "History of City Linked, Dec. 31, 1933, 7-C.
14. The offending foundry, built in 1876, moved to the eastern edge of downtown, where it grew into Alamo Iron Works. The old site was later used for two public library buildings, the second since incorporated into the Briscoe Western Art Museum.
15. McDowell, "San Antonio's Mills on the River;" Fisher, *C. H. Guenther & Son*, 24, 27. Guenther chose a prime site where the river flowed southwest, then sharply doubled back to the northeast to form a peninsula before again heading south. Guenther dug a millrace from the river's higher parallel segment down to the lower, the fall of the water turning his millwheel. Other mills close to the center of town were the Spanish-era Molino Blanco, to the north on the site of Central Catholic High School; the 1871 Alamo Mill, near Avenue B and Eighth Street; and Guenther's 1868 Upper Mill, at Washington and Beauregard streets upstream from his main mill.
16. Steinfeldt, *San Antonio Was*, 103.
17. McDowell, "San Antonio's Mills on the River;" *Express*, "Brig. Gen. Rochenbach Returns," Sept. 11, 1928, 11.
18. Santleben, *A Texas Pioneer*, 129–30; *Light*, "When Boats Dotted," May 22, 1910, 8; *Express*: "Twenty-Three Bridges," Aug. 19, 1911, 18; "Bridge Built in 1870 Still in Service," Nov. 4, 1927, 8.) Photographs of the original Navarro Street/Mill Bridge show it with a King Bridge & Manufacturing Company plaque dated 1870.

19. *Light*, "When Boats Dotted," May 22, 1910, 8.

20. "San Antonio, Texas," "Berlin Bridges and Buildings," 126.

21. "Bridge Built in 1870 Still in Service," *Express*, Nov. 4, 1927, 8.

22. "San Antonio, Texas," "Berlin Bridges and Buildings," 126–27; Express, " 'Letters of Gold Bridge' Moved," Dec. 16, 1925. Berlin parabolic truss bridges were also installed at Augusta (1890), Crockett (1891) and Market (1890) streets. San Antonio's Berlin bridges were apparently unique in the company's prodigious output by having decorative posts some 15 feet high at each corner. Such posts, topped with finials, survive on the Augusta Street Bridge. (Victor Darnell, in discussion with the author, Nov. 15, 1996.)

   Commerce Street's Berlin bridge was replaced with a concrete bridge in 1914 and moved to Johnson Street in the King William area. During work on the river channel, the bridge was taken down and placed in storage, where most of its parts—including three of its four spires—were inadvertently destroyed. New spires were cast when the bridge was recreated as a pedestrian bridge across the river at Johnson Street when channel work was completed in the 1960s. The Berlin bridges at Augusta and Crockett streets remained in place after the flood of 1921. The other two were moved and replaced with concrete bridges. The Market Street Bridge was reassembled to replace a wooden bridge at South Presa Street. The St. Mary's Street Bridge, rebuilt across the river in Brackenridge Park, is described as the only lenticular thru truss bridge surviving outside the Northeast. (Carolyn Peterson, "Letter to the Editor," San Antonio Conservation Society News, Nov. 1994; "Brackenridge Park Bridge," http://www.bridgemapper.com/bridge_detail.php?ID=465, retrieved May 16, 2013.)

23. *Express*, "Sunday Scenes," Jan. 26, 1903, 2; "History of City Long Linked," Dec. 31, 1933, 7-C; *Light*, "When Boats Dotted San Antonio River," May 22, 1910, 8. In 1883 the owners of two rowboats announced plans to add "a small-sized, low pressure steamboat" to carry twenty-five to fifty passengers from Houston Street around the Great Bend to the Navarro Street/Mill Bridge, but no indication that their plans were carried out can be found. (*Express*, "A Steamboat for San Antonio," Sept. 18, 1883, 4.)

24. Finis Collins, in discussion with the author, May 24, 2014. Finis Collins, a noted San Antonio artist, is a great-grandson of Finis F. Collins.

25. *Express*, "Rise of River and Creeks," Sept. 18, 1921, 1-A. The depth of water within the church is sometimes reported as nine feet, a level termed "almost incredible" by later engineers, though they agreed that the floodwaters of 1819 did reach "a very remarkable height." (Metcalf & Eddy, "Report to City of San Antonio," 12.)

26. *Express*, "Rise of River and Creeks," Sept. 18, 1921; Metcalf & Eddy, "Report to City of San Antonio," 7, 12–13.

27. Metcalf & Eddy, "Report to City of San Antonio," 12–13; Albert Maverick, "Notes on the Flood of 1921," author's collection. Instead of building a dam at Olmos Creek, a counterproposal was made to divert its floodwaters in a channel west and south to Alazan Creek and thus bypass the center of town. Another deluge, in 1866, sent floodwaters as high as six feet on streets near the river. (Corner, *San Antonio de Bexar*, 155; "The Deluge," *Daily Herald*, Sept. 1, 1866, 3.)

28. Ibid; "Report of G. Sleicher, F. Giraud and V. Considerant" in Metcalf & Eddy, "Report to City of San Antonio," 3, 327–36; Corner, *San Antonio de Bexar*, 133. The Boston engineering firm studying San Antonio flood control in 1920 praised the engineers' work: "In view of the small amount of information available and the paucity of hydraulic knowledge generally at the time of the 1865 report, it is remarkable for its intelligent grasp of the situation and for the breadth of view shown in the measures recommended."

29. *Express*, "Low State of the River," Aug. 23, 1887, 5.

30. *Light*, "The San Antonio River," Aug. 18, 1887, 4; Ewing, "Waters Sweet and Sulphurous," 13n9. San Antonio's first municipal sewage system was authorized in 1894 and completed in 1900.

31. *Light*, "When Boats Dotted," May 22, 1910, 8; *Express*, "History of City Long Linked," Dec. 31, 1933, 7-C. A noted contemporary of Blankenship was "a Pennsylvania Dutchman named Bender," who had a furniture store near the river at Commerce and Presa streets. "So fond was Bender of fishing in the river," one writer reported, "that when the spirit moved him he closed up his store, hung a sign out, 'gone fishing,' and until he returned to his store he was to be found along the banks of the river pulling in large trout and perch." (*Light*, "San Antonio in Olden Days," Jul. 10, 1910, 30.)

32. Ewing, "Waters Sweet and Sulphurous," 10–11.

33. McLean, *Romance of San Antonio's Water Supply*, 9–10; Ewing, "Waters Sweet and Sulphurous," 12–13; Morrison, *The*

City of San Antonio, 101. Soon after its strike, the Crystal Ice Company purchased its major competitor, the San Antonio Ice Company on Losoya Street. Their combined daily capacity reached 65 tons. Making the 1891 Water Works strike were brothers Moses Campbell Judson—later Water Works superintendent—and John William Judson, who were beginning their long careers in South Texas drilling. (Green, *Place Names of San Antonio*, 55.)

34. *Express*, "Will the River Run Dry?," Oct. 26, 1922, 8-A.
35. *Express*, "The San Antonio River," Aug. 23, 1887, 7.

Chapter 2:
BUILDING THE RIVER PARK

1. T. U. Taylor, "The Water Powers of Texas," U.S. Geological Survey Water Supply and Irrigation Paper (1904), 105, in Ewing, "Waters Sweet and Sulphurous," 16; *Express*: "To Beautify The City's River," Jul. 4, 1900, 5; "Sunday Scenes On The San Antonio River," Jan. 26, 1903, 2.
2. *Express*, Feb. 27, 1903, 1, 7.
3. *Express*: "Citizens Stop Ruin," Aug. 20, 1904; "City May Enjoin," Jul. 15, 1905, 10.
4. *Express*, "Old Spanish Manner," Sept. 4, 1904, 11; "San Antonio River Assumes," Oct. 15, 1905, 17.
5. *Express*: "Citizens Stop Ruin," Aug. 20, 1904.
6. Phelps, "Shading the Future," 112. Phelps's column features George M. Braun recalling a conversation with his uncle Adolph Schattenberg—Gustav Schattenberg's grandson—who told Braun "about how he went with Uncle George Steudebach up to the Guadalupe and Cypress Creek to get these cypress trees that we have along the San Antonio River now."
7. *Light*, "Landing of King Selamat," Apr. 25, 1905, 5; *Express*: "Greatest Carnival," Apr. 25, 1905, 5; "San Antonio River Assumes Ancient Importance," Oct. 15, 1905, 17. The king, David J. Woodward, was in a line of kings designated "Selamat," tamales spelled backwards.
8. *Express*, "Memorial Day Fittingly Observed," May 31, 1905, 5.
9. *Express*: "Venetian Carnival," Apr. 20, 1907, 6; "Canoeing on the San Antonio River," 4.
10. *Light*: "All Are Glad," Apr. 19, 1910, 1; "Civic Pageant An Object Lesson," Apr. 19, 1910, 4; "River Illumination," Apr. 23, 1910, 5.
11. *Express*: "Public Wants River," Feb. 20, 1910, 3; "Plans For Improving River," Mar. 20, 1910, 1-A; *Light*: "Work Starts," Mar. 27, 1910, 26; "River Illumination," Apr. 23, 1910, 5. Also beautified were the quarter-mile from the northern Navarro Street to Augusta Street bridges, 600 newly terraced feet beside the Ursuline Academy and the area below the new St. Mary's School on St. Mary's Street, across from the church. Improvements on the southern leg of the Great Bend past the Water Works were made later.
12. *Express*, "Water Rights Settled," Nov. 16, 1911, 16.
13. *Express*, "Urges Sanitation Now," Aug. 12, 1910. The writer, A. D. Powers, noted that when he arrived in San Antonio he was surprised that his rent was so low for what seemed like "such a splendid place." "I know now why the rental was small," he wrote. "The property is on the San Antonio River. At night when the wind stops blowing it is impossible for us to forget that we live on the 'beautiful' San Antonio River. It stinks to heaven, but I don't imagine it smells like anything in heaven—it would rather remind you of the other place."
14. Wilson, *The City Beautiful Movement*, 1–5, 302–305. The City Beautiful Movement was at its peak nationally from 1900 to 1910.
15. Booth, Johnson, and Harris, *The Politics of San Antonio*, 12–13; *Express*, "Final Rally," Feb. 4, 1911. From 1910 to 1920 San Antonio's population nevertheless grew another 67 percent, to some 161,000, continuing the strain on municipal infrastructure.
16. *Express*: "Citizens Pitch," Oct. 19, 1910, 1; "Final Rally," Feb. 4, 1911.
17. *Express*: "Commission Charter Defeated," Feb. 5, 1911, 1; "Returns Are Canvassed," Feb. 7, 1911, 18.
18. Coppini, *From Dawn to Sunset*, 176–177; *Express*: "Billboard Men Complain," Oct. 14, 1911, 16; "Ordinance Is Criticised," Dec. 25, 1911, 16; "Coliseum Site," May 4, 1913, 5-B; "Workers Are For City Federation," May 27, 1913, 9; "Clean-Up Pictures," Jun. 7, 1913, 20; Bartholomew and Associates, "A Comprehensive City Plan for San Antonio," 225.
19. *Express*: "Start the Big Idea," Feb. 5, 1911, 1-A; "The Big Idea," May 18, 1913, 1-A.
20. *Express*: "Start the Big Idea," Feb. 5, 1911, 1-A; "Will Improve The River," Sept. 27, 1911, 11; "The Big Idea," May 18, 1913, 1-A.
21. *Light*: "Francis Bowen Suggests," Feb. 27, 1903, 4; "Fought Riot On Bridge," Jun. 26, 1910, 7.

22. Simpson, a 1905 graduate of the Massachusetts Institute of Technology, returned to his native San Antonio, helped organize the Alamo Canoe Club on the river, and built a cedar-framed, canvas-covered canoe he could paddle the six miles from Brackenridge Park to the Arsenal Street bridge when the river was up. In 1909 he formed, with his brother Guy, what became a distinguished engineering and construction firm. (*Express*, "Canoe Fleet," Sept. 20, 1908, 24; "Canoeing on the San Antonio River," *The Passing Show*, July 27, 1907; Steadman, "A History of the W. E. Simpson Company," 1.)

23. W. E. Simpson, "Report On The Design Of A Conduit" in Metcalf and Eddy, "Report to City of San Antonio," 143–150.

24. *Express*: "Public Baths," Aug. 6, 1911, 15; "Will Improve The River," Sept. 27, 1911, 11.

25. *Express*: "Pump Will Be Installed," Sept. 30, 1911, 16; "City Employees Will Receive," Oct. 3, 1911, 5; "Start Pump Saturday," Oct. 6, 1911, 11; "Snags Will Be Removed," Oct. 8, 1911, 10-A; "For Improving The River," Dec. 29, 1911, 14.

26. *Express*: "Start Pump Saturday," Oct. 6, 1911, 11; "Water Pumped," Oct. 9, 1911, 12; "Million Gallons Pumped," Oct. 12, 1911, 13; "River Is Slowly Rising," Oct. 14, 1911, 16; "River Is Underground," Oct. 18, 1911, 5.

27. *Express*, "Irrigation Ditches Dry," Oct. 22, 1911, 39-B.

28. *Express*: "City Employes Will Receive," Oct. 3, 1911, 5; "Mayor Is Willing," Oct. 24, 1911, 5; "For Improving The River," Dec. 29, 1911, 14; "For Clearing The River," Feb. 12, 1912, 12; "Rates For A New," Feb. 20, 1912, 7.

29. *Express*, "Make City Beautiful," Sept. 1, 1912, 1.

30. *Light*, "The San Antonio River," Aug. 18, 1887, 4; Ewing, "Waters Sweet and Sulphurous," 13n9. San Antonio's first municipal sewage system was authorized in 1894 and completed in 1900.

31. *Express*, "Refuse In River," Sept. 20, 1912.

32. *Express*, "Free Bath House," Sept. 2, 1912, 1.

33. *Express*: "Plan To Change," Sept. 6, 1912, 14; "San Antonio River," Sept. 8, 1912, 1.

34. Wilson, *The City Beautiful Movement*, 260; *Express*: "Council Provides," Sept. 4, 1912, 16; "To Write Parts," Sept. 7, 1912, 16; "Refuse In River," Sept. 20, 1912; "To Invite City Planner," Oct. 4, 1912, 7; "Will Raise Fund," Oct. 19, 1912, 5. Two other leading planners were considered—Frederick Law Olmsted Jr. of Boston and John Nolen of Cambridge, Mass.

The committee also sought the advice of Chicago architect Marion West, who was doing work in Galveston. (*Express*, "City Plan Meeting," Jan. 21, 1913, 11.)

35. *Express*: "Surkey Seeks To Restore," Jun. 27, 1913, 18; "Building Surkey Seawalls," Aug. 16, 1913, 16; "Surkey's River Beautiful," May 20, 1915, 25.

36. *Light*, "Bowen's Island," Mar. 22, 1912, 3; *Express*, "Bowen's Island Measure," Feb. 4, 1913, 9. In return for title to the old riverbed, Ward donated land for widening both South St. Mary's and West Nueva streets, built sidewalks and curbs along both streets and absolved the city from any damages incurred in the process.

37. *Light*, "Sans Souci-Coliseum Stock," Apr. 21, 1912; *Express*: "Shorten The River," Oct. 29, 1912, 11; "Suggested Canal," Oct. 30, 1912, 16; "Coliseum Site," May 4, 1913, B-5.

38. *Express*: "Mayor Gus Jones' Death," Apr. 8, 1913, 1; "Faults Of City," May 31, 1913, 1.

39. *Express*: "Victory For Brown," May 14, 1913, 1; "Bond Issue Will Not Be Greater," May 31, 1913, 1; "Bond Issue For $3,350,000," Jun. 3, 1913, 1; "Surkey Seeks To Restore," Jun. 27, 1913, 18; "Building Surkey Seawalls," Aug. 16, 1913, 16; *Light*, "A Fortune Spent," Nov. 19, 1914, 15. In 1917, retaining walls were extended north of the Ursuline Academy with stones from San Antonio's first high school, then being razed. (*Light*, "Extend River Walls," Feb. 5, 1917.)

40. Coppini, *From Dawn to Sunset*, 204; Booth and Johnson in *The Politics of San Antonio*, 13–14; *Express*: "San Pedro Park Has Water," Aug. 18, 1913, 12; "Spring Is Flowing," Aug. 26, 1913, 5.

41. Ellsworth, *Floods in Central Texas*, 10.

42. *Express*: "Farmers and Railroads," Oct. 2, 1913, 1; "Overflow Water Fills," Oct. 3, 1913, 7.

43. *Express*: "River on Rampage," Oct. 2, 1913, 2; "Fire Chief Used," Oct. 3, 1913, 5; "Four Drown," Oct. 3, 1913, 7; "Saving the Fish," Oct. 12, 1913, 2.

44. *Express*, "Four Drown," Oct. 3, 1913, 1, 7.

45. Ellsworth, *Flooding in Central Texas*, 1.

46. *Express*: "Loss Small," Dec. 5, 1913, 1; "Militiamen's Good Work," Dec. 5, 1913, 5; "Effects of Flood," Dec. 6, 1913, 3.

47. *Express*: "Loss Small," Dec. 5, 1913, 1; "Damage Is Not Great," Dec. 6, 1913, 3; "Overflow Water Fills," Oct. 3, 1913, 7.

48. *Express*: "Loss Small," Dec. 5, 1913, 1; "The Reason," Dec. 6, 1913, 1; "Rail Service," Dec. 6, 1913, 3; "Today's Express And Its Dress," Dec. 7, 1913, 1.

49. Ellsworth, *Flooding in Central Texas*, 1; *Express*: "Loss Small," Dec. 5, 1913, 1; "Tries to Swim Stream," Dec. 6, 1913, 3.

50. *Express*: "Floods Toll," Oct. 24, 1914, 1; "Rescue Fails When Home Topples," Oct. 24, 1914, 4; "Flood Claims Nine Lives," Oct. 25, 1914, 4.

51. *Express*: "Gray Is Coming," Dec. 7, 1913; "Flood Proves Need of Dam," Oct. 25, 1914, 4, 1; *Light*, "Gray Has No Plan," Jan. 11, 1914, 1.

52. *Express*: "Loss Small," Dec. 5, 1913, 1; "Flood Carries Away," Dec. 6, 1913, 3.

53. *Express*, "Dig Up Many Old Relics," Jul. 5, 1914, 3.

54. Coppini, *From Dawn to Sunset*, 205. The fountain was donated by the San Antonio *Express*. The city planned to pay for the statue of Jones but family members objected to the use of public funds, believing the statue should instead be funded by donations from private citizens. The sides of the still-empty northern alcove were removed in 1940 for stairway entrances to the River Walk. The four decorative pilasters disappeared during the 1950s.

55. *Light*, "It Will Be Called," Nov. 19, 1914, 16; Express, "Commerce Street Is Dedicated," Nov. 22, 1914, 4-B; Carl Moore and Claude Aniol, "75th Anniversary Historical Report," *The Wheel*, 88, no. 36, Rotary Club of San Antonio, Mar. 8, 2000.

56. San Antonio Chamber of Commerce, San Antonio, 3.

57. *Express*, "Lends Touch of Beauty," Mar. 10, 1918, 12-A. The addition was financed by the estate of the late George M. Maverick, developer of that block of Houston Street. Its style led to its being called "the Chinese balcony." Reports sometimes garble the structure as a former "Chinese restaurant" built by George Maverick, who died five years before it was constructed.

58. Frary, "The River of San Antonio," *Architectural Record*, April 1919, 380–81.

Chapter 3:
THE FLOOD OF 1921

1. Unisys Weather, "1921 Hurricane/Tropical Data for Atlantic," http://weather.unisys.com/hurricane/atlantic/1921/index.html.

2. Metcalf and Eddy, "Report to City of San Antonio," ii, iv, 112a.

3. *Express*: "Walls Pierced By Openings," Dec. 9, 1913, 1; "Expert's Report Shows Olmos Dam," Dec. 10, 1913, 1.

4. *Express*: "Straighten-River Plan Idle Talk," Dec. 7, 1913, 4-B; "Not A Doubt Of Safety Of Dam, Says Pancoast," Dec. 12, 1913, 1.

5. *Express*, "Flush Gates Are Closed," Dec. 11, 1913, 5. A week after the December 1913 flood, the city sealed gates from the river into the old Alamo Acequia at the northern edge of the city and removed the small dam to limit flooding in adjacent neighborhoods along River Avenue, now Broadway.

6. *Express*: "City May Build Retaining Walls," Jun. 12, 1917, 18; "Condemnation Of Soledad Property," Jul. 24, 1917; San Antonio City Commissioners Minutes, Book B, 467–468, 514.

7. *Express*: "$3,950,000 Bond Issue Election," Jan. 24, 1919, 1; "Bond Issue Approved," Jul. 26, 1919, 1; "City Designates Auditorium Site," Jun. 1, 1920.

8. Metcalf & Eddy, "Report to City of San Antonio," 2–3, 135–137.

9. Metcalf & Eddy, "Report to City of San Antonio," ii, 25, 105.

10. Metcalf & Eddy, "Report to City of San Antonio," ii, 27, 53, 122–134. Of the six cutoffs recommended, four were north of downtown: below Josephine Street, shortening the river by 1,200 feet; Ninth Street, 2,450 feet; above McCullough Avenue, 950 feet; and above Navarro Street—the cutoff already planned for Municipal Auditorium—saving 1,495 feet. South of downtown, a fifth cutoff at Durango Street would save 670 feet and the sixth, above South Alamo Street, would save another 285 feet. Two nearby dams would be removed and tributary channels modified.

11. Metcalf & Eddy, "Report to City of San Antonio," iii–iv, 4, 42–44, 135; *Light*: "Would Cut Out Big Downtown Bend," Jun. 18, 1920, 11; "River Project To Be Started," Nov. 5, 1920, 10.

12. Metcalf & Eddy, "Report to City of San Antonio," 32, 109. Bridges also needed to be reconstructed or replaced, since barriers could be formed by trestle-style bridges whose trusses caught debris in floodwaters and became dams. Some built at angles to the river deflected floodwaters into the city, and those on piers narrowed the channel.

13. *Light*, "River Project To Be Started," Nov. 5, 1920, 10.

14. C. H. Guenther & Son, Inc. to Mayor and Commissioners, Nov. 27, 1920, and Feb. 10, 1921, letters in archives of C. H. Guenther & Son, Inc., San Antonio, Texas; *Express*, "River Will Have," Mar. 13, 1921, 1-A.

15. *Express*, "River Will Have," Mar. 13, 1921, 1-A.

16. *Express*: "City-Wide Protest Greets Plan," Apr. 1, 1921, 13.

17. Metcalf and Eddy, "Report to City of San Antonio," ii, iv, 112a.

18. Bartlett, "The Flood of September, 1921," 357.

19. *Light*, "37 Bodies Found," Sept. 10, 1921, 1; *Express*, "Known Flood Dead," Sept. 11, 1921, 1; Bartlett, "The Flood of September, 1921," 357; Ellsworth, *Floods in Central Texas*, 9–11.

20. Ellsworth, *Floods in Central Texas*, 36–37; *Express*, "Known Flood Dead," Sept. 11, 1921, 1.

21. *Light*, "37 Bodies Found," Sept. 10, 1921, 1; *Express*, "Known Flood Dead," Sept. 11, 1921, 1; Forman, *We Finish to Begin*, 41–43; Fisher, *Saint Mark's Episcopal Church*, 58.

22. *Light*, "37 Bodies Found," Sept. 10, 1921, 1; *Express*, "Known Flood Dead," Sept. 11, 1921, 1; *New York Times*, "40 Known Dead," Sept. 11, 1921, 1.

23. *Express*, Sept. 11, 1921, "Millions Damage Done," 1; Albert Maverick, "Notes on the Flood of 1921," author's collection.

24. *Express*, "Millions Damage Done," Sept. 11, 1921, 1.

25. *Express*, "Known Flood Dead," Sept. 11, 1921, 1; *Light*, "38 Bodies," Sept. 11, 1921, 1; "Soldiers and the Flood," *The Trail*, Sept. 16, 1921, 3.

26. *Light*, Sept. 10, 1921, "37 Bodies Found," 1; *Express*, "Known Flood Dead," Sept. 11, 1921, 1. Another dog awoke a household on Alazan Creek in time for them to escape floodwaters. Six months later that dog led a Humane Society parade. (*Express*, "Dog That Saved Lives," Mar. 22, 1922, 7.)

27. *Express*, "Property Loss," Sept. 11, 1921, 4; *New York Times*, "40 Known Dead," Sept. 11, 1921, 1.

28. Bartlett, "The Flood of September, 1921," 357; Ellsworth, *Floods in Central Texas*, 5, 9–10.

29. Ellsworth, *Floods in Central Texas*, 11. Unofficial totals of rainfall nearby reached 38 inches.

30. Forman, *We Finish to Begin*, 41.

31. *Express*: Sept. 11, 1921, 1: "Millions Damage Done," "Civilian Shot;" *The Trail*, "Soldiers and the Flood," 3.

32. *New York Times*, "40 Known Dead," Sept. 11, 1921, 1.

33. Ellsworth, *Floods in Central Texas*, 5; *Express*, "Millions Damage Done," "Known Flood Dead," Sept. 17, 1921, 20; Bartlett, "The Flood of September, 1921," 358. Ellsworth's breakdown reports 15 deaths on San Pedro Creek near South Flores and Mitchell streets, 10 on San Pedro Creek between West Commerce Street and the mouth of Alazan Creek; 20 on Alazan Creek between West Commerce Street and the mouth of San Pedro Creek; 3 on Apache Creek between Elmendorf Lake and South Brazos Street near Tampico Street; 3 on the San Antonio River at Newell Avenue; and 1 south of San José Mission. Ellsworth put the total known dead from the storm throughout Texas at 224, including 159 along the Little River and San Gabriel River in Williamson and Milam counties.

34. *Express*, "Laborer Returns," Oct. 14, 1921, 2.

35. *Express*: "2,000 Victims," Sept. 11, 1921, 1; "$18,000 Is Given," Sept. 12, 1921, 1; "One More Street," Sept. 17, 1921, 20.

36. [Quiroga], *La Tragedia de la Inundacion*, 50–53.

37. *Express*: "Millions Damage Done," Sept. 11, 1921, 1; "New Week Ushers Fight," Sept. 12, 1921, 1; "Rest Sector During Flood Clean-Up," Oct. 2, 1921, 12-A; *Light*, "Property Loss," Sept. 11, 1921, 4; *The Trail*, "Soldiers and the Flood," 3, 13. "It was the first real chance the soldier had to become acquainted with San Antonio," observed the Second Division's weekly magazine, *The Trail*, in a souvenir flood edition. "The days of the war, with patriotism at fever heat, seemed restored. Business men and gentle ladies missed no chance to get the sentry at his post a glass of cooling refreshment or to place their cars at the disposal of any man in uniform who needed 'a lift.' There was a smile and a kindly word for them all."

38. *Express*: "Known Flood Dead," Sept. 11, 1921, 2; "$18,000 Is Given," Sept. 12, 1921, 1.

39. *Express*, "San Antonio Able to Care," Sept. 12, 1921, 2.

40. Ellsworth, *The Floods in Central Texas*, 5; *Express*: Sept. 12, 1921, 1: "New Week Ushers Fight," "Business as Usual," "Water Should be Available," "Street Car Crews Run;" Bartlett, "The Flood of September, 1921," 361.

41. *Express*: "Cleanup And Reconstruction," Sept. 12, 1921, 1; "Streets Will Be Cleared," Sept. 16, 1921, 20; "One More Street Open," Sept. 17, 1921, 20; "City Prepares To Resurface," Sept. 20, 1921, 20; "Only Two Blocks Remain Closed," Sept. 20, 1921, 20; "Lasting Streets Built," Apr. 18, 1922, E-5; "Streets Soon Will Lose Flood Traces," Oct. 9, 1921, 4. Over the strenuous objection of City Engineer D. D. Harrigan, North Flores Street property owners convinced the city to advertise for bids for old-style wooden paving blocks for streets on which substantial portions of such blocks remained. Harrigan relented when the property owners agreed to pay for any costs beyond those of the more modern blacktop materials being used elsewhere. (*Express*, "N. Flores Favors," Oct. 7, 1921, 9.)

42. *Express*: "Emergency Food Distribution Ends," Sept. 22, 1921, 22; "Lasting Streets Built," Apr. 18, 1922, E-5.

43. *Express*: "Homes To Get Salvaged Lumber," Sept. 16, 1921, 20; "San Fernando's Congregation Will Dedicate," Oct. 22, 1921, 2; "Immigrants' Son Recalls Prejudice," Sept. 11, 2005, 1-K; *The Trail*, "Here Is Your Chance!!," 1.

44. Ellsworth, *Floods of Central Texas*, 1.

45. Bartlett, "The Flood of September 1921," 358, 368.

46. *Express*, "Flood Restoration," Oct. 17, 1921, 1. Attitudes began to change six years later after flooding on the Mississippi, the nation's worst natural disaster until the New Orleans flood of 2005, left more than one million people homeless. The Flood Control Act of 1928 began the shift to public shouldering of responsibility for causes and effects of natural catastrophes.

Chapter 4:
TAMING THE RIVER AND THE GREAT BEND

1. *Light*, "River Project To Be Started," Nov. 5, 1920, 10; Bartlett, "The Flood of September 1921," 366. At the time the city adopted the Metcalf & Eddy plan, there was skepticism that officials had the will to carry out the full program. After the flood, Metcalf & Eddy's Charles Sherman, who had worked closely with city officials on the study and sensed their reactions, revealed himself in a report by Terrell Bartlett to have been one of those skeptics. The firm's engineers were pleased that fragmentary accounts of the enormous flood in 1819 had survived to give them a benchmark against which to measure future major floods, but Sherman, for one, feared that since the lesser floods of 1913 were "so much in excess of any flood within the memory of the people of San Antonio," the city would conclude that efforts to prevent such floods as those would be adequate. Then, he suspected, Metcalf & Eddy recommendations would be scaled back, the key dam would not be built and San Antonio would be left still without adequate protection.

2. *Express*, "Realtors To Tell," Oct. 9, 1921, 5.

3. *Express*: "City To Build," Mar. 12, 1922, 12; "Public Improvements," Apr. 18, 1922, E-7; "30th Bridge," Apr. 25, 1922, 13; "Rains Hamper," June 18, 1922, 5; "Bridge at Navarro," Dec. 12, 1922, 9; "San Antonio, City of Bridges," Feb. 5, 1928, 1-A. Available records identify no architect of the new Mill Bridge, despite its unusually handsome design. Bridges were usually designed by the contractor doing the work. In this case that was the company headed by San Antonio's versatile Terrell Bartlett, the noted hydraulics, irrigation and structural engineer who also prepared the definitive paper on the 1921 flood. It can thus be assumed that the designer was a talented engineer in Bartlett's firm.

4. *Express*: "Letters-of-Gold Bridge," Dec. 16, 1925, 8; "San Antonio, City of Bridges," Feb. 5, 1928, 1-A.

5. *Express*, "Retention Dam To Protect City," Sept. 22, 1921.

6. *Express*: "Property Owners Will Be Asked," Sept. 17, 1921, 1, 20; "Three Methods," Oct. 9, 1921, 14.

7. *Express*: "Survey Of Olmos," Sept. 27, 1921, 7; "Three Methods," Oct. 9, 1921, 14. Three businessmen and four engineers were named to a Flood Prevention Committee. The businessmen were attorney Harry Rogers, banker Franz C. Groos and department store owner Nat Washer. Engineers were W. B. Tuttle, Edwin P. Arneson, Willard Simpson and Clinton H. Kearney. Ex-officio members were Mayor Black, Bexar County Judge Augustus McCloskey, Col. Edgar Jadwin of the U.S. Army Corps of Engineers at Fort Sam Houston, City Engineer D. D. Harrigan and Chamber of Commerce President Morris Stern. (*Express*, "Property Owners Will Be Asked," Sept. 17, 1921, 20.)

8. *Express*, "Property Owners Will Be Asked, Sept. 17, 1921, 20.

9. *Express*, "C. F. Crecelius Recommended," Aug. 24, 1924, 8.

10. *Light*, "American Military Engineers," Oct. 19, 1925, 1; *Express*, "Olmos Detention Dam," Dec. 12, 1926, 26.

11. *Express*: "Engineer Begins Studying," Sept. 3, 1924, 20; "River Channel Work," Jan. 9, 1926, 1; "Work Begins," Jan. 12, 1926, 4; "2,100-Foot River Bend," Jun. 1, 1926, 6.

12. *Express*: "Two Bends," Jun. 8, 1926, 8; "Old Mill Wrecked," Aug. 19, 1926, 5.

13. *Express*, "City Buys River Channel Land," Mar. 16, 1926, 9. Who owned abandoned land of former river bends was soon decided by the Texas Supreme Court. The city filed suit against a developer who attempted to circumvent the city's claim to land once occupied by a river bend south of town and tried to buy the abandoned land directly from the state. The court ruled that while an 1837 Texas law generally gave the state title to abandoned property along with the ability to sell it, San Antonio maintained title to the riverbed, abandoned or not, under terms of its land grant from the King of Spain in 1730. To prevent future challenges, the city set about

better surveying its river lands. (*Express*: "City Given Right," Mar. 10, 1929, 13; "City Will Mark," Apr. 23, 1929, 15.)

14. *Express*: "Ornamental Fountains," Oct. 26, 1924, 2; "River Lighting Ordered," Jun. 9, 1926, 24; "Three Plans," Jun. 16, 1926, 9; "River Lighting," Jul. 3, 1926, 20.

15. Fisher, *Saving San Antonio*, 3–8, 210–11; *Express*, "Queen's Pageant on River," Nov. 13, 1924, 11. In September 1924, members presented city council with a puppet show written by the society's first president, Emily Edwards, entitled "The Goose That Laid the Golden Eggs." The unique puppets, some designed to resemble council members, debated the importance of preserving the city's unique aspects represented by six golden eggs. The river was a subcategory of the egg marked "Beauty." A rewriting of the script in the 1950s to emphasize a new threat to the river led to the erroneous belief that saving the river was also the theme of the 1924 presentation.

16. Fisher, *Saving San Antonio*, 183–84.

17. *Express*, "$175,000 Voted," Jun. 15, 1926, 1.

18. *Express*: "New Channel To Cost $250,000," Jul. 14, 1926, 7; "Flood Channel Waits," Jul. 30, 1926, 6; "Overflow Channel Plans," Jan. 13, 1927, 5; "Street Will Top," Jul. 2, 1927, 6; "50 Foot Channel, Crecelius," Oct. 18, 1927, 11; "City Will Rent Channel Lots," Nov. 20, 1927, 11.

19. *Express*: "Flood Channel Plans," Jun. 23, 1927, 22; "Street Will Top," Jul. 2, 1927, 6; "Mayor Outlines Plans," Aug. 9, 1927, 8.

20. *Express*: "Section of River Cut-Off," Sept. 27, 1927, 24; "Wider Overflow Channel," Oct. 2, 1927, 8.

21. *Express*: "Section of River," Sept. 27, 1927, 24; "Wider Overflow Channel," Oct. 2, 1927, 8.

22. *Express*, "City Will Not Change Plans," Oct. 11, 1927, 8.

23. *Express*: "50 Foot Channel," Oct. 18, 1927, 11; "Contract Let For New Channel," Oct. 20, 1927, 22; "Work On Cut-Off Channel," Jan. 24, 1928, 10; Metcalf & Eddy, "Report to City of San Antonio," 54.

24. *Express*: "Bond Issue For Library," Jan. 17, 1928, 8; "Cut-Off Channel Decision," Jan. 26, 1928, 7; "Channel Width Still Unsettled," Feb. 8, 1928, 10; "Channel Width," Feb. 9, 1928, 9.

25. *Express*: "Channel Width," Feb. 9, 1928, 9; "City Urged To Keep Crecelius," Feb. 14, 1928, 8; "Crecelius Salary Cut," Feb. 28, 1928, 6; "Flood Prevention Office To Close," Aug. 31, 1928, 15; "Crecelius Quits," Sept. 1, 1928, 7; *Light*: "Cre-celius Job In Air," Feb. 14, 1928, 1; "Resignation Refused," Feb. 15, 1928, 1; "Man Fatally Hurt," Oct. 3, 1929, 1.

26. *Express*: "City Ready to Call," Aug. 12, 1928, 1-A; "Flood Prevention Work," Oct. 26, 1928, 6; "2 Firms Named," Nov. 15, 1928, 10. In a budget-cutting move the next year, the city again consolidated the flood prevention office with the city engineer's office, eliminating twenty-nine of the flood prevention office's thirty employees. (*Express*, "200 Employees," May 26, 1929, 2-A.)

27. *Evening News*, "River Bed Would Enrich," Feb. 15, 1928, 1.

28. *Evening News*, "River Bed Would Enrich," Feb. 15, 1928, 1; *Light*, "River Land," Feb. 15, 1928, 2-A; *Express*, "Big Bend Not To Be Eliminated," Feb. 16, 1928, 9.

29. *Express*, "'Big Bend' Not To Be Eliminated," Feb. 16, 1928, 9.

30. *Evening News*, "River Bed Would Enrich," Feb. 15, 1928, 1; *Express*, "'Big Bend' Not To Be Eliminated," Feb. 16, 1928, 9. In recent decades, City Hall has been made the scapegoat for a plan to eliminate the Great Bend. No firm evidence, however, has yet been advanced to support that case, nor has documentation been offered to further define the women's "counter-movement." No mention of eliminating the Great Bend appears in minutes of city commissioners or the City Federation of Women's Clubs. Although Conservation Society minutes of the time are missing, contemporary histories of the society by its members make no reference to such an effort, as they would have had the uproar been as extensive as it was later made out to have been. The lack of authoritative accounts left those in later decades to stitch together a "series of ingenious conjectures and amusing fables" in the belief that they were reporting actual history. (Fisher, *Saving San Antonio*, xv, 210–11.)

31. *Express*: "City Buys," Mar. 16, 1926, 9; "Church Built In 1886," Nov. 5, 1927, 6; "Alamo Widening Project," Dec. 12, 1928, 11. East of the neighborhood, details were being completed in 1928 to widen South Alamo Street. The east-west Nueva Street was already being widened through southern La Villita. The tallest building in San Antonio, the thirty-story Smith-Young Tower/Tower Life Building, rose at the west, where a new bridge across the cutoff channel would reconnect Villita Street with Dwyer Avenue.

32. *Express*: "City Commission Promises," Dec. 12, 1928, 11; "Losoya Extension," Mar. 26, 1929, 22; "Street Will Be Built," Mar. 29, 1929, 28.

33. *Express*: "Street Will Be Built," Mar. 29, 1929, 28; "Losoya Extension Plan," Apr. 14, 1929, 1-A.

34. *Light*, "Losoya River St. Killed!," Apr. 12, 1929, 1; *Express*: "Suspended Street Project 'Ditched,'" Apr. 13, 1929, 24; "Losoya Extension Plan," Apr. 14, 1929, 1-A.

35. *Express*, "Losoya Street Extension," Oct. 4, 1929, 1-C.

36. *Express*: "Famous Old Lawyers' Office Building," Jan. 20, 1927, 6; "River Wall Extended," Apr. 6, 1927, 9; "Home Firm Given," Mar. 20, 1929, 28; "Big Bend Cut-Off Work," Mar. 30, 1929, 22. Another landmark that would have been in the path of the bypass channel was the 1859 Greek Revival Market House, already razed for the widening of Market Street. Behind the Market House location, the channel took the site of the Spanish-era Casas Reales, the council house that was the scene of a noted fight between San Antonians and Comanches in 1840.

37. Fisher, *Saving San* Antonio, 191; *Express*: "Wider River Channel," Sept. 10, 1929, 7; "Man Fatally Hurt," Oct. 3, 1929, 1; "Mayor Is Opposed," Oct. 20, 1929, 1-A; "Concrete River Channel Doomed," Oct. 22, 1929, 24; "Channel Project Checks," Oct. 23, 1929, 15; "Plans For River Ready," Oct. 26, 1929, 24.

38. Fisher, *Saving San* Antonio, 191; *Express*: "Wider River Channel," Sept. 10, 1929, 7; "Mayor Is Opposed," Oct. 20, 1929, 1-A; "Concrete River Channel Doomed," Oct. 22, 1929, 24; "Channel Project Checks," Oct. 23, 1929, 15; "Plans For River Ready," Oct. 26, 1929, 24.

39. Metcalf & Eddy, "Report to the City of San Antonio," 53; *Express*: "$10,000,000 Buildings," Aug. 12, 1928, 1-C; "City To Condemn Land," Oct. 16, 1928, 28; "Wider River Channel," Sept. 10, 1929, 7. San Antonio's population was soaring by more than 40 percent from 161,000 to end the decade at 230,000, and the skyline was expanding outward and upward. By mid-1928 fifteen construction projects were underway at a cost of $10 million, a record expected to double within six months.

40. *Express*: "90-Foot Channel," Aug. 16, 1928, 6; "New Taxable Values," Mar. 30, 1929, 3-C; "12 Acres On River," Jul. 21, 1929, 1-C; Metcalf & Eddy, "Report to City of San Antonio," 61a–62.

41. *Express*: "Mayor To View," Oct. 3, 1929, 10; "Club Women Fight," Oct. 4, 1929, 28; "Women's Clubs to Oppose," Sept. 8, 1929, 1-A; "Wider River Channel," Sept. 10, 1929, 7; "Second Protest," Oct. 5, 1929, 10.

42. *Express*: "City Commission To Decide," Jan. 21, 1930, 26; "Mrs. W.E. Pyne Federation Head," Feb. 21, 1930, 5; *Light*: "S.A. Clubwomen Unite," Sept. 8, 1929, 1; "City Accepts Swiss Plaza," Jan. 27, 1930, 1. This was not the only deal the city made. Pioneer Flour Mills donated a strip of land to widen the channel in exchange for the city's widening South Alamo Street near its plant and replacing two wooden railroad bridges with steel ones. (*Express*: "City Will Build Bridges," Jul. 27, 1929, 6.)

43. *Express*, "49 Committees Report," May 15, 1928, 10. Six weeks before the convention, the Texas Game, Fish, and Oyster Department's director of natural resources praised San Antonio's compliance with new antipollution laws, saying that the river through San Antonio was "the cleanest in Texas." (*Express*, "San Antonio Praised," Apr. 6, 1928, 4.)

44. *Express*: "Walk To Be Built," Jan. 27, 1928, 9; "Trash Removed," Apr. 4, 1928. The Old Spanish Trail Association was formed to promote paving the old trail from San Diego, California, through San Antonio to St. Augustine, Florida, now the basic route of Interstate 10. Its river committee members, headed by the wife of attorney John L. Browne, included the wives of architect Atlee Ayres and sculptor Gutzon Borglum, plus artist Mary Bonner.

45. Fisher, *Saving San* Antonio, 187, 209; *Express*: "River Will Be Lighted," Mar. 25, 1927, 9; "River Lighting Conferences," Jan. 25, 1928, 8; "New River Lights," Feb. 15, 1928, 15; "River Lighting To Be Changed," Mar. 22, 1928, 9; "Flood Lights for Illumination," Mar. 24, 1928, 2; "Monks Lauded," Apr. 5, 1929, 10.

46. Bartholomew, "A Comprehensive City Plan for San Antonio," vii; *Express*, "City Starts Big Bend Beautification," Apr. 9, 1930, 13.

47. *Express*, "Mrs. W.E. Pyne Federation Head," Feb. 21, 1930, 5.

48. Bartholomew, "A Comprehensive City Plan," 326; *Express*: "River Flow Jazzed Up," Aug. 6, 1927, 4; "Grass on River Banks," Aug. 16, 1928, 3; "Artists Advised To Paint River," Apr. 6, 1929, 10.

Chapter 5:
DEBATING THE RIVER PARK

1. *Express*, "San Antonio Has 17 of 135 Skyscrapers in State of Texas," Nov. 10, 1929, 15-C. Skyscrapers were defined as buildings with more than ten stories.

2. Fisher, *Saving San* Antonio, 134–35; *Express*: "Mayor Names Plan Body," Dec. 7, 1928, 10; "Street Layout In San Antonio," May 26, 1929, 1-A.

3. Hugman, "Oral History," 2.

4. Zunker, *A Dream Come True*, 95.

5. Hugman, "How Paseo del Rio," 10; *Express*, "Business Group Looks Ahead," Oct. 30, 1938, 1-A; Ellen Ugoccioni, "The City of Coral Gables: Still an Oasis," *Florida History and the Arts*, Summer 2004; "The History of Coral Gables Venetian Pool," http://www.venetianpool.com/History.html.

6. Hugman, "Speech," 19–20. Aragon links with Spain, but Romula appears geographically only as a Roman city in present-day Romania. In reminiscences a half-century later, Hugman tended to omit specifics and garble nuances, requiring a careful reading of his accounts. He repeatedly referred, for example, to Mrs. Lane Taylor as president of the Conservation Society at the time of his visit in 1929, although she was then only chairman of the society's river committee (Mrs. Perry Lewis was president), implying an outsize role of that society in promoting his proposal.

7. Hugman, "How Paseo del Rio," 4; C. M. Chambers, "To Whom It May Concern," May 29, 1929, letter copy in San Antonio Conservation Society library.

8. Fisher, *Saving San Antonio*, 194; Hugman, "Oral History," 18; *Express*, "Preliminary Steps," Jun. 29, 1929, 8; *Light*, "Unique S.A. Asset," Jun. 30, 1929, pt. 7, 1.

9. Hugman, "Speech," 12–13. In 1985, owners of the building cut a pass-through to open the rear of the building for riverside dining on just such a patio as Hugman had envisioned.

10. Hugman, "Speech," 5–6.

11. Fisher, *Saving San Antonio*, 194; *Express*, "Preliminary Steps," Jun. 29, 1929, 8; *Light*, "Unique S.A. Asset," Jun. 30, 1929, pt. 7, 1. Hugman was careful to stress economic benefit: "We must not forget that San Antonio is the 'Winter Playground of America,' and its historic traditions and natural beauty must be sacredly preserved if we would build the right foundation for steady growth and future interest. In all of our great America we cannot find another city with history quite so laden with interest. The blood stained Alamo, the old cathedral and the missions with their incomparable beauty lend to our city a poignant charm. All of these are properly appreciated, but there is one great asset of San Antonio that is not being capitalized—its beautiful winding river."

12. *Express*, "Prize City Plan Idea," Jul. 16, 1929, 28.

13. *Express*: "Prize City Plan Idea," Jul. 16, 1929, 28; "City Plan Expert," Jul. 19, 1929, 24.

14. *Express*: "Women's Club Members," Oct. 18, 1929, 8; "Landscape Architect To Develop," Oct. 18, 1929, 8; "Landscape Architect Employment," Nov. 16, 1929, 24.

15. Garvin, *The American City*, 443–45. *Express*: "City Planner Views River," Dec. 19, 1929, 26; "Planner Studies River," Dec. 20, 1929, 15; Bartholomew, "A Comprehensive City Plan," 322. Bartholomew's position as the nation's first full-time city planner was in Newark, New Jersey. He served as director of planning for St. Louis from 1916 to 1953 and was appointed to federal planning committees by presidents Herbert Hoover, Franklin Roosevelt and Dwight Eisenhower.

16. *Express*, "River Boulevard," Jun. 6, 1918, 2-A.

17. Bartholomew, "A Comprehensive City Plan," 279–83, 321–28.

18. *Light*, "City Passes Zoning Law," Jan. 27, 1930, 1.

19. Hugman, "Oral History," 4; Seguin Walnut Branch Master Plan, 5, http://www.seguintexas.gov/images/uploads/Master%20Plan%20Report_FINAL.pdf, retrieved Jun. 14, 2014.

20. *Express*: "Springtime," Mar. 17, 1935, 1-A; "Rock Work Adds," Aug. 4, 1935, 1-A; "Rubiola Backs River," Jul. 10, 1935, 16. The cascade was originally built in 1924 by Dr. and Mrs. Lee Rice, apparently as a gift to St. Mary's College.

21. *Express*: "Dam And Cutoff Control," Jun. 14, 1935, 1; "Not A Gondola In Sight," Jul. 1, 1936, 18. Riverside tenants were tracked in city directories.

22. Fisher, *Saving San Antonio*, 228–29.

23. Hugman, "Oral History," 4–5.

24. Hugman, "Speech," 10.

25. *Express*: "Beautifying River," Jul. 6, 1935, 5; "Rubiola Backs River," Jul. 10, 1935, 16; "Architect Tells of River's Beauty," Oct. 11, 1935, 18; "River Downtown To Be Lighted," Apr. 8, 1936, 16.

26. Fisher, *Saving San Antonio*, 105–6.

27. *Express*: "Boats Christened," Apr. 21, 1936, 6; "Venetian Night Attracts," Apr. 22, 1936, 3; *Light*, "Venice in Old San Antonio," Apr. 21, 1936, 9-A.

Chapter 6:
THE VENICE OF AMERICA

1. Hugman, "Oral History," 5; *Express*, "Extensive Beautifica-tion," Apr. 24, 1938, 7-A. In addition to chairman Jack White, committee members were attorney Claude V. Birkhead, Dr. Frederick G. Oppenheimer, San Antonio Printing Co. Presi-dent Luther B. Clegg, investor Lawrence J. Hart, attorney La-mar G. Seeligson, St. Mary's University President Rev. Alfred Rabe, Our Lady of the Lake College Chaplain Rev. Walter A. Arnold, San Antonio Music Co. President Isaac Bledsoe, D. A. Powell, insurance executive James H. Turner, engineer John K. Beretta and Judge Conrad A. Goeth.
2. *Express*, "Extensive Beautification," Apr. 24, 1938, 7-A.
3. *Express*, "Business Group Looks Ahead," Oct. 30, 1938, A-1.
4. *Light*, "City Rejects River Plans," Apr. 28, 1938, 6-B; Im-provement District," Sept. 13, 1938, 8-A; *Express*, "Funds Raised," May 22, 1938, 1-C. In mid-1939 the name of the Works Progress Administration was changed to Work Proj-ects Administration.
5. *Express*, "Funds Raised," May 22, 1938, 1-C; *News*, "River Beautification," Aug. 1, 1938.
6. *Express*, "New River Improvement District," Sept. 18, 1938. The city's last previous improvement district, created in 1919, was formed by a neighborhood in the southern part of the city to raise funds to pave streets, the most common use of the technique. Improvement districts fell out of use after new legislation permitted the city to charge property owners directly for two-thirds of such costs.
7. *Express*: "New River Improvement District," Sept. 18, 1938; "Bonds Approved," Oct, 26, 1938, 1; "Work on River," Nov. 13, 1938; *Light*: "Improvement District," Sept. 15, 1938, 8-A; "River Liason Group," Nov. 10, 1938; *News*, "Work On Beau-tifying," Oct. 26, 1938. Six Central Improvement Committee members had been on Jack White's Beautification Associa-tion committee created nine months earlier: Carryovers were Jack White, D. A. Powell, Claude V. Birkhead, Isaac Bledsoe, Dr. Frederick G. Oppenheimer and Rev. Walter A. Arnold. New were attorney Wilbur W. Matthews and banker Walter W. McAllister.

One of Robert Hugman's appealing stories is about how Jack White engineered the critical tax vote, though Hugman's account does not square easily with statistics reported in the press. Said Hugman in an oral history forty years later: "As they made the surveys to find eligible voters, they found that there were only five legitimate votes in the district—people who lived on the[ir] property. . . . At this point in time they did not have the bond election with five voters when they knew that three of them were opposed to it. An old bachelor and two old maids living over the Blackstone Auto Garage on St. Mary's Street were those who opposed the proposition. Now, a local law states that if you own property of any kind you would be eligible to vote. So Mr. White got a number of people living in his hotel to register and vote in this election because they had even so little as a watch. . . . So, when they had the election and there were, I believe, 74 votes for and two votes against, I assumed one of the old ladies was sick that day since there were two negative votes instead of three." (Hugman, "Oral History," 7–8.)

Conflicting with this story are contemporary news reports stating there were 107 eligible voters who represented eight percent of the district's property owners but owned two-thirds of the district's appraised real property, a percentage valued at $20 million. If, in fact, there were only five residents living on their real property, the property value owned by each would have had to average $4 million. If the "old bachelor and two old maids" living above the garage were impoverished, the remaining two "legitimate" residents would each have to have lived on their own real estate worth an average of $10 million—today's equivalent of $165 million—which strains credibility. It may well be that some Plaza Hotel guests were found eligible to vote under such a loophole and that a few did, though, if so, the precise numbers seem lost to history.
8. Maverick's son, Maury Maverick Jr., said he was told the first story by Louis Lipscomb. It is sometimes reported as having occurred when Maverick was mayor and Lipscomb was his police commissioner, though by the time the two held those offices the river was already funded and the project was well underway. The son said he had also heard the second story, but could not recall from whom. (Maury Maverick Jr., in discussion with the author, Sept. 22, 1996.)
9. *New York Times*, "Gondolas For Texans," Feb. 12, 1939.
10. *Express*, "Business Group Looks Ahead," Oct. 30, 1938, A-1.
11. Hugman, "Speech," 14; *Express*: "E. P. Arneson Funeral,"

Dec. 8, 1938; "Triple Check," Dec. 16, 1938, 8. Before being executed, plans had to be approved by the Central Improvement Committee, then by the city council and finally by the city's flood prevention engineers. Consulting engineer Walter Lilly later supervised preparation of San Antonio's second master plan, which he completed in 1951 during the administration of Mayor Jack White. ("San Antonio Master Plan," http://www.salsa.net/aiasa/sa-mastp.html.)

12. Work Projects Administration, *Along the San Antonio River*, 12–13, 15.

13. Hugman, "Oral History," 9, 15; *Light*, "River Beauty Project," Mar. 29, 1939; *Express*, "Trees Being Preserved," Jun. 14, 1939, 10.

14. Hugman, "Oral History," 10; Work Projects Administration, *Along the San Antonio River*, 12–13, 15.

15. Hugman to Green, Feb. 1, 1940, letter copy in San Antonio Conservation Society Library.

16. Work Projects Administration, *Along the San Antonio River*, 12, 20; Zunker, *A Dream Come True*, 155.

17. Work Projects Administration, *Along the San Antonio* River, 13, 33; Hugman, "Speech," 16–17.

18. Hugman, "How Paseo del Rio," 10; Fisher, *Saving San Antonio*; 193; Work Projects Administration, *Along the San Antonio River*, 22. New stairways to the River Walk were self-supporting and structurally unattached to bridges, preventing separation due to dual actions of vibrations at street level and the movement of water-soaked earth below.

19. Hugman: "How Paseo del Rio," 8; "Oral History," 10–11.

20. Zunker, *A Dream Come True*, 114.

21. *Express*: "City To Place," Sept. 17, 1939, 1-A; "Water Fills River," Dec. 24, 1939, 1-A.

22. *Express*, "Trees Being Preserved," Jun. 14, 1939, 10; *Milwaukee Journal*, "Hoosier Vagabond," Dec. 21, 1939.

23. Hugman, "Oral History," 16; Fisher, *Saving San Antonio*, 196; *Light*: "Rock Work On River Rapped," Dec. 21, 1939, 13-A.

24. Fisher, *Saving San Antonio*, 196.

25. Ayres to Green, Feb. 1, 1940, letter copy in Conservation Society Library.

26. Hugman to Green, Jan. 31, 1940, letter copy in Conservation Society Library.

27. Hugman, "Oral History," 12; *Express*, "Buenz to Boss River," Mar. 22, 1940, 8. Hugman's fee was 2.5 percent of the total cost of the project, not to exceed $6,600, today's equivalent of $110,000. (Zunker, *A Dream Come True*, 110.)

28. Maverick to Green, Feb. 19, 1940, letter copy in Conservation Society Library.

29. Hugman: "Oral History," 13; "Speech,"16.

30. *Light*, "Architect May Fight City," Mar. 22, 1940, 14-A; Hugman: "Oral History," 13; "How Paseo del Rio," 12; Zunker, *A Dream Come True*, 116. Nor had Hugman received much outside input. Bridges made high for gondolas aside, Hugman said "the only suggestion I had during the preparation of my plans from anyone was that the bridges be made high enough so we could have the river parade, have the floats on the river." (Hugman, "Oral History," 12.)

31. *Express*, "Buenz to Boss River," Mar. 22, 1940, 8; Hugman, "Oral History," 13.

32. Hugman, "Oral History," 13; "How Paseo del Rio," 12.

33. Hugman, "Speech," 16–17.

34. Fisher, *Saving San Antonio*, 207, 348.

35. *Express*, "River Beautification Project," Mar. 14, 1941, 1-A; Work Projects Administration, *Along the San Antonio River*, 31–32. Hugman designed the maintenance boat so that at night a deck could be drawn over the irrigation gear and form an upper level for musicians cruising the river.

36. Graham, *History of The Texas Cavaliers*, 11, 53; *Express*, "50,000 See Fiesta," Apr. 21, 1941, 1. Member Bill King is credited with the inspiration for Cavaliers sponsorship, and was the group's first river parade chairman.

37. Graham, *History of The Texas Cavaliers*, 53–57; *Express*, "50,000 See Fiesta," Apr. 21, 1941, 1. Fifty of the plywood boats, measuring six by twenty feet, were built by WPA arts and crafts workers on the two lowest floors of the Smith-Young Tower/Tower Life Building beside the river.

38. *Express*, "50,000 See Fiesta," Apr. 21, 1941, 1. For the parade, Richard Friedrich purchased several paddleboats left from San Francisco's international exposition two years earlier.

39. Graham, *History of The Texas Cavaliers*, 57–58.

40. *Express*, "50,000 See Fiesta," Apr. 21, 1941, 1.

Chapter 7:
DISUSE AND RESCUE

1. Fisher, *Saving San Antonio*, 221–223. In 1947 the Conservation Society moved the event from the River Walk up to La

Villita, where the next year it was named A Night in Old San Antonio and grew to a four-night feature of Fiesta Week.

2. *Light*, "Glamour Out In War Bond Sales," Apr. 19, 1943, 2-A; Lomax, *San Antonio's River*, xxvi.

3. *Light*, "First New River Boat," Aug. 12, 1945, 6-A; Lomax, *San Antonio's River*, 79–80, 81.

4. Lomax, *San Antonio's River*, 79–80, 81.

5. Bill Lyons, in discussion with the author, Nov. 27, 1996. At first the restaurant was indoors. An outdoor patio was soon built at a level higher than the River Walk, still subject to slight overflowing from imprecise gate control, since maintaining a precise water level along the Great Bend was not yet perfected. Finally, tables beneath umbrellas were added along the River Walk itself.

6. *Express*, "S.A.'s Casa Rio renewed at 46," Oct. 16, 1992, 7-C; *Express Images*, "Keepers of the Flame," Sept. 29, 1996, 4. One source reports the boat concession being run in 1948 by "the San Antonio River Company, a private concern originally from St. Louis, Missouri." (Lomax, *San Antonio's River*, 83.)

7. Breeding, *Flood of September 1946*, 1, 3, 8. The rainfall beneath the center of the storm was 16 inches, with 7 to 8 inches over northwestern San Antonio.

8. Breeding, *Flood of September 1946*, 8.

9. *Express*, Feb. 23, 1951; *Light*: "Flood Spurred Start," Jan. 1, 1961, 12-A; "Placid S. A. River," Jan. 2, 1961, 29; "Construction Just Beginning," Jan. 3, 1961, 2; San Antonio River Authority, *San Antonio River Authority 1937-1987*, 1, 3, 5, 8. Some work was supervised by the San Antonio River Canal and Conservancy District, predecessor of the San Antonio River Authority and a carryover from the last grand scheme to straighten and deepen the entire San Antonio River as a barge canal to the Texas coast. The district was chaired by Col. W. B. Tuttle, who had planned the Fiesta river parade in 1907.

10. *Light*, Dec. 13, 1957, 28.

11. "Establishments Off Limits in San Antonio," Office of the Provost Marshal, San Antonio Military Police, Fort Sam Houston, Dec. 20, 1945; *News*, "3 Held in River Assault," Oct. 11, 1962; *Express*, "Police Float Down River Beat, Jun. 24, 1964.

12. Fisher, *Saving San Antonio*, 221, 224, 263. The properties, both limestone block structures built in the mid-nineteenth century, were the Dashiell House at 511 Villita Street and, two doors up at the northwest corner of Villita and South Alamo streets, the two-story Bombach Building, since 1967

the Little Rhein Steakhouse, set up by Heinie Mueller and sold to Frank Phelps.

13. Fisher, *Saving San Antonio*, 263.

14. "To the Stockholders and Directors of Endowment, Inc.," Nov. 15, 1951, petition copy in San Antonio Conservation Society Library; Fisher, *Saving San Antonio*, 210.

15. David Straus, in discussion with the author, Jun. 24, 2014.

16. Fisher, *Saving San Antonio*, 264; *Express*, "City Wins Fight," Oct. 27, 1951; *News*, "Society Loses," Jun. 4, 1952, 22.

17. *Express*, "River Bend Park," Jun. 1. 1961, 1.

18. Ford to Chamber, May 30, 1961, letter copy in San Antonio Conservation Society Library.

19. David Straus, in discussion with the author, June 24, 2014.

20. Straus to Guerra, Sept. 14, 1992, copy in UTSA Archives, David Straus Papers, Box 5; Ordinance 302382, 1962, copy in UTSA Archives, David Straus Papers, Box 1.

21. River Walk Commission Minutes, June 1, 1962, in UTSA Archives, David Straus Papers, Box 2. Other initial members were F. M. Davis of the H. B. Zachry construction company, real estate broker C. W. Fenstermaker, designer Roger Rasbach, Gene Sommerhauser of Lone Star Brewing, insurance executive A. H. Cadwallader and Straus. Atlee Ayres served on the River Walk Commission until 1967 and continued to practice as an architect until his death two years later at the age of 96.

22. In addition to Wagner and Torres, architects on the committee were O'Neil Ford, Edward Mok, Brooks Martin, Arthur Mathis, Thomas Pressly and Boone Powell. Allison Peery joined later. Consulting from city government were planner Larry Travis and Bill Hunter, special projects engineer. (River Walk Commission Minutes, Jan. 23, 1963, in UTSA Archives, David Straus Papers, Box 2; Wagner, "Planning for the Development," 5.)

23. Wagner, "Planning for the Development," 3–4; *Express*, "River Bend is Renamed," Apr. 16, 1963, 3-B.

24. Wagner, "Planning for the Development," 5.

25. George, *O'Neil Ford, Architect*, 158. The project's site, owned by Nick Catalani, was ultimately used for the Hilton Palacio del Rio Hotel.

26. Holmesly, *HemisFair '68*, 66–67; *Express*, "Dixieland Night Club," Apr. 4, 1963, 14-F.

27. *Light*, "Restaurant Hailed," Jun. 6, 1964, 7; Holmesly, *HemisFair '68*, 62.

28. David Straus, in discussion with the author, June 7, 2006.

29. *Light*, "River Architect Flays Power Barges," Nov. 5, 1972, 17-A; Hugman to Straus, May 30, 1977, letter copy in UTSA Archives, David Straus Papers, Box 1; David Straus, in discussion with the author, Jun. 24, 2014.

30. *Express*; "Downtown HemisFair Site," Jul. 4, 1963, 1; "Taxi Contract," Jan. 28, 1967. The 350-room El Tropicano Motor Hotel opened on Lexington Avenue at the northern end of the River Walk in 1962.

31. Fisher, *Saving San Antonio*, 300; *Express*, "All Seven Bond Issues Carry," Jan. 29, 1964, 1.

32. Fisher, *Saving San Antonio*, 313.

33. Zunker, *A Dream Come True*, 156; Fisher, *Saving San Antonio*, 313.

34. Huxtable, *New York Times*, "HemisFair, Opening Tomorrow," 49; Black, "San Antonio's Linear Paradise, *AIA Journal*, July 1979, 36.

35. Montgomery, "HemisFair '68, " *Architectural Forum*, October 1968, 88. A marina for storing boats and barges was built at the extension's east end. Project architect for the extension was Allison Peery and landscape architect was James Keeter. Engineers were Haggard, Groves and Associates. Contractors were Darragh and Lyda, Inc. and H. A. Lott, Inc.

Chapter 8:
CROWN JEWEL OF TEXAS

1. The River Walk was number one when the Tourism Division of the governor's office began doing surveys in 1998. Since dropping behind the Alamo in 2003, it has bounced back and forth on various polls. In 1995 the American Volkssport Association named a two-hour stroll along the River Walk as second in walking routes only to a trail along the Hudson River at West Point. Boat tours make similar rankings.

2. Sinclair Black, "San Antonio's Linear Paradise," *AIA Journal*, July 1979, 30; *An Evaluation of Expansion Opportunities for the Henry B. Gonzalez Convention Center* (Washington, D.C.: Urban Land Institute, 1995), 8.

3. Fisher, *Rosita's Bridge*, 32. Rosita's father and two uncles were WPA workers on the River Walk project.

4. *Singapore River Development Plan* (Singapore: Urban Redevelopment Authority, 1992), 10; *Express*: "Richmond likes Riverfront," Dec. 8, 1993, 1-D; "S.A.–Israel river teamwork contin-

ues," May 6, 2010, C-2; San *Antonio Business Journal*, "River Walk now serves as model," Apr. 19, 1996, 14; "Monterrey adding Alamo City touch," Sept. 20, 1996, 1; *New York Times*, "Gentrification Moves In," Nov. 28, 2005, A-19. A group from Indianapolis returned to lower the White River fourteen feet through the center of its city. Back to Virginia went planners of the $34 million Richmond Riverfront, fifteen feet below street level along abandoned Civil War–era stone-lined canals and locks. "We were incredibly impressed," said the chairman of the Miami River Revival Committee as he returned to Florida to promote a $500 million river project. Others came from Sacramento, Phoenix, Minneapolis, Kansas City, Louisville, Charlotte, Oklahoma City. From Hull, Quebec, came Canadians planning a French village along their new Brewery Creek River Walk.

5. City of San Antonio Ordinance 41341, Oct. 12, 1972, copy in UTSA Archives, David Straus Papers, Box 1.

6. *Express*, "S.A.'s Casa Rio renewed at 46," Oct. 16, 1992, 7-C; *Express Images*, "Keepers of the Flame," Sept. 29, 1996, 4. One source reports the boat concession being run in 1948 by "the San Antonio River Company, a private concern originally from St. Louis, Missouri." (Lomax, *San Antonio's River*, 83.)

7. Zunker, *A Dream Come True*, 124. Paul Silber's younger son, John, was a longtime president, then chancellor of Boston University.

8. Boone Powell, in discussion with the author, Nov. 23, 1996. Also honored at the event, as later River Walk activists, were Walter Mathis, Jimmy Gause, David Straus and James L. Hayne.

9. *Light*, "River Architect Flays Power Barges," Nov. 5, 1972, 17-A; Hugman to Straus, May 30, 1977, letter copy in UTSA Archives, David Straus Papers, Box 1; David Straus, in discussion with the author, Jun. 24, 2014.

10. *Light*, Dec. 13, 1957, 28.

11. Carson and McDonald, *A Guide to San Antonio Architecture*, 38; Straus to River Walk Commissioners, Dec. 10, 1986, copy in UTSA Archives, David Straus Papers, Box 1. Some observers noted that the Hyatt Regency's design did not, however, comply with the city ordinance requiring new River Walk buildings to be "in keeping with early San Antonio architecture."

12. Fisher, *Saving San Antonio*, 221, 224, 263. The properties, both limestone block structures built in the mid-nineteenth

century, were the Dashiell House at 511 Villita Street and, two doors up at the northwest corner of Villita and South Alamo streets, the two-story Bombach Building, since 1967 the Little Rhein Steakhouse, set up by Heinie Mueller and sold to Frank Phelps.

13. "Downtown Renaissance Looks to Retail 'Eden' on the Riverwalk," *Texas Architect*, Sept.-Oct. 1988, 9; "Just add water," *Architectural Record*, March 1989, 100; Fisher, *Saving San Antonio*, 491. The mall was attracted through efforts of Mayor Henry Cisneros and City Manager Tom Huebner and planned since 1980 by Florida-based Edward J. DeBartolo Corp. and Allied Stores. Restaurants went at river level, most retail outlets at street level and above. Design was by Urban Design Group and Communications Arts of Tulsa, and work involving water by San Antonio's Ford, Powell and Carson. The Marriott Rivercenter was designed by Baltimore's RTKL. It exceeded by eleven stories the Smith-Young Tower, since renamed the Tower Life Building, San Antonio's tallest building since it was built in 1929.

14. *Express*, "Center of Attention," Nov. 25, 2001, 1-H. Lead architects for the project were Steve Tillotson and John Kell of Kell Munōz Architects and Ken Fowler of the landscape architecture firm Rialto Studios.

15. Fisher, *Saving San Antonio*, 439; *Express*, "A work in progress," Jul. 5, 2001, 1-B. The San Antonio Conservation Society contributed $150,000 to help match a federal Economic Development Administration grant for building the wall.

16. *Express*: "Ousted owners lament," Jan. 10, 2006, 1-E; "Battle for the River Walk," Mar. 12, 2006, 1-K; "River Walk clamp on chains eyed," Apr. 16, 2006, 1-A.

17. *Express*, "River Walk clamp on chains eyed," Apr. 16, 2006, 1-A.

18. *Express*, "Down by the river," May 12, 2001, 1-E. Initial River Commission appointees were Darryl Bird, Pearl Brewery CEO; Lynda Billa Burke, former San Antonio city councilwoman; A. J. Rodriguez, Hispanic Chamber of Commerce president; Lionel Sosa, former advertising and marketing executive; Julian Trevino, former San Antonio Independent School District chairman and El Mirador Restaurant owner; Ed Whitacre, former chairman of AT&T and of General Motors; and Lisa Wong, owner of Rosario's and Acenar restaurants.

19. *Express*, "Giving credit to McCormick," Aug. 16, 2009, 4-G.

20. *Express*: "Let there be Lights," Nov. 29, 1996, 1-C; "The Light Stuff," Nov. 29, 2002, 1-B; "Price tag nears $1M," Jul. 7, 2012, 1. Also during the Christmas season, at the Arneson River theater carolers perform on Saturday afternoons and at night the Alamo Kiwanis Club, sponsor of the summertime Fiesta Noche del Rio, holds a Fiesta Navidad del Rio. At Rivercenter Mall, boats portraying vignettes of the Christmas story enter the lagoon for a pageant. After Christmas, college bands from the Alamodome's Alamo Bowl contestants hold floating pep rallies. The River Walk Holiday Festival concludes on New Year's Eve with entertainment at Rivercenter Mall and strolling musicians, performers and bands on barges.

21. *Express*, "Changed River Walk awaits disabled," Dec. 21, 2009, 1. The 2006 project was overseen by FisherHeck architects Lewis S. Fisher and Charles John.

22. *Express*: "O'Malley barge group sinks rival," Mar. 10, 1995, 1; "Awash in years of change," Nov. 21, 2004, 1-B.

23. *Express*, "Brothers run aground," Jul. 14, 1998, 1-B.

24. *Express*: "S. A. sues 4 River Walk firms," Apr. 2, 1998, 1-A; "River Walk dispute settled," Aug. 14, 2001, 1-B.

25. Regnier to Phelps, Nov. 15, 1977, letter copy in UTSA Archives, David Straus Papers, Box 1.

26. Holmesly, *HemisFair '68*, 66–67; *Express*, "Dixieland Night Club," Apr. 4, 1963, 14-F.

27. Two miles north, Olmos Dam was found to be not as sound as once thought. An engineering study in 1974 praised the "unusually competent attention" to its concrete and placement, but concluded that if such storms as those of 1921 and 1946 were to occur directly over the Olmos Creek watershed, the dam could become unstable and tip over. Under the U.S. Army Corps of Engineers, the dam was partially reconstructed by 1982. The roadway was diverted from along the top to ground level below the dam and replaced with a curved concrete cap to serve as a spillway. A new concrete slope strengthening the downstream side replaced most of the original decorative arches. Since new construction in the drainage area far above had increased the volume of storm runoff, the dam was further strengthened in 2010–11 by a series of sixty-eight cable tendons anchored to bedrock and sealed within the dam. (Hensley-Schmidt, *Olmos Dam Inspection*, 4, 8, 38, 51–52; *Express*, "Olmos Dam Gets Upgrade," Dec. 9, 2010, 1.)

28. *Express*, "Lady Eco to speed up," June 23, 2006, 1-B. The $100,000 barge was designed by John Olthius's San An-

tonio–based Aqua Sweepers International. Contributing funds was the San Antonio Parks Foundation, headed by River Oversight Committee co-chair and former mayor Lila Cockrell. Implementation was under River Operations Supervisor Lincoln St. George.

29. *Express*: "New park links," Oct. 1, 2001, 3-B; "River link evolves," Oct. 14, 2001, 1-H; "River Walk link," Oct. 21, 2004, 1-B.

30. *San Antonio Business Journal*, "San Antonio leaders dedicate," Dec. 13, 2010.

31. *Express*: "River Walk area is closed," Nov. 19, 1998, 1-B; "River upgrade gets under way," Jan. 31, 2001, 8-B; "Revamped river," Mar. 19, 2002, 1-B; "Changes true to spirit," Apr. 7, 2002, 1-H. Beneath bridges, mosaic tile murals were done by Oscar Alvarado. Punched-metal light fixtures were designed by Judith Maxwell. Landscape architect for the project was Bender Wells Clark Design.

Chapter 9:
REACHING NORTH AND SOUTH

1. *Express*, "A Vision for the River," Dec. 9, 2007, X-4.

2. "How City Leaders Turned a Grand Vision Into Reality," http://tpr.org/post/how-city-leaders-turned-grand-vision-reality-museum-reach, retrieved Aug. 3, 2014.

3. Irby Hightower, in discussion with the author, Aug. 8, 2014.

4. In taking a relatively conservative approach to spending its substantial flood control tax revenues, Bexar County specified that the project must be undertaken north and south concurrently, that the city must also appropriate funds, that the River Authority find federal dollars and that the county would commit funding only at the same rate as city and federal funding. A hurdle in scheduling funding was that federal funds were appropriated only annually and the city could only use bond funds appropriated in advance. Adding difficulty was that all commitments had to be reduced in proportion to the least amount committed by an entity, amounts committed by year and not by project phase. (Irby Hightower, in discussion with the author, Aug. 8, 2014.)

The San Antonio River Foundation was established in 2003 by the San Antonio River Authority to raise private funds for river enhancements not covered by public funds. Its first chair was Sally Buchanan. She was succeeded by Edward E. Collins,

Nick Hollis and Frates Seeligson Jr. Executive directors have been Martha Oesterreich, Gayle Spencer, Catherine Cooke, Kim Abernethy and Estela Avery.

5. "How City Leaders Turned a Grand Vision Into Reality," http://tpr.org/post/how-city-leaders-turned-grand-vision-reality-museum-reach, retrieved Aug. 3, 2014.

6. *Express*, "A Vision for the River," Dec. 9, 2007, X-4. Defeat of a 2000 bond issue proposal to raise the sales tax to help finance $30 million in river improvements was attributed to fears that developers would benefit disproportionately to the city.

7. *Express*, "San Antonio's 'own little Panama Canal,'" May 5, 2009, 1-A.

8. *Express*, "SAMA puts on new face," Apr. 5, 2009, 1-A.

9. *Express*: "Forgotten piece of history," Feb. 7, 2008, 1-A; "Wave of change looms," May 9, 2009, 1-A.

10. *Express*, "City's ambitious project," Dec. 16, 2007, 1-A

11. *Express*: "Visitors, officials mark," May 30, 2010, 9-B; "Success seen," May 30, 2014, 1-A.

12. *Light*, "Fishing for S. A. Pearls," Jul. 12, 1937, 3-A.

13. "Mission Reach Restoration and Recreation Project," http://www.sanantonioriver.org/mission_reach/mission_reach.php#education, retrieved Aug. 5, 2014.

14. SWA Group, *San Antonio River Improvements Project Concept Design*, 14.

15. *Express*, "River project to turn back clock," Jan. 8, 2004, 8-B.

16. Commissioners Court was led by County Judge Nelson Wolff and Commissioner Sergio "Chico" Rodriguez in proposing the "visitor tax," a financing tool combining a 1.75 percent hotel/motel occupancy tax and a 5 percent short-term car rental tax. River Oversight Committee member Milton Guess secured support of local tourism, hotel/motel and rental car industries, helping the proposition overwhelmingly pass without opposition.

17. *Express*: "River work's price," May 21, 2009, 1-A; "New boss," Jun. 3, 2009, 1-A.

18. *Express*: "3rd victim of weekend floods," May 27, 2013, 1-A; "Mission Reach's role," Jun. 13, 2013.

19. The study, completed in April 2013 and updated the next year on the Museum Reach, was by Dr. Steve Nivin, assistant professor of economics at St. Mary's University. He projected another $1 billion in investment along the Museum Reach and Museum Reach and that employment and incomes would "expand significantly."

Bibliography

Baker, T. Lindsay. *Building the Lone Star*. College Station: Texas A&M University Press, 1986.

Bartholomew, Harland, and Associates. *A Comprehensive City Plan for San Antonio*. St. Louis, 1933.

Bartlett, C. Terrell. "The Flood of September, 1921, at San Antonio, Texas." *Transactions of the American Society of Civil Engineers* 85 (1922): 354–77.

Booth, John A., David R. Johnson, and Richard J. Harris, eds. *The Politics of San Antonio: Community, Progress and Power*. Lincoln and London: University of Nebraska Press, 1983.

Black, Sinclair. "San Antonio's Linear Paradise." *AIA Journal* (July 1979): 30–38.

Breeding, Seth D. *Flood of September 1946 at San Antonio, Tex*. Geological Survey Circular 32. Washington: United States Department of the Interior, Nov. 1948.

Burkhalter, Lois W., painted by Caroline Shelton. *San Antonio: The Wayward River*. San Antonio: Trinity University Press for Paseo del Rio Association, 1979.

Burleson, Clyde W. and E. Jessica Hickman. *The Panoramic Photography of Eugene O. Goldbeck*. Austin: University of Texas Press, 1986.

Bushick, Frank. *Glamorous Days in Old San Antonio*. San Antonio: The Naylor Company, 1934.

"Canoeing on the San Antonio River," *San Antonio: The Passing Show* 1, no. 37 (July 27, 1907): 4–5.

Carson, Chris, and William McDonald. *A Guide to San Antonio Architecture*. San Antonio: San Antonio Chapter of the American Institute of Architects, 1986.

Coppini, Pompeo. *From Dawn to Sunset*. San Antonio: The Naylor Company, 1949.

Corner, William. *San Antonio de Bexar*. San Antonio: Bainbridge & Corner, 1890.

Cox, I. Waynne. *Historic Overview and Archival Archaeological Investigation for the San Antonio River Improvements Project: Houston to Lexington Segment*. San Antonio: Center for Archaeological Research, University of Texas at San Antonio Archaeological Survey Report No. 299, 2000.

_____. *The Spanish Acequias of San Antonio*. San Antonio: Maverick Publishing Company, 2005.

Ellsworth. C. E. *The Floods in Central Texas in September 1921*. Geological Survey Water-Supply Paper 488. Washington: Department of the Interior, 1923.

Everett, Donald E. *San Antonio: The Flavor of Its Past, 1845–1898*. San Antonio: Trinity University Press, 1975.

Everett, Richard. "Things In and About San Antonio." *Frank Leslie's Illustrated Newspaper* VII, no. 163 (Jan. 15, 1859): 95–96, 102–3.

Ewing, Thomas E. "Waters Sweet and Sulphurous: The First Artesian Wells in San Antonio." *Bulletin of the South Texas Geological Society* 60, no. 6 (Feb. 2000): 9–22.

Fisher, Lewis F. *Crown Jewel of Texas: The Story of San Antonio's River*. San Antonio: Maverick Publishing Company, 1997.

_____. *C. H. Guenther & Son at 150 Years: The Legacy of a Texas Milling Pioneer*. San Antonio: Maverick Publishing Company, 2001.

_____. *River Walk: The Epic Story of San Antonio's River*. San Antonio: Maverick Publishing, 2007.

_____. *Saint Mark's Episcopal Church: 150 Years of Ministry in Downtown San Antonio, 1858–2008*. San Antonio: Maverick Publishing Co., 2008.

_____. *Saving San Antonio: The Precarious Preservation of a Heritage*. Lubbock: Texas Tech University Press, 1996.

Fisher, Lewis F., and Maria Watson Pfeiffer. *Traditions and Visions: San Antonio Architecture*. San Antonio: AIA San Antonio, 2007.

Fisher, Mary McMillan. *Rosita's Bridge*. San Antonio: Maverick Publishing Company, 2001.

Forman, Josephine. *We Finish to Begin: A History of Travis Park Methodist Church*. San Antonio: Travis Park United Methodist Church, 1991.

Fox, Ann A., and Lois M. Flynn and I. Waynne Cox. *Archaeological Studies for the San Antonio Channel Improvement Project, Including Investigations at Guenther's Upper Mill (41BX342)*. Report No. 136. San Antonio: University of Texas at San Antonio Center for Archeological Research, 1987.

Frary, I. T. "The River of San Antonio." *Architectural Record* 45 (Apr. 1919): 380–81.

Frost, Susan Toomey. *Colors on Clay: The San José Tile Workshops of San Antonio.* San Antonio: Trinity University Press, 2009.

Garvin, Alexander. *The American City.* New York: McGraw-Hill, 1996.

George, Mary Carolyn Hollers. *O'Neil Ford, Architect.* College Station: Texas A&M University Press, 1992.

Gould, Stephen. *The Alamo City Guide.* New York: Macgowan & Slipper, Printers, 1882.

Graham, Henry. *History of the Texas Cavaliers, 1926–1976.* San Antonio: Texas Cavaliers, 1976.

Guerra, Mary Ann Noonan. *The San Antonio River.* San Antonio: The Alamo Press, 1987.

Gunn, Clare A., David J. Reed and Robert E. Couch. *Cultural Benefits From Metropolitan River Recreation— San Antonio Prototype.* Technical Report No. 43. College Station: Texas Water Resources Institute, Texas A&M University, June 1972.

Hensley-Schmidt, Inc. *Olmos Dam Inspection For City of San Antonio, Texas.* Chattanooga, 1974.

Holmesly, Sterlin. *HemisFair '68 and the Transformation of San Antonio.* San Antonio: Maverick Publishing Company, 2003.

Hugman, Robert H. H. Bexar County Historical Commission Oral History Interview with Doris Dupre, 1977. University of Texas at San Antonio Institute of Texan Cultures Oral History Collection.

_____. "How Paseo del Rio." Delivered at Arneson River Theater bells dedication, Nov. 1, 1978. Typescript in San Antonio Conservation Society files.

_____. River Walk architectural drawings (prints). San Antonio Conservation Society Library.

_____. "Speech to San Antonio Historical Association," 1975. Bexar County Historical Commission Oral History Program, University of Texas at San Antonio Institute of Texan Cultures Oral History Collection.

Huxtable, Ada Louise. "HemisFair, Opening Tomorrow, Isn't Texas-Size, But It's Fun." *New York Times,* Apr. 5, 1968, 49.

Industries of San Antonio, Texas, The. San Antonio: Land & Thompson, 1885.

Knight, Larry. "Defining American in San Antonio in the 1850s." *Southwestern Historical Quarterly* CIX, no. 3 (Jan. 2006): 319–35.

Lomax, Louise. *San Antonio's River.* San Antonio: The Naylor Company, 1948.

Lovelace, Eldridge. *Harland Bartholomew: His Contributions to American Urban Planning.* Urbana: University of Illinois Dept. of Urban and Regional Planning, 1993.

McDowell, Catherine. "San Antonio's Mills on the River," 1974, ms. in San Antonio Conservation Society Library.

McLean, Bert J. *The Romance of San Antonio's Water Supply and Distribution.* San Antonio: San Antonio Printing Co., 1927.

Metcalf & Eddy. *Report to City of San Antonio, Texas, Upon Flood Prevention.* Boston, 1920.

Montgomery, Roger. "HemisFair '68, Prologue To Renewal." *Architectural Forum* (Oct. 1968): 88.

Morrison, Andrew. *The City of San Antonio.* St. Louis: George W. Englehardt and Company, 1889.

Newcomb, Pearson. *The Alamo City.* San Antonio: Standard Printing Company Press, 1926.

Olmsted, Frederick Law. *A Journey Through Texas.* New York: Dix, Edwards & Co., 1857.

Phelps, Christi. "Shading the Future," *San Antonio Monthly Magazine,* Jan. 1987: 112.

Pfeiffer, Maria Watson. "Brackenridge Park: A History." http://www.brackenridgepark.org/Resources/Documents/brackenridge%20park%20history.pdf.

[Quiroga, José]. *La Tragedia de la Inundacion de San Antonio.* San Antonio: Libreria de Quiroga, [1921].

Ramsdell, Charles. *San Antonio: A Historical and Pictorial Guide.* Austin: University of Texas Press, 1959.

Report of the Widening of Commerce Street A.D. 1914. San Antonio: Passing Show Printing Co., 1915.

San Antonio. San Antonio: [San Antonio Chamber of Commerce, 1915].

San Antonio City Commissioners Minutes, 1915–30. City Clerk's office, San Antonio.

San Antonio, City of, and San Antonio River Authority. *Conceptual Plan for the San Antonio River from Nueva Street to U.S. Highway 281.* San Antonio, 1993.

San Antonio Express.

San Antonio Light.

San Antonio River Authority. "San Antonio River Authority." www.sara-tx.org.

San Antonio River Authority. *San Antonio River Authority, 1937–1987.* San Antonio: San Antonio River Authority, 1988.

San Antonio River Foundation. "San Antonio River Foundation." www.sariverfoundation.org.

"San Antonio, Texas." *Berlin Bridges and Buildings,* Berlin Bridge Co., East Berlin, Conn. 1, no. 9 (Dec. 1898): 126–28.

Santleben, August. *A Texas Pioneer.* I. D. Affleck, ed. New York: Neale Publishing Company, 1910.

"Scenes in Flood Relief Work at San Antonio, Texas." *The Red Cross Bulletin,* Washington DC 5, no. 39 (Sept. 26, 1921): 5.

Sibley, Marilyn McAdams. *George W. Brackenridge, Maverick Philanthropist.* Austin and London: University of Texas Press, 1973.

Skidmore, Owings & Merrill, Marshall Kaplan, Gans, and Kahn. *San Antonio River Corridor.* San Francisco, 1973.

"Soldiers and the Flood." *The Trail, Published in the Interest of the Second Division,* Camp Travis, Tex. 1, no. 37 (Sept. 16, 1921): 1–15.

Spofford, Harriet Prescott. "San Antonio de Bexar." *Harper's New Monthly Magazine,* Nov. 1877: 831–50.

Steadman, Doug. "A History of W. E. Simpson Company from 1909 to 1993." San Antonio, 1993.

Steinfeldt, Cecelia. *Art for History's Sake: The Texas Collection of the Witte Museum.* San Antonio: The Texas State Historical Association for the Witte Museum, 1993.

_____. *San Antonio Was: Seen Through a Magic Lantern.* San Antonio: San Antonio Museum Association, 1978.

Stothert, Karen E. *The Archaeology and Early History of the Head of the San Antonio River.* Southern Texas Archaeological Association Special Publication No. Five, Incarnate Word College Archaeology Series No. Three. San Antonio: Southern Texas Archaeological Association in cooperation with Incarnate Word College, 1989.

Straus, David J., Papers. University of Texas at San Antonio Library Archives.

SWA Group and others. *San Antonio River Improvements Project Concept Design,* 2001.

Wilson, William H. *The City Beautiful Movement.* Baltimore and London: Johns Hopkins University Press, 1989.

Work Projects Administration Writer's Program in the State of Texas, comp. *Along the San Antonio River.* American Guide Series. San Antonio: City of San Antonio, 1941.

Zunker, Vernon G. *A Dream Come True: Robert Hugman and San Antonio's River Walk,* rev. ed. San Antonio: N.p., 1994.